To my parents and the other parent figures in my life:

Tom and Una Bruce, Bob and Lillian Barker, John and Edna Stroud, and Peter and Margery Rowland

Contents

Preface to the third edition

It is now just over ten years since the first edition of this book was published. What has happened over that period? In most ways progress has been startling. Since then, the *International Journal of Nonprofit and Voluntary Sector Marketing* has been launched in this country; non profit marketing articles appear regularly in the *Journal of Marketing* and the *European Journal of Marketing;* three more charity marketing books have been published in the UK; a masters degree in marketing and fundraising has been launched; and NCVO holds successful annual conferences on the subject, which are regularly over subscribed – all evidence that interest and commitment is growing at a rapid pace.

But whether it is because it is a dark afternoon, or because it is true, I feel a huge drag on acceptance of marketing in our sector, caused by public misconception of the subject – which I put down to the losing battle commercial marketers and their representative bodies are having in maintaining ordinary people's belief in the breadth and morality of marketing. When I started my career in the 1970s, being known as a marketer engendered approbation; now it requires a defensive explanation as to why I am involved in something so narrow cast and unethical. In the 1970s producers used to say 'we have to advertise it better'. Now they say 'we have to market it better', equating marketing with the last, separate and rather vulgar stage of developing a product. This usage is even rampant in business schools across the UK. Even more worrying, I sense marketing has increasingly been associated with unethical behaviour, often imagined but no less damaging for all that. The high profile usage of the term by the industries of drinks, tobacco, football and politics has certainly not helped – encouraging the view of marketing which I sometimes describe as 'selling people things they don't need at prices they cannot afford'.

So what do we charity marketers do? I think we can help in our small way. First, we are using marketing for obvious good (although even we need to be vigilant over our fundraising marketing ethics). Second, we are pushing back marketing frontiers with our widespread and continuous addressing of multiple target groups/constituencies with differing needs and wishes, some of which pay money and some of which do not, but all of which pay hidden prices. And third, we have the zeal and freshness of new converts to a cause, who are bringing new thinking with new territory. But I do appeal to the overwhelmingly dominant branch of our profession in the commercial world to relaunch the product that is marketing.

This third edition has been carefully updated and so readers can be confident that some of the best and newest references are included. However, it is reassuring for our emerging specialism that so much of the earlier writing has stood the test of time. The book is re-structured into three parts. The third part, which is entirely new, contains chapters on relationship marketing and partnership marketing, including cause related marketing (CRM). The chapter on income and fundraising generation has been extensively updated, and all the chapters include revisions. People familiar with commercial marketing can skip Chapter 2.

In an attempt to reclaim and make clear the breadth and depth of the marketing contribution, I have once again modified the title. This is intended as a public signal of the fundamental contribution of marketing to the effective running of voluntary and community organisations in order to meet the needs of beneficiaries.

All the thanks and appreciation recorded in previous prefaces remain undiminished, especially to the people in Unilever who first taught me about marketing. I wish to add special thanks to colleagues in ICSA, to Susan Richards and Clare Grist Taylor for asking me to do this third edition and to Phil Brown, Kevin Eddy, Kate Ellison, Jacki Reason and Simon Bailey. Ten years is a long time in the life of a business school and my thanks go to the new dynamic leaders helping us to make an impressive impact – David Rhind, David Currie, Steve Haberman, Henrietta Royle and Georges Selim. This has also been an inspirational 18 months in the life of VOLPROF, now transformed into the Centre for Charity Effectiveness, and my thanks go to the Worshipful Company of Management Consultants, particularly John Mclean Fox, Patrick McHugh, Gareth Rees, Barrie Collins, William Barnard, Allan Duigood and Allan Williams. Their contribution has been critical, not least because it has given me the space to work on this edition. The quadrupling in size and impact of the Centre has also been through the contribution of my Centre colleagues Caroline Copeman, Sue Douthwaite, Denise Fellows, Andrew Forrest, Mary Harris, Jenny Harrow, John Hailey, Karen Hickox, Adah Kay, Peter Grant, Ruth Lesirge, Paul Palmer, Atul Patel and Ian Williams, whose cheerful companionship have aided this writing commission. Lastly, but pre-eminently, I have had unfailing support from Tina, my partner for life.

Thanks once again to ICSA for asking for a third edition – I hope you have a good read!

Ian Bruce
May 2005

Abbreviations

4Ps	Produce, Price, Promotion, Place
AIDA	Attention, Interest, Desire, Action
AOP	Association of Optical Practitioners
BA	British Airways
BCO	British College of Optometrists
BCODP	British Council of Organisations of Disabled People
BPA	British Parachute Association
BVS	Broad Voluntary Sector
CAF	Charities Aid Foundation
CRC	Cancer Research Campaign
CDI	Comprehensive Disability Income
CRM	Cause Related Marketing
DARAC	Disability Access Rights and Advice Service
DBC	Disability Benefits Consortium
DCC	Disability Charities Consortium
DDA	Disability Discrimination Act
DfES	Department for Education and Skills
DIG	Disability Income Group
DLA	Disability Living Allowance
DTI	Department of Trade and Industry
DWP	Department for Work and Pensions
FMCG	Fast-moving consumer goods
FODO	Federation of Dispensing Opticians
GDP	Gross Domestic Product
IANSA	International Action Network on Small Arms
ICRF	Imperial Cancer Research Fund
LEA	Local Education Authority
NACRO	National Association for the Care and Resettlement of Offenders
NCH	National Children's Home

NCVO	National Council for Voluntary Organisations
NOPWC	National Old People's Welfare Council
NSPCC	National Society for the Prevention of Cruelty to Children
NVS	Narrow Voluntary Sector
OFSTED	Office for Standards in Education
ONS	Office of National Statistics
PR	Public Relations
PRO	Public Relations Officer
RADAR	Royal Association of Disability and Rehabilitation
RCSB	Royal Commonwealth Society for the Blind/SightSavers
RNIB	Royal National Institute of the Blind
RNID	Royal National Institute for Deaf People
RNLI	Royal National Lifeboat Institution
RPI	Retail Price Index
RSB	Royal Society for the Blind
RSPB	Royal Society for the Protection of Birds
RSPCA	Royal Society for the Prevention of Cruelty to Animals
SDU	Service Delivery Unit
SWOT	Strengths, Weaknesses, Opportunities, Threats
TEC	Training and Enterprise Council
USP	Unique Selling Proposition
VSO	Voluntary Service Overseas
WWF	World Wildlife Fund (now Worldwide Fund for Nature)

PART I

The Philosophy, Framework and Tools

1   What is charity marketing?

Introduction

I am a passionate believer in marketing and in applying a marketing approach to the voluntary sector. This is in part because I was trained as a manager by Unilever, where marketing was, and still is, the 'way we do it round here'. But the main reason for my continuing passion is that marketing is philosophically and practically well suited to the voluntary and public sectors. What a gift to find a technique that has as its philosophy a dominant ethos of starting with the needs of the consumer, rather than the concerns of the provider. And doesn't it also just feel right to have a practical process that starts from where the consumer actually is, rather than where we would like them to be? Such a philosophy and practice rings all sorts of bells in my background and current life. For me, as a child of the 1960s, a marketing approach has similarities with community work and community development – giving a major role in the creation and delivery of services to people who were previously regarded as passive recipients. Being married to a Froebelian educator whose core philosophy and practice is the dictum 'begin where the learner is' (Friedrich Froebel 1782-1852) has produced an unexpected harmony between an educator and a manager.

What is marketing?

Essentially, marketing is a way of fitting together the planning and implementation of goods, services or ideas in a practical but sophisticated way, and in a way that emphasises the needs of the customer, client or person in need rather than simply trying to improve the efficiency of existing processes or ways of doing things. So much of voluntary sector activity development takes place in what the commercial world would call a product- or production-orientated way. Superficially this can increase efficiency, but the risk in this rapidly changing world is that the product or process becomes increasingly less relevant or appropriate to what customers or clients need and want.

Consumer satisfaction

The majority of definitions describe marketing as an activity to help the organisation achieve its goals by providing consumer satisfaction. This description should reassure the charity reader because it describes the key role of the organisation. But it also establishes the key focus on the customer/user/client/patient. In this book I use the term 'customers' to cover all of a charity's target groups and, when appropriate, divide this term into 'beneficiaries' and 'supporters' (see page 35). However, at best the selection of the appropriate term is a matter of sensitivity and at worst it is a matter of fashion. Too much concentration on terms, in my experience, simply holds up discussion of the more fundamental issues.

Negative associations

But for many people the term 'marketing' has negative associations. It describes a process for selling people things they do not need. For those with a centre-to-left political orientation it is associated with an intensely capitalist and commercial environment that is antithetical to the public and not-for-profit sector. For those with a centre-to-right view, it is generally more acceptable, but its application in the public and voluntary sector can seem irrelevant or inappropriate. Even where marketing is accepted, it is often only readily associated with areas such as fundraising and public relations (PR).

So, if the term starts with such a bad press, why continue to use it in the public and voluntary sectors? Over the last fifty years the approach, practice and techniques of marketing have transformed the commercial world and its provision of goods. It is also now significantly affecting the world of services. Our world needs to take advantage of these advances. But should we use a new name? I think not. There have been attempts in the public and voluntary sector to use the term 'public relations' as an alternative (Bruce 1973), but PR also has negative overtones and is too narrow a concept. Professional practices (such as lawyers and architects) tried a similar approach by substituting the term 'practice development', but this did not catch on (A. Wilson 1984, pp. xi–xiv).

Value-neutral

Marketing as a term and a process is value-neutral. It can be used for good or ill. It can and has been applied not only in the commercial world, but also in the not-for-profit world, and even in the former planned economies of Eastern Europe.

Despite its 'discovery' for the non-profit sector by Kotler and Levy as long ago as 1969, marketing has only achieved a modest penetration into public and not-for-profit organisations in the United Kingdom. As a rough benchmark, best practice is probably at the quality and penetration levels experienced in the commercial world in the 1960s. Over the last few years it has begun to influence strategic planning, service provision and campaigning but, as suggested above, in the main it is only extensively applied in fundraising and PR (Hankinson 2000). However, best practice in these two areas (such as direct mail) is extremely impressive and can teach the commercial world a thing or two.

Definitions

There is a whole host of definitions of marketing. Most of the more sophisticated ones could be applied to the public and voluntary sector. The one quoted below is by Philip Kotler, Professor of International Marketing at Northwestern University, United States. Kotler has the longest-standing interest of any academic in the field of public and not-for-profit marketing. He developed an early version of the following definition in the 1970s, which has essentially stood the test of time.

> 'Marketing is the analysis, planning, implementation, and control of carefully formulated programmes designed to bring about voluntary exchanges of values with target markets to achieve institutional objectives. Marketing involves designing the institution's offerings to meet the target markets' needs and desires, and using effective pricing, communication, and distribution to inform, motivate, and service the markets.'
>
> (Kotler and Fox 1985, p. 7)

This comprehensive, albeit tightly packed, definition is helpful because it identifies the different elements of marketing, which helps to indicate how it can be applied in the charity sector. Kotler uses the term 'offering' in place of 'product' – the generic term for physical goods and services. In this book I use 'product' to cover a charity's physical goods, services and ideas. Where it is important to draw particular attention to the type of product, I use the terms 'physical product', 'service product' and 'idea product'.

Andreasen and Kotler (2003) have defined marketing management as:

> 'The process of planning and executing programs designed to influence the behavior of target audiences by creating and maintaining beneficial exchanges for the purposes of satisfying individual and organisational objectives.'

(p. 39)

Case examples

The following four short case examples exemplify what the different elements in the definition can mean in practice. While two of the four have been taken from social services and education, they could equally have been taken from health, transport, the arts or sports. The social services study is of a voluntary visiting service for older people run by a local charity, but could also have been a study of a service for families under extreme stress or any other personal social service. The example from education is a school run by a national charity, but again any education service may have been selected. The fundraising example is a charity dinner, but could have been big-gift fundraising, a jumble sale or any other fundraising method. A pressure group involved with the arts forms the final case example, but once again could just as well have been drawn from a number of areas, including social welfare or the environment.

CASE EXAMPLE: A VOLUNTARY VISITING SERVICE FOR OLDER PEOPLE

Introduction

In this example we look at a marketing approach to service delivery. It involves a checklist of analysis, planning, implementation and control necessary for a successful service; and achieves all of this with a very strong emphasis on the needs and desires of service recipients. Equally important, it involves a lot of common sense. References to the terms in Kotler's definition above are italicised.

Analysing

The social services department, whether as purchaser or provider, has an *institutional objective* of helping older people to stay independent in the community for as long as possible. *Analysis* of local and national research among older people shows that those who live alone, or who have a dependent spouse, can become isolated and rapidly spiral down into high levels of dependency. The *target market* is therefore identified as over-75-year-olds living alone, over-75-year-olds with a dependent spouse, and over-65-year-olds with a health problem or a disability. The *needs and desires* of this target group are obviously many and varied. However, research shows that, to a lesser or greater extent, people want to be able to share their concerns and worries, and be able to ask for help when necessary. They want to be able to do this with someone they know and trust, but they also want to feel that the person can get something done in the official structure.

Meeting needs

It could be argued that in an ideal world, this would be a question of a social worker calling in once a week, but the *analysis* and *planning* immediately indicate that this would be impossible within the given resources. Research and knowledge of other local authority provision suggests that visiting schemes (the *product* or, more specifically, *service product*) using volunteers might well meet social services' objectives, provided that there is a *carefully formulated programme* which is well *planned* and subsequently *controlled* and evaluated. Research shows that the interaction between volunteers and clients is the key to success or failure. In other words, the programme has to enable a *voluntary exchange of values* that is satisfying to both parties. If this does not happen, either the exchange will become sterile, or one

cont.

CASE EXAMPLE: A VOLUNTARY VISITING SERVICE FOR OLDER PEOPLE continued

of the two parties will drop out. In this service the volunteers therefore also become a *target market* with *needs and desires* that have to be met. Early retired people are identified as potential volunteers because the visiting scheme gives them an important role in the community but does not give them the feeling of an open-ended commitment, which may drain them.

In this situation it is felt that charging (*pricing*) for the service is not appropriate to the quasi-friendship relationship and would hinder the *voluntary exchange of values* (although both volunteers and those visited are paying a 'price' of loss of free time and loss of privacy, which the benefits must outweigh). However, the remaining elements of what is called the marketing mix – *communication, and distribution to inform, motivate and service the markets* – are particularly problematic in a voluntary visiting service.

Distribution and communication

Starting with *distribution*, what size of geographic or population area should the scheme serve? Should it be delivered directly by social services or contracted out to a voluntary organisation? These and other issues concerned with the distribution of the service will need to be carefully formulated for the programme to work. In this example the marketing mix needs to be applied to the volunteers as well as to the people being visited, but we shall concentrate on the latter. *Informing*, let alone *motivating* older people to become involved, takes a lot of planning. The former can be achieved through publicising the programme via churches, day centres, clubs and leisure interest groups that often involve older people, such as bingo halls and bowls clubs, but informing people is not enough. They have to be sufficiently *motivated* to want to take up the service. Word-of-mouth recommendations from people already involved become crucial in promoting this type of service. Similarly, recommendations from doctors, social workers and health visitors can be very important in motivating people to ask for the service.

Delivery

Perhaps most important of all is the *effective servicing* of the *market*. If the recipients do not get an effective service and see obvious benefits, the exercise is clearly a complete waste of time. Structures and

cont.

> **CASE EXAMPLE: A VOLUNTARY VISITING SERVICE FOR OLDER PEOPLE continued**
>
> processes have to be developed so that voluntary visitors can trigger a process of wider service and delivery if the older person appears to want this. At the level of quasi-friendship, the voluntary visitor has to be at least prepared, and probably trained, in order to deliver the service in a way in which both sides gain satisfaction.

Some readers may still be thinking that a strong user orientation with careful planning and implementation procedures are obvious and so much like common sense that marketing, as defined above, is simply making the whole process far too technical and sophisticated. This can be disproved quite simply by Shenfield and Allen's impressive research of voluntary visiting schemes (Shenfield and Allen 1972).

Voluntary visiting schemes were springing up across the country. Research showed that a majority were ill conceived and badly implemented. Some of the key problems were:

- the planners had not identified the main target groups that needed/wanted visiting (the *target market*);
- they did not analyse or understand the *needs and desires* of either the people being visited or the volunteers, and so there was either a non-existent or unsatisfactory *exchange of values*;
- there was no *control of the programmes*, in the form of monitoring and evaluation.

As a result of not adopting a marketing approach, many schemes were set up which visited the wrong people, delivering a 'service' that was unappreciated and, even worse, went on for many years involving the time and energy of volunteers who felt guilty about throwing in the towel.

CASE EXAMPLE: A SCHOOL FOR CHILDREN WITH SPECIAL EDUCATIONAL NEEDS

Introduction

From the 1920s onwards the Royal National Institute of the Blind (RNIB) set up an increasing number of residential homes called Sunshine Homes for Blind Babies. In their heyday there were nine such homes ('service products'), taking children from the age of two years.

Two key social policy changes in the external environment resulted in the number of schools being reduced to one by 2000. The first was the growing view that it was undesirable for blind children, certainly as young as two years old, to be taken away from the family environment and placed in residential institutions. The second, in part a concomitant of the first, was the growing view that young blind children should and could be educated locally, and as a consequence necessarily included in educational settings with sighted children.

At first these changes were seen as indicators that the role of these schools should diminish and eventually disappear. However, the marketing approach produced a radically different view, and as a result a radically different service product. RNIB encouraged changing social policy views, which shows an essential difference between commercial and social marketing. In the former world it is highly unlikely that you would see the parent company encouraging policy shifts that would damage one of its leading products.

Meeting organisational objectives

RNIB's educational objective was, and is, to ensure that young blind people get the best possible education. Experience in parts of Scandinavia had shown that changing to a completely integrated system, while having many advantages, had one particular disadvantage – the dissolution and eventual degradation of any specialist knowledge of particular educational needs of visually impaired children. In other words, as the separate schools for educating visually impaired children disappeared, specialist staff either retired or were distributed around the country, so specialist knowledge became dissipated and eventually began to reduce.

RNIB's approach was different. First, while it was losing or encouraging the loss of its singly disabled blind children, it identified a new need – namely the education of multi-disabled blind children. These were young people who, in addition to having a visual impairment, had

cont.

9

CASE EXAMPLE: A SCHOOL FOR CHILDREN WITH SPECIAL EDUCATIONAL NEEDS continued

one or more other difficulties, such as a severe learning difficulty and/or severe behavioural problems. Severe learning difficulties or behavioural problems alone would have meant that they would not fit into the existing network of local special schools, but the overlay of severe disability made the educational challenge that much more complex and appropriate for the special knowledge and skills of the Sunshine School. Second, the service developed an outreach arm, helping with the assessment of singly disabled blind children and giving advice to mainstream education.

The RNIB's schools' name had become both a strength and a weakness. It was changed from Sunshine Home for Blind Babies into Sunshine House School. The Sunshine House Schools also moved away from the exclusively residential form of service delivery. First, weekly boarding (going home at weekends) was introduced wherever possible. Second, the number of day pupils was increased via the use of taxi services. The location of two of the schools close to the M25 was a distinct advantage, which was exploited.

Communication
The change in the service and its method of delivery was significant, but the challenge of getting this new form across to intermediary customers – local education authorities (LEAs) – and to the parents of visually impaired children was a major task. Sunshine House School heads invited local education special needs advisers to visit the schools; RNIB's own education advisers made the revised form of service more widely known; more active PR was employed, partly for fundraising purposes but also in order to get the new form of service across, and the parents of newly visually impaired children were welcome to visit the school on a regular basis, both to sample the school and to make contact with other parents. The latter was particularly important because there are relatively few blind children, and parents can easily feel isolated.

Pricing
The price of the service was also radically revised. The declining numbers of children in the remaining schools had initially encouraged RNIB to keep the price artificially low. At a time when it was increasing

cont.

CASE EXAMPLE: A SCHOOL FOR CHILDREN WITH SPECIAL EDUCATIONAL NEEDS continued

school fees in its other schools, it felt it could not afford to raise prices in the Sunshine Homes. However, the recruitment of children with far greater educational challenges and the provision of an educational service appropriate to their needs gave the logical basis for fairly significant price rises. LEAs, which paid the fees, were prepared to accept quite significant fee charges for children they felt they could not educate locally; this was in contrast to being unprepared to pay the earlier, relatively low prices for singly disabled children, when LEAs felt that they did not need to pay such charges when they could educate the children in their own locality. Individual pricing was also introduced so that LEAs funding less severely disabled children were not subsidising those sending more severely disabled children.

Pricing the outreach service has, however, proved problematic. LEAs have not been used to such services and, while they were prepared to spend tens of thousands of pounds on fees for children to attend a special residential school, they have proved remarkably reluctant to pay the few hundred pounds per day required for specialist advice and assessment. This is in part because LEAs have different budget heads, and partly because the increase in outreach service coincided with the relative pressure on local government income, both from central government and via local taxation.

It is important to point out that these changes took nearly ten years to identify and implement. In the early stages, they were not even identified as part of a marketing process, although in essence that is what they were; nor were they planned or implemented holistically. This is because, although RNIB is probably the leader among British charities trying to introduce a marketing approach to services, it was at that time still in the early stages of development. Nevertheless, the changes did take place in an evolutionary and complementary fashion. As we shall see later, they also took account of all of the elements of what is known as the 'marketing mix' (Borden 1964, pp. 2-7). In Chapter 2 we shall see the marketing mix as it functions in the commercial sector. In Chapter 4 we shall look at its contribution to the charity sector.

CASE EXAMPLE: A FUNDRAISING EVENT

Introduction

Charities put on a huge range of special fundraising events such as local or national theatre first nights, film premières and ticketed receptions. One of the most basic and frequently used is a fundraising dinner. What is not widely known is that, unless these events are organised from a professional marketing viewpoint, they may only just break even, and on occasions can lose money. These are many reasons why these events can be relatively unsuccessful. These include:

- insufficient analysis and planning;
- poor implementation;
- offering things that are not attractive to the people the charity is hoping to attract;
- poor promotion and/or incorrect pricing, which results in too few people turning up to make a profit;
- enticing too heterogeneous an audience (for example, inebriated Hooray Henries insulting abstemious, rich, regular donors).

The list is endless and the cost of failure is both short and long-term. Not only does the event lose money, but it may make it virtually impossible for subsequent events to be put on successfully.

The following example is a major and quite sophisticated one, but it is not unusual among larger charities. Its purpose is to show the marketing approach in action.

Fundraising dinner

Each year a major national charity is selected to receive the proceeds of an Ascot race day. The day usually offered is one the race organisers know will not conventionally attract a large attendance; the understanding is that the charity will bring in additional punters, and benefit as a result. However, careful analysis of previous events shows that they are complicated to organise and raise relatively small sums. The charity decides to have an associated fundraising dinner, a product it is well used to organising.

Analysis and planning

The dinner will be putting forward all three basic products – an idea product ('come to the dinner and you will be helping the charity's beneficiaries through your expenditure'); a service product ('pay for the

cont.

12

CASE EXAMPLE: A FUNDRAISING EVENT continued

ticket and come along and have a wonderful meal in good company');
and a physical product ('come along and bid for items in the auction
which will go at very keen prices'). Delivering three such different
products at once is an unusual challenge for a commercial marketer.
Clearly a credible idea product (the charity's purpose) is an underlying
essential. The service product is essential to attract people and make a
modest amount of money. The physical product, the auction, is crucial,
because this is where the majority of money will be raised. In the
charity auction, the goods are valuable, but donated, and the auction
audience is prepared to bid amounts only a little below, and sometimes
considerably above, market value.

Target market

There are, broadly speaking, two target markets: the volunteer
organisers of the dinner, who come from the leadership of the racing
fraternity; and the people attending the dinner, especially those who
can be expected to bid for the expensive items.

   The voluntary organising committee membership is attracted by a
conventional method of persuading a leading aristocrat, well known in
the racing fraternity, to chair the committee. Organising committee
members and/or their partners are leading race horse owners, who
enjoy each other's company, gain pleasure from contributing to an
important charity and enjoy the more intimate social preserves of the
chair. They offer the charity advice on a venue that will be attractive to
their peers and what prices to expect at the auction. They also bring in
the donated auction items and, equally importantly, sell the tickets. (It
is not unusual for charities to organise first-class special events but be
unable to attract sufficient numbers of people.)

Products

The service product of the dinner is fairly straightforward, and is not
detailed here other than to say that the three remaining elements of the
marketing mix, *pricing*, communication (*promotion*) and distribution
(*place*), have to be effectively worked out in relation to the diners'
anticipated needs and desires. However, as this is a service product, a
fifth element of the marketing mix, namely *people*, is crucial. Services
in general, and fundraising services in particular, only work effectively

cont.

CASE EXAMPLE: A FUNDRAISING EVENT continued

when the participants have a natural affinity. They effectively help to create the product through their approach, attitude and behaviour.

The physical products of the event, the auction items, are arguably the most crucial in fundraising terms. The key items to be auctioned, it is decided, are nominations (where the owner of a thoroughbred stallion allows one relatively short opportunity for the purchaser's mare to be impregnated). The organising committee, through its contacts, gains offers of four nominations, two to be auctioned at £60,000 and two at £40,000, the prices related to the quality of stallions on offer.

Consumers

The next vital ingredient for marketing success is to attract sufficient numbers of diners who would be motivated to bid for the nominations. So, within the target market of diners in general, there is an absolutely crucial submarket of people prepared to bid up to £60,000 for a nomination. Once again the organising committee, with its contacts, come up trumps. However, a *carefully formulated programme* comes in again because a successful auction requires more than a rich, motivated audience and a good product: it requires a professional auctioneer, and a master of ceremonies to create the right kind of atmosphere. The committee achieved this through their contacts in Sotheby's and Christie's, and they persuaded one of the leading television racing commentators to speak.

What could have been a fairly mediocre dinner, raising very little money, but requiring a lot of organisational effort, was transformed into a prestigious event that raised nearly £400,000. This was achieved due to careful analysis of previous Ascot race days, and careful planning, implementation and control (right down to making sure that the auction purchasers wrote out a cheque on the same evening), with three carefully formulated product offerings. The target markets were carefully subdivided and the 'needs and desires' of each group identified and met. In addition to the standard four 'Ps' of product, price, promotion and place, the fifth one of 'people' was added because of the service nature of the event.

CASE EXAMPLE: AN ARTISTS' PRESSURE GROUP CAMPAIGN

Introduction

The Arts Council was established primarily to subsidise the performing arts so that art in all its various forms could be available to a wide cross-section of people. This meant that the bulk of the financial subsidies did, and still do, go to those responsible for the performing arts (theatres, galleries, orchestras) rather than to the artists who create the original work (painters, composers, playwrights).

A group of artists had got together to try to persuade the Arts Council to amend its policy, and provide more financial help and encouragement to individual creative artists who, they argued, were creating the arts of the future. Informal discussions had largely failed, on two counts. First, the Arts Council argued that it was the responsibility of performing organisations to encourage and put on the work of new artists, and second, the Council did not really 'rate' new, largely unknown artists, who were not part of their central remit. The campaign had relied on informal contacts between unequal partners (the Council and the unknown artists), the goodwill of the Council (which had run out, regarding the unknown artists as somewhat 'potty' and self-seeking), and a somewhat superficial analysis of the patterns of Arts Council expenditure on individual artists (which the Council had dismissed as spurious).

The leading artist involved, David Castillejo, decided he needed more broadly based help with the campaign. He drew together an organising group consisting of an established and respected composer, the Dean of the Royal College of Art, a young practising painter who also happened to be a member of the House of Lords, and a marketing expert. Together they set up a formal pressure group, which they called Artists Now.

Analysing and planning

Given that negotiations with the Arts Council had effectively broken down and, in the eyes of the Arts Council, the arguments had been disproved, it was necessary to go back to the drawing board. The Arts Council's key argument was that the performing organisations it funded would be satisfactorily supporting living creative artists of today and that Castillejo's argument that less than 0.5 per cent of the Council's expenditure went directly to artists was misleading.

cont.

CASE EXAMPLE: AN ARTISTS' PRESSURE GROUP CAMPAIGN continued

Offerings

The pressure group therefore decided that its offering or *idea product* should be two-fold: first, an analysis of how the major recipients of Arts Council funds supported living artists; and second, the development of a number of proposals as to how money and support might be devoted to living creative artists. There followed a very careful programme of analysis using the national press whereby the performances and annual reports of all the major Council-subsidised companies (orchestras, theatres, galleries) were analysed to establish what percentages of performances and exhibitions involved the work of living and dead artists respectively (painters, composers, writers). This gave the pressure group access to information not available to the Arts Council. It established that the figure of Council financial support going to living artists only rose from 0.5 per cent to less than 2 per cent of total Arts Council expenditure. Further, the group developed a range of ideas as to how budding individual creative artists could be helped with their careers, for example through playwrights or composers being given access to performance possibilities.

Programme

So the pressure group now had a *carefully formulated programme*, but it still had no way of getting into serious negotiations with the Arts Council over the evidence and the proposals. Rather than go back into private discussions with the Arts Council, which gave the Council all the cards, it was decided to launch the report via the media, and so put the debate into the public domain. This, it was argued, would establish a more equal partnership, and would force the Arts Council to have to respond publicly. Artists Now felt it had an 'offering' which was effectively *priced* and was capable of *communicating* and *distributing* to the target market.

The report, 'Patronage of the Creative Artist', was launched with a suitable press release, embargoed for midnight on a Sunday, and distributed well in advance. The report got coverage in every serious national newspaper, on Radio Four's 'Today' programme and on five other national radio programmes, two of them about the arts.

cont.

CASE EXAMPLE: AN ARTISTS' PRESSURE GROUP CAMPAIGN continued

Results

In so far as the *target market* was other creative artists, the campaign was very successful and gained a lot of support through the national publicity. However, the key target market was the Arts Council and its administrators, and such a public method of negotiation, while it was effective at *informing* the Council, was not designed to *motivate*. So the establishment made one or two relatively minor concessions, as it always does when under some public pressure, but the campaign of 'hearts and minds' was lost. It is also interesting to note that these concessions were largely achieved by what commercial marketers would call *'personal' selling*. In short, the concessions were achieved by subsequent private discussions, not between the public leadership of Artists Now and the Arts Council, but through the personal promotion of the more established members of Artists Now, the Dean of the Royal College of Art and the established composer.

Conclusion

I hope these examples have made Kotler's definition more concrete and have given some small taste as to how a marketing approach can be a helpful analytical and implementation tool for the full range of charity activity.

The next chapter goes to the source of marketing, the commercial world, prior to Chapter 3, which proposes a philosophy and techniques, albeit in an adapted form, for the charity sector.

2   Classical marketing

Introduction

This chapter describes the classical marketing models as applied to:
- physical goods;
- services (to a lesser extent);
- and (as we shall see later) ideas.

This is a basic description of the tools of marketing, and will be familiar to business students and others acquainted with commercial marketing.

It might seem logical to start with the definition, but here we hit a problem: there are so many! Crosier (1975) reviewed over fifty definitions, which he classified into three major groups: those that regard marketing as a 'process'; those that see it as a 'concept or philosophy of business'; and those that regard it as an 'orientation'.

Kotler's definition, given in the previous chapter (see page 4), is probably the most useful and comprehensive to apply in the charity world, and arguing for and against different commercial definitions is outside the purpose of this book. In essence, marketing is producing and delivering goods, services and ideas from a consumer rather than a production standpoint.

Graphical representations of marketing abound in the literature. Inevitably, they are somewhat crude and do not take account of all the intricacies of real life. However, they do give us a clear framework.

Figure 2.1 (opposite) represents the main elements of the core of marketing. Around this core, which tends to concentrate on individual products in particular customer groups, there are several other concepts and realities that affect it, including the impact of the changing social, political, technical and economic environment.

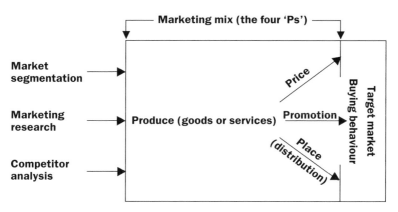

Figure 2.1 Classical core marketing model

Before looking at the different elements of the marketing core, an example of how they fit together and interact might be useful.

CASE EXAMPLE: UP-MARKET CREDIT CARD

Let us take an example of an up-market credit card. In terms of marketing jargon, it is a *product* even though the credit card is probably 90 per cent a service and only 10 per cent a physical good. It is physical in that you have a plastic card that performs rather practical miracles inside shops, hotels, etc, but essentially it is a financial service.

The marketing manager of this up-market credit card has *segmented* her market (all adults) by socio-economic groups. Her *target market* is in the two upper socio-economic groups – those with the highest incomes. *Marketing research* among a representative sample of the target markets has shown a significant correlation between certain attitudes towards the credit card and the likelihood of people taking it up. Put crudely, possession of the credit card is a sign of status.

The marketing manager has done a *competitive analysis* of other cards on the market, which has helped her to undertake a fairly sophisticated SWOT analysis (strengths, weaknesses, opportunities and threats) of her own product. This has been the basis of a review of the marketing mix (the term commonly used to describe the individual elements of product, price, promotion and place). She has identified that one of the USPs (unique selling propositions) of her card is its high status. Unfortunately, in terms of expanding sales, the card is only

cont.

CASE EXAMPLE: UP-MARKET CREDIT CARD continued

available to account holders at a small, up-market banking chain. (The fourth 'P' – place – is quite a difficult term to grasp. Many writers on marketing turn 'place' into 'distribution' – how the product is distributed.) She decides there is a major opportunity to expand sales if the card is made available to people who do not have ordinary accounts at the bank. However, she wants to maintain the distinctive *differentiation* of her product (its high status) and decides therefore to charge a much higher entry fee (*price*) for non-account holders than for account holders. In order to *promote* this product's enhancement she purchases a number of names from up-market mailing lists and carries out a discrete test market direct mail campaign.

I chose the above example partly because it will help us to lay out what the Americans call our emotional baggage. Marketing a high-cost status symbol to rich snobs is hardly likely to appeal to would-be voluntary sector marketers but, as we saw in Chapter 1, marketing is value-neutral. It can be used for good or ill. It can be used for what most readers of this book would regard as high-priority activity, such as ensuring that appropriate and effective overseas aid is engendered and delivered; or it can be used for what some people might regard as low-priority activity, such as marketing top-of-the-range credit cards. As far as the voluntary sector is concerned, what matters is that it works and helps us to achieve our objective, which is to meet need.

Having taken the credit card as an example of the use of the key tools for marketing, the remainder of this chapter runs through each of the core marketing elements. It is difficult to know where to start because the different elements interact and change and modify as they integrate. However, given our subject, the market and how we can segment it is as logical a place to start as any.

Market segmentation

While the basis of marketing is to produce products your customers need and want, most companies or organisations are not starting from scratch – they already have a range of products and services. Therefore the technique of dividing, or segmenting, the potential market into groups of people to see whether they are more or less likely to buy the existing or proposed product was developed. Credit for the origination of this idea and technique of market segmentation is attributed to Pigou (1932, chs VIII, XI and XII) and Chamberlin (1938).

The key to successful market segmentation is to divide the market up according to attributes that are likely to make sense in terms of the product's attractiveness, but at the same time to divide it up in such a way that it is possible to reach the segment with your product. In other words, you may discover a segment of the market panting to buy your product, but if you have no physical way of reaching it, then it is all rather academic. For example, when fabric conditioners first came on the market, research showed that the most likely purchasers were flexible innovators. But, given that there was no mass circulation/mass audience medium reaching this group, the soap companies had to hit housewives with expensive TV advertisements in order to reach the target purchasers and, as a consequence, the brands had to be repositioned.

Methods

Ways of segmenting the market have become increasingly sophisticated. This is in part because of increased data collection, and in part because of the sophisticated cross-tabulations that can now be done quickly and easily by computer. The traditional bases for segmentation are:

- geographic (region, density, climate);
- demographic (age, sex, family size, income, occupation, social class);
- psychographic (lifestyle, personality);
- behaviouristic (behaviours exhibited towards the product – purchasing rate, usage rate, particular benefits sought).

With new census data and more sophisticated computer programs combining the first two categories, geodemographics has made a big impact. Relationship segmentation is now also important and useful (especially in fundraising), riding on the back of relationship marketing.

Marketing research

Segmentation and marketing research are symbiotic. If we identify a market segment which is a likely, valuable purchasing source, then we need to do research among actual and potential consumers to find out more. Similarly, research on the product among consumers and how they use or do not use it, and how they like or do not like it, will help us greatly with effective market segmentation. Such research should at least be exploratory and, at best, identify correlations (such as the fact that credit cards tend to be purchased by upper socio-economic males aged 35-45 years); or even better, go further and reveal *why* they purchase.

Marketing managers new to the job quite often assume that very little consumer information is available and can easily rush into proposals for marketing research. However, this is the second stage. The first stage is to find out what is known already, and here the technique used is desk research, such as what sales records tell us about seasonality, average volume of sales, frequency and loyalty of purchaser; whether customer records reveal sex, age and geographic representation. Once this information has been gathered, you are in a position to decide what else is needed.

In terms of a framework of questions, Blyth (1989) gives a useful *aide-mémoire*:

1 Who are you?
2 What do you buy?
3 How much do you buy?
4 What do you pay?
5 Where do you buy it?
6 When did you buy it?
7 What else could you have bought?
8 Why?

He then argues that from this list you can infer answers to the following:

9 What will you buy next?
10 What if (for example) price/advertising/distribution/packaging/product specifications are changed?

Five steps of marketing

Dibb *et al.* (2001, p. 172) describe the five steps of the marketing research process as follows:

1 Defining and locating problems.
2 Developing hypotheses.
3 Collecting data.
4 Analysing and interpreting research findings.
5 Reporting research findings.

Data can be gathered in a variety of ways. Although seldom acknowledged, reinterpretation of personal experience is frequently used. More objectively, *desk* marketing research, as mentioned above, is a crucial starting point. *Qualitative* marketing research, sensitively done, can be crucial. Here we gain insights into the user group in some depth, but we cannot be sure how widely applicable these conclusions and insights might be. Such research normally takes the form of in-depth interviews with individual or groups of potential or actual customers. *Quantitative* market research is by far the most expensive but can be incredibly effective, provided that a representative sample can be drawn or later constructed. As the name implies, one can begin to quantify some of the hypotheses about a product and the reasons for its success or failure and, more importantly, hypotheses about how sales can be improved.

Competitor analysis

Even in the commercial world there is a tendency for marketing managers to concentrate too much on their own product and fail to recognise competitors' impact on sales. Competitor analysis tends to go wider than core marketing issues. Certainly competitors have to be evaluated according to marketing issues such as market share, distribution strengths, geographic coverage, price competitiveness and sales competitiveness. However, a good competitor analysis will also look at competitors' manufacturing capacity, their financial position and their organisational strengths or weaknesses.

Strategy

The most widely quoted expert on competitive strategy is Porter (1985). He created a model, which is shown in Figure 2.2.

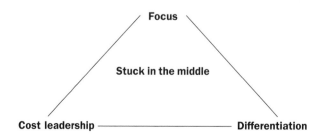

Figure 2.2

Porter argued that the successful product needs to be close to an apex, rather than 'stuck in the middle'.

- *Differentiation* means having a product that is clearly differentiated from others in the market and is seen to have real advantages. Bird's Eye fish fingers are set apart from the competition by the avuncular Captain Bird's Eye who reassures consumers that eating Bird's Eye fish fingers is wholesome and good fun.
- *Cost leadership* may mean low price, but not necessarily. It may mean that the product or product range is so dominant in the market-place that it sets the guideline price and achieves economies of scale to allow the company to plough large profits back into new product development and launch. IBM was a classic example of this in the 1980s.
- *Focus* is an approach to be adopted by smaller companies in the market that do not have the capacity to become market leaders. Essentially, a focus strategy is to concentrate on providing a product to a well-defined group of customers with a well-defined need. For example, Cussons Imperial Leather soap has competed successfully against bigger brands, albeit on a smaller scale, for decades. It has a focus or niche, for purchasers aspiring to an up-market toilet soap that reassures the purchaser and gives a coded message to visitors. This particular competitive strategy assumes some importance for voluntary sector organisations, as we will see later in this book.

Product

The term 'marketing mix' was introduced in Chapter 1 and its crucial contribution is shown in Figure 2.1. It is attributed to Borden (1964, pp. 2–7) and was popularised by McCarthy (1981, pp. 42–3) into the four 'Ps' of product, price, promotion and place. Doyle (2003) reframes McCarthy's key components of product as:

- brand;
- quality;
- design;
- features;
- variety;
- packaging;

- service and support;
- guarantees.

Within certain limits all these attributes are clearly variable. It is the marketing manager's job to adjust these features to take account of the needs and wants of the target market, bearing in mind marketing research findings and what the competitors are doing. In marketing language, product is a generic term covering *physical goods* (soap powder, televisions, cars) and *services* (fast-food restaurants, hotels, air travel). Later we shall see that in the voluntary sector the third category of product, namely *ideas*, assumes a far greater importance than in the commercial sector.

Goods

Although the term 'product' is generic, it is no coincidence that in a lay person's mind it is equated with physical goods. Companies selling fast-moving consumer goods (FMCGs), such as frozen foods, toiletries and soap powders, were arguably first into the commercial marketing field and still have a dominant position in it. Although it is beginning to change, the vast majority of marketing books have either an explicit or implicit focus on the marketing of physical goods. However, because the service sector is growing fast and is becoming dominant, the situation is changing under the leadership of services marketers such as Berry, Bitner, Booms, Crosby, Gronroos, Gummeson, Lovelock, Parasuraman, Shostack, Stephens and Zeithaml (listed in the references). Services can be further split into two; namely non-professional services (such as fast-food restaurant chains, hotel groups, financial services) and professional services (such as architectural and law firms). Attention to this latter area is fairly new, and is in part prompted by deregulation (for example, law firms can now advertise). It is useful to note the lack of popularity of marketing terms in the professional services area, a relevant point for the voluntary sector. Indeed A. Wilson (1984) managed to write a book on marketing for professional practices where, in three pages of contents, the word 'marketing' is hardly mentioned.

Services

Building on earlier work, Zeithaml *et al.* (1985 and 2006) and Zeithaml and Bitner (2003) summarised a number of characteristics that distinguish services from goods:

- intangibility – it is often not possible to experience services (through taste, feel, sight) before they are purchased;
- inseparability – services often cannot be separated from the person or the seller;
- heterogeneity – it is often difficult to achieve standardisation of output in services;
- perishability – services cannot be stored (a spare room in a hotel for one week represents capacity loss forever).

All these service characteristics create marketing challenges needing solutions that differ, in the main, from those applied to physical goods. For example, there has to be a greater focus on benefits from the service; service reputation is absolutely critical; personnel need careful selection and training; standards need to be monitored regularly and frequently.

Price

Doyle (2003) reframes McCarthy's elements within price as follows:

- list price;
- discount;
- trade margins;
- payment terms;
- trade-ins.

Baker (1991 and 2003) quotes several studies which indicate that pricing is only a middle-order critical factor in the success of a product. However, its ranking may well vary in relation to macro-economic factors (in recession, price will be more critical) and a product's life cycle. For example, a highly innovative new product with major advantages over competitors is likely to command a premium price in its early stages. As volume builds (and costs come down) and other copycat products come on the market, its price is likely to drop – although packaging and features may need to change in order to avoid antagonising earlier purchasers. Pricing of video cameras and personal computers over the last twenty years has exhibited this life cycle phenomenon.

Of the elements in the marketing mix, price is usually the most flexible tool of intervention, with more immediate impact than other elements. Price comparison between similar products is one of the most immediate and absolute comparisons that the potential customer can apply to a buying decision. A change in price is likely to have an immediate impact. However, a price change also has a very major impact on profitability. Simon (1989) gives six reasons for price being an important element in the marketing mix:

1 Price elasticity is twenty times greater than advertising elasticity (a 1 per cent price change has a sales effect twenty times as big as a 1 per cent change in advertising expenditure).
2 The sales effect of a price change is often immediate, and so measurable, while changes in other mix variables are usually lagged and difficult to quantify.
3 Price changes are easy to effect compared with other mix variables.
4 Competitors react more quickly to price changes.
5 Price does not require an initially negative cash flow, unlike other marketing expenditures such as advertising, which also have a lagged impact.
6 Price and the product are the only two mix elements that feature significantly in strategic planning concepts.

Price is one of the most difficult conceptual and practical elements of the marketing mix when it comes to not-for-profit marketing. Blois (1987 and 2003) argues that Borden (1964) stressed that his concept of the marketing mix was a flexible one and therefore it is quite possible to think of a marketing mix with no 'P' for price. However, we shall discuss this later.

Promotion

The elements within promotion are sometimes called the promotional mix, namely:

- advertising;
- personal selling;
- sales promotion;
- public relations.

Advertising is probably the best-known element, given that we all experience it daily. Dibb *et al.* (1991 and 2001) describe advertising as a 'paid form of non-personal communication about an organisation and its products that is transmitted to a target audience through a mass medium such as television, radio, newspapers, magazines, direct mail, public transport, outdoor displays, or catalogues'. Advertising is highly flexible in its application, in that broadly based mass markets as well as tightly targeted audiences can be addressed. It is also attractive because the message can be delivered exactly as the promoter wishes, which is not the case with, for example, public relations.

Personal selling is, as its name implies, a direct contact with the potential purchaser and can be 'in person' or over the telephone. It is more expensive per customer contact than advertising, but is usually more effective.

Sales promotion, say Dibb *et al.* (1991, p. 404, and 2001) is 'an activity or material that acts as a direct inducement, offering added value, or incentive for the product, to resellers, sales persons or consumers'. In FMCGs this is most commonly recognised as 'money off' for supposed 'good value' offers, provided that so many coupons or package tops are sent with the order for the offer. Promotion is a tactical weapon in the selling process to encourage either the consumer to increase consumption temporarily or indeed the retailer to stock more heavily. Over-promoting a product can often give the impression of desperation and may encourage people to think that the product has insufficient inner value.

Public relations uses many of the media employed by advertising – television, radio, newspapers or word of mouth – through editorial channels. Unlike advertising, it is 'free' in that space is not paid for. However, the promoter has far less control over an accurate interpretation of the message. Obviously news reporters want to put their own angle on the story, and in many cases the story is not covered at all. The kind of message that the product promoter wishes to put across is seldom of great interest to the editor.

Place

The term 'place' is used in order to maintain the consistency of the widely used four 'Ps'. However, I find it one of the least descriptive headings in the marketing mix, and on occasions just plain confusing. The term 'distribution' rather than 'place' is often used and is probably easier to understand.

Doyle (2003) reframes McCarthy's list of elements of place as follows:

- distribution channels;
- coverage;
- assortments;
- location;
- inventory (stock);
- transport.

In essence, place is meant to identify how we are going to get the product from wherever it is being manufactured or constructed (in the case of services) to the end consumer. Traditionally in the area of FMCG marketing it has been the Cinderella element of the mix – handled by the operations side of the business and associated with warehouses and diesel fumes rather than the glamour of advertising agencies.

However, if place (distribution) is ignored for too long, or if it is not thought through carefully at the beginning of a new product launch, the results are disastrous – the product does not reach the customer. Distribution is particularly challenging for small and medium-size companies with growing products. At one time, trying to find a retailer who sold Teasmaids was like looking for a needle in a haystack.

When we look at the application of marketing in the voluntary sector, it will be seen that lack of attention to place (distribution) in the marketing mix is often the cause of products (goods/services/ideas) not reaching their target market.

Consumer buying behaviour

The majority of commercial marketing texts (including Dibb *et al.* 1991 and 2001) describe the buying decision-making process as a flow diagram as shown in figure 2.3 (overleaf).

It is widely acknowledged that the process is much more complicated than this simple model would suggest, with greater or less concentration on each of the stages, and complicated loop-backs to an earlier part of the process. However, Foxall (1987 and 2003) reports that while consumers *claim* to like more rather than less information, they do not use it extensively and do not necessarily make more rational decisions. In particular, he reports that even when relatively expensive, infrequently purchased consumer durables are bought, customers are often quite cavalier in their purchasing behaviour. For example, when purchasing an expensive DVD recorder they often only visit one retail outlet and

Problem recognition

Information search

Evaluation of alternatives

Choice/purchase

Post-purchase evaluation

Figure 2.3

consider only one brand, using price and their own and the shop staff's view of the reputation of suppliers in order to make a purchase. The description, translated into a social marketing context, is a familiar one. Donors often contribute on a less than rational basis. Clients, often under real pressure, take up the first service they come across.

Factors

Personal experience immediately suggests that there is a myriad factors that affect buying decisions. Marketing authors such as Dibb *et al.* (1991 and 2003) have attempted to group these into personal, psychological and social factors. Baker (1991 and 2003) groups them into psychological and social influences. Of all the areas of commercial marketing, I find the literature on consumer buying decisions the least satisfactory. At its most basic, it seems to be over-dominated by lists of factors that *might* influence behaviour, but it is difficult to predict which factors will be dominant and what the interaction between them will be. A typical list of factors affecting the buying decisions includes culture, social class, other demographic factors (such as age, sex, race, income, family life cycle and occupation), reference groups and lifestyle. There are also psychological influences such as perception, motivation, attitudes and personality (see Hibbert and Horne 1996).

Role of the manufacturer/service deliverer

The majority of the basic marketing texts pay very little attention to the interaction between marketing and manufacturing, and not much more to the interaction of marketing and service construction/delivery. In my experience one of the hardest parts of marketing in the FMCG field is trying to stop the manufacturing/production side of the business adding 'knobs' to the product that one feels are not wanted by the customer, and, much more frequently, trying to persuade the manufacturer/producer to add those 'knobs' that the manufacturing arm feels are not necessary/too expensive/too difficult.

In the field of services marketing the relationship with the person running the service (such as the hotel manager) is even more critical because the service is constructed and marketed simultaneously. Introducing or maintaining a marketing approach in this situation is often extremely difficult. Once again, we shall return to this subject in relation to the voluntary sector.

Conclusion

Marketing dominates the field of fast-moving consumer goods and there is a mass of literature to support the would-be marketer in this area. Marketing is now established in the field of services and is becoming dominant in certain sectors, such as mass delivery services (for example fast-food chains). However there is much less literature available to support the services marketer. Relationship marketing (see Chapter 11), has sprung to prominence and is particularly useful to our sector.

For voluntary sector personnel, there are a number of basic, very clear commercial marketing texts that elaborate the field (these include Dibb *et al.* 2001, Kotler *et al.* 2002, Baker 2003, and Zeithaml *et al.* 2006).

The rest of this book looks at marketing when applied to the charity world, to help us in our prime task of meeting broadly social needs. Although it seems at first sight unlikely, the philosophy and practice of commercial marketing, suitably adapted, can help us to become more effective in our work of identifying and meeting need.

Key points

Commercial marketing theory and practice involves the interaction and integration of a number of core elements:

- **Segmentation** – dividing up the market according to geographic, demographic, psychographic, behaviouristic or other criteria in order to understand and assess the likely demand for the product.

- **Marketing research** – best carried out in stages, first collecting data on what is already known, in order to establish what further information is required – looks especially at consumer buying behaviour.
- **Competitor analysis** – evaluating the impact of competitors, including assessing market share and strengths and weaknesses (for example in distribution, pricing, geographic coverage and manufacturing capacity).
- **Marketing mix** – the four Ps: product (includes goods, services and ideas), price, promotion (covers advertising, personal selling, sales promotion and public relations) and place.

3 Fundamentals of a charity marketing approach

Who are we here for?

At its most straightforward, we are here to help the beneficiaries explicitly or implicitly identified in our charitable purposes. As a first level of analysis that is quite useful: the Royal National Institute for Deaf People (RNID) was established to provide services for deaf people; Shelter, for homeless people; Age Concern Southwark, for older people in Southwark, and so on.

Primary purpose

However, is the primary purpose to focus on today's beneficiaries or on future generations? For example, Cancer Research UK operates largely to find a cure for cancer: this means helping future generations rather than present one and, technically, not helping cancer patients at all because the discovered cure will prevent cancer. How does the Royal Society for the Protection of Birds (RSPB) achieve a balance between its activities to save existing birds (for example through oil clean-up operations) and activities to reduce pollution and guarantee future bird stocks? There are many charities where the end beneficiaries are not clearly spelt out. Is an arts charity, set up to promote modern music, primarily aiming to support contemporary composers producing modern music or is it aimed at audiences who like modern music?

Layers of complexity

Even where the end beneficiaries appear to be very clearly identified, such as with the RNID, there are additional layers of complexity. First, there is the balance, as described above, between the interests of today's deaf people (services) and preventing deafness in the future (prevention research). Second, how do you define deafness? Does the charity only help people who are totally deaf, or does it encompass people who 'only' have a hearing loss? If it does help people who have hearing problems, where is the cut-off point, and is this cut-off point measured medically (say, 60 per cent hearing loss) or functionally (someone who is profoundly deaf may cope quite well by being very able at lip reading, whereas someone with a comparatively minor hearing loss may not be able to cope at all socially or economically)?

Then, there are the myriad charities that have gained charitable status under the legal categories of education or religion. Charities in these categories (unlike the relief of poverty) allow an enormous flexibility in deciding a charity's customer group.

Thus it is clear that deciding who a charity's 'customers' are is absolutely crucial if the organisation is to have clarity of purpose, work effectively, stay within the legal limits of its 'purposes', decide how to apply its resources and, most important of all, provide effective help in the area of need.

Customers

Charities must interact with, and meet the needs and wants of a wide variety of groups. These typically include beneficiaries, funders, trustees and the Charity Commission. What inclusive term can we use? Drucker (1990, p. 83) calls them constituencies. Gwin (1991, p. 43) calls them constituent groups. Kay (1993) calls them stakeholders. Despite being politically fashionable it does not seem realistic to claim that beneficiaries have a 'stake' to the extent that an individual beneficiary can exert any rights arising out of that stake; similarly with individual donors, unless they are major donors. In terms of stakeholder theory, beneficiaries and donors may have legitimacy but they seldom have power. Representatives of these groups may have both legitimacy and power and therefore qualify as stakeholders. The term constituency (but not constituent group) conveys appropriate meaning. However, I prefer 'customer' because it brings home the importance of recognising that each of the disparate customer groups of beneficiaries, funders, trustees, staff and regulators have needs and wants which need to be met or at least accommodated. But terminology should not dominate the important business of meeting needs and wishes, and those who are wedded to the term 'stakeholder', broadly defined, can read 'stakeholder' each time this book uses 'customer'.

Beneficiaries

While the individual charity's target groups might be clearly specified, for example older people with a hearing loss, charity marketing has to have some terms that allow general discussion. Commercial marketing often uses the term 'consumer', but this does not always sit easily in the charity world. Social welfare charities often talk of clients. Educational charities talk of students. In health care charities it is normally patients. Arts charities talk of audiences or patrons. An environmental charity might refer to them as members. A local charity might use the term 'residents' or 'Londoners'.

So what generic term can we use to cover those who benefit from a charity's fundamental aims? Rados (1981, p. 14) uses the term 'clients'. While this can work well with social welfare charities, it does not sit comfortably with educational, environmental and religious charities. 'Users' as a term is attractive but does not include a major segment of charity customers who benefit from but do not use a charity's product. This is particularly true of pressure group activity on behalf of large numbers of beneficiaries – Age Concern may, through its campaigning, achieve a benefit for many more older people than actually use its services or even have any contact with it.

The term I prefer is 'beneficiaries', deriving from the word 'benefit'. This can be used generically to cover a wide range of people such as clients, patients, students, audiences and members. It can also accommodate future generations of customers as well as those who do not actually 'use' or 'consume' but do benefit. Applying a marketing approach to products for not-for-profit beneficiaries is crucial, but is used much less than in the fields of general fundraising and public relations (Bruce 1994; Ali 2001; Pyne and Robertson 1997; Hankinson 2000).

Supporters

Support comes from individuals, groups or organisations in the form of money, gifts in kind or (unpaid) professional, skilled or unskilled time. While there can often be considerable overlap between charities' beneficiaries and supporters (resource providers), there are also many occasions when they are separate, with different needs and wants, and in charity marketing terms must be identified separately. The most obvious group of supporters are *donors*, who might be individuals, companies, trusts or government departments. But there are also *volunteer fundraisers* (such as volunteers who place and collect charity collecting boxes, or who organise coffee mornings or jumble sales) and *voluntary service workers* (such as voluntary visitors to a charity's residential home; volunteers who repair talking book machines in blind people's homes; volunteers in playgroups). Another supporter group, quite often ignored, is what I would call *advocates*. These are people relatively unconnected with the charity who voluntarily speak up on its behalf and for its cause. For example, an advocate may be an individual (who may or may not be a donor or voluntary service worker) who writes to the local MP on a particular issue directly or indirectly at the behest of the charity; or, less formally, it may be the woman in the sub post office putting money in a collecting box for NSPCC and saying to a friend 'I always support NSPCC because it does such good work with children'. Lastly there are the *purchasers*, who will typically be statutory authorities. The term *supporters* covers those who back the charity – through donations, voluntary fundraising, voluntary service, advocacy or purchasing on behalf of a third party.

Regulators

External *regulators* can usefully be regarded as a separate target group, albeit only addressed infrequently. Charity services may be inspected by local authority departments (such as education or social services), the Charity Commission or the Home Office. Less formal regulation comes through groups such as the National Council for Voluntary Organisations. Even local communities can be informal regulators, for example, residents opposing the building of a home for disabled people in 'their' street.

Stakeholders

The last target group of people crucial to a charity marketing approach, especially where the charity is providing services, is *stakeholders*, who include trustees, representatives of beneficiaries and staff. Commercial service marketers always emphasise the importance of staff in the marketing mix. Indeed, two of the leading service marketing writers, Berry and Parasuraman (1991), devote a whole chapter in their book on service marketing, 'Marketing to Employees' (pp. 157–72). For the term to be meaningful, stakeholders are those who have legitimacy and power (Mitchell *et al.* 1997) over the running of the charity. So beneficiaries are not stakeholders in any legal or realistic sense, but *representatives* of beneficiaries, recognised by the charity, are. However, stakeholder theorists would include (beneficiary) customers as stakeholders.

So, for a discussion of marketing in charities, it is useful to divide customers into *beneficiaries*, *supporters*, *regulators* and *stakeholders*. Each of these four groups will have subgroups that will need to be specified; examples are given in Table 3.1 (overleaf).

Intermediaries

Intermediaries – people not directly connected to the charity who can improve both beneficiaries' benefits and the resources gained from supporters – are crucial to charity marketing. In the beneficiary field of activity, intermediaries have been the subject of increasing attention. Pressure group work is a prime example, where many charities spend considerable energy in trying to persuade intermediaries such as policy-makers to make decisions that will help their beneficiaries (such as improving social security for single parents). As well as pressure group work, increasing numbers of charities (for example Age Concern, Barnardo's, RSPB and RNIB) have set up (indirect) services aimed at influencing other providers (intermediaries) to the charities' beneficiary groups. These providers might be statutory services such as local authorities, or commercial companies such as retailers and public utilities. For example, RNIB runs advisory, training and consultancy services aimed at NHS ophthalmology services, social services departments, local education authorities, public utilities and commercial companies in order to advise these services on how they can better serve the needs of blind and partially sighted people. An example of intermediaries in the supporter field would be chief executives of commercial companies where a charity was trying to gain access to significant payroll giving opportunities from a company's workforce.

Table 3.1 Voluntary organisation customer groups with examples

Beneficiaries	Supporters	Stakeholders	Regulators
Clients	Donors	Staff	Charity Commission
Students	Volunteer fund-raisers	Representatives of beneficiaries	Local authorities (e.g. inspection of homes, schools)
Patients	Voluntary service workers	Committee members	Local community
Users	Advocates		
Purchasers	Purchasers		
Local public			
Members			
Audience			
Patrons			
Beneficiary intermediaries	**Supporter intermediaries**	**Stakeholder intermediaries**	**Regulator intermediaries**
Statutory providers	Religious leaders	Staff managers	MPs
Statutory purchasers	Company chief executives	Union representatives	Home Office
Commercial providers	School head teachers	Committee leaders	Local councils
Family purchasers			
Other voluntary organisation providers			
Policy-makers			
Decision-makers			

Here the chief executive would be persuaded to encourage the staff publicly to make monthly donations out of their pay packet.

So it can be seen that charities have wide-ranging target markets. Multiple constituencies, says Drucker (1990, p. 83) make managing a charity very difficult. This is a distinguishing feature between charities and businesses, which have fewer constituencies. Similarities between businesses and charities are reviewed by Leat (1993).

Customer take-up behaviour

Commercial marketing tends to use the term 'customer buying behaviour', but for the charity sector I use the term 'customer take-up behaviour'. Many transactions in the not-for-profit sector, such as recruiting volunteers or free services to clients, cannot easily be described as 'buying'. Even where money changes hands, buying does not seem an apt description. For example, if charity beneficiaries buy goods or services, they are often at non-market, or heavily subsidised rates. Also, while I argue that a supporter is 'buying' an idea, it still seems a far cry from a comparable commercial purchase.

Because charities have such a bewildering variety of customers, take-up behaviour in the marketing process is extremely complicated. This complexity is all the more difficult to handle because there are disagreements among theorists in this area in commercial marketing. So how do we approach this complexity?

Social and psychological influences

All the social and psychological factors that influence commercial buying decisions (mentioned in Chapter 2) are relevant in the charity marketing setting, but unfortunately are probably even less understood in terms of their practical impact on take-up behaviour. In charity marketing we need to spend a lot more time understanding customers' psychological interaction with our goods, services and ideas, their motivations for taking them up or not, the impact of their personality, and their attitudes. Also, while the social factors affecting take-up are quite crude – culture, social class, reference groups and the whole gamut of socio-demography – they are also very important. If the voluntary sector does not get better at taking account of these factors, charities in particular will retain too much of their Victorian heritage of forcing themselves onto relatively small minorities, while having very little contact with the majority of their target groups – potential beneficiaries and supporters.

However, charities quite often have one or more factors of the beneficiary transaction process defined for them because of their legal purposes. For example, the key attributes of beneficiaries of Marie Curie Cancer Care, Age Concern and a charity housing advice centre are fairly easily defined. Subfactors associated with the key attributes, such as the time since onset of cancer and its location and spread; numbers and needs of older people; and homeless versus poorly housed people, are often very pertinent.

However, broad categories only take us so far. In the next section we look at what it is that turns a potential charity customer into an actual customer.

Voluntary exchanges

Andreasen and Kotler (2003, pp. 93–94), Kotler and Andreasen (1991, pp. 121–34) and Lovelock and Weinberg (1984, pp. 43–64; 1989, pp. 37–43) apply traditional exchange theory used in commercial marketing to our field. They use the idea of voluntary exchanges between the not-for-profit organisation and its customers to explain take-up behaviour. Marketing is concerned with increasing the number and quality of the voluntary exchanges.

At a simplistic level, an exchange results in costs and benefits to each party. Classical theory suggests that when the benefits to each party outweigh the costs, then a voluntary exchange will take place. It should be noted that the central role of exchange in marketing has been challenged. Clarke and Mount (2001) argue that exchange theory arises out of the 'neo-classical economics', where the focus is on the individual.

> 'Decisions on consumption are made by the individual and not by collectives. There can be no socially motivated or socially determined consumption [in neo-classical economics].'
>
> (p. 81)

However, Clarke and Mount do not use this argument to rule out marketing in the non-profit world, where they say it plays a 'useful' role; their main purpose is to prompt a rethinking of the main theoretical assumption underpinning marketing theory generally and to call for other theory to be developed.

Costs and benefits

So continuing with this dominant exchange theme, what are the costs and benefits associated with not-for-profit exchanges? Lovelock and

Weinberg (1984, p. 47; 1989, p. 39) list five categories drawn from commercial marketing and apply them to the not-for-profit world:

- *sensory* benefits (how does the product feel, sound, smell or taste?);
- *psychic* benefits (how does the product stimulate a positive psychological state of mind?);
- *place* benefits (how does the product become more attractive because of where and how it is sold or passed on?);
- *time* benefits (how long does it take to find and get hold of the product?);
- monetary benefits (does the product save money in the medium term; is it likely to have a higher resale value over time; does it enhance a person's earning power?).

These categories can be translated by mirror image into costs and can provide a useful checklist for helping a not-for-profit organisation make sure that it has covered all the pros and cons of any product it is delivering.

Adapting to the not-for-profit context

However, for charities which, in extreme cases, can literally be dealing with the life or death of beneficiaries, and regularly deal with products that dramatically change a beneficiary's quality of life, these categories, and the order in which they appear, come across as superficial. They appear to have been constructed at the behest of the cosmetics marketing manager focusing heavily on sensory, psychological and convenience factors. Taking account of the much more dramatic impact of many charity products and of Maslow's Hierarchy of Needs (Maslow 1943), I would construct the following list of costs and benefits that need to be evaluated for a charity product. Such products could be physical goods, services or ideas, and could be aimed at any intermediary or end customer group – beneficiaries, supporters, stakeholders or regulators. While virtually all the following benefits will apply to each kind of product and customer group, the mix will vary: benefits/disbenefits will assume greater or lesser importance in encouraging a transaction between customer and charity.

- *Physical benefits/disbenefits*. Will it keep the beneficiary alive and relatively well? Benefits include: will it keep them longer in their own home rather than in an institution; will it enable them to get

out of the house when previously they could not; will the supporter
get a well-constructed item through its purchaser catalogue; do
staff have satisfactory equipment? Disbenefits can literally be the
opposite. For example, will it put a person's life at risk (hand-
gliding); will it require them to be institutionalised for lengthy
periods in order to aid recovery (hospital drug recovery
programmes, residential rehabilitation for disabled people)?

- *Quality-of-life benefits/disbenefits*. Will the product increase or
  decrease the beneficiary's range of life opportunities? For example,
  vocational training for a disabled person would increase his or her
  range of employment opportunities; providing talking books would
  increase a blind person's daily enjoyment); is the work programme
  organised so that it not only helps beneficiaries but also gives staff a
  better quality of work life?

- *Psychological benefits* (equivalent of Lovelock and Weinberg's
  psychic benefits). These are different from quality-of-life benefits in
  that they have less basis in physical reality. For example,
  membership of an organisation entitling members to put letters
  after their name or wear badges publicly on their lapels (such as
  professional associations or Rotary); supporter or staff association
  with a group that has a high status, perhaps with royal involvement
  and patronage; beneficiaries being offered more involvement in a
  service, thus improving self-esteem; acceptance of a pressure group
  demand, thus enhancing the status of the decision-maker within
  their organisation.

- *Access benefits and disbenefits*. How physically accessible is the
  product to beneficiaries (for example posting talking books directly
  to blind people's homes as opposed to placing them in their local
  library); how psychologically accessible is the product to
  beneficiaries (for example Alcoholics Anonymous where it is a
  requirement that one admits to being an alcoholic before joining,
  as opposed to other organisations where it is not); how physically
  or psychologically accessible is the supporter programme (for
  example, are events wheelchair accessible; do the procedures
  inhibit minority groups?).

- *Time benefits/disbenefits*. How much time must the supporter
  devote (for example how many committee meetings); how long is
  the beneficiary's rehabilitation course; how much overtime do staff

have to work? Arguably this is part of access but it is an important subhead of that category in that so many charity products are time-consuming.

- *Monetary benefits/disbenefits*. How much does it cost; is it worth it; can beneficiaries afford it; can supporters afford the price (for example of a fundraising dinner, or the frequency of direct mail solicitations); is an intermediary prepared to spend their budget in this way (for example, one residential school placement will cost as much as three placements in local mainstream schools)?
- *Sensory benefits/disbenefits*. For example, the disbenefits of care homes that smell of urine and overly antiseptic hospitals, and the benefits of good food at charity dinners.

The above list is important in any theoretical consideration as to whether a voluntary transaction between a customer and a charity is to take place; it is also useful as a checklist in designing and assessing new goods, services and ideas, and assessing continuing ones. Examples include assessing a residential rehabilitation service that is resulting in psychological over-dependency of beneficiaries or a centrally located facility that is being under-utilised because of transportation difficulties and physical access problems for disabled people, or where a pressure group proposal is rejected because it was too expensive in year one, but could have been phased in over five years. All the charities concerned would have done well to consider the above checklist in some detail. To fail to do so is to risk being an enthusiastic amateur who ends up with what they feel is a good product but which is under-utilised or even rejected.

Relationship marketing and the customer

The 1980s saw a major shift in commercial marketing away from a concentration on the isolated transaction towards developing a continuing relationship with the customer to promote a series of transactions (see Chapter 11). Such a relationship approach, done well, brings loyalty and prevents switching to competitors, and keeping an existing customer is far less costly than recruiting a replacement. (Dwyer *et al.*1987). This approach in fundraising, pioneered by Burnett in 1992 (see Burnett 2002), has increasingly been developed by non-profit marketers, especially in the fundraising field. Part III of this book returns to the important contribution of relationship marketing to voluntary and community organisations.

Marketing information and research

Why marketing research?

Marketing research is at the heart of charity marketing. It is the prime tool used in understanding the needs of customers, and in particular beneficiaries. Espy (1993, p. 90) argues that marketing research helps organisations to reach out to actual and potential consumers, to understand their wants and needs, and assess their satisfaction with existing products. If we want charities to be needs-led rather than process or resources-driven, we must undertake a significant amount of marketing research. For example, RNIB spends approximately £200,000 per year in this field. As a passionate marketer, two of the projects that have given me most satisfaction in the voluntary sector have been initiating and directing three major needs surveys, one on older people with Age Concern England, and two on blind and partially sighted people with RNIB (Bruce *et al.* 1991, and Bruce and Baker 2001; 2003). All three had a major impact on service design as well as being powerful campaigning tools. Less obviously they changed attitudes inside the agencies, making them more customer focused.

Customer groups

Marketing research is, essentially, gathering information about actual and potential intermediary and end customers, and reflecting these findings and conclusions onto the design and delivery of our physical, service and idea products. This research needs to be undertaken among all the customer groups – beneficiaries, supporters, stakeholders and their intermediaries. The only group that cannot easily be formally researched are some regulators, but even there informal sounding out is important.

Of the customer groups, research among actual and potential beneficiaries is the bedrock that both supports work directed at them and informs work with other customer groups. The RNIB needs surveys referred to above not only helped modify services to blind and partially sighted people, but have also been fundamental to pressure group work, public relations and fundraising. For example, one provided crucial evidence for convincing civil servants that a new social security allowance should be designed so that it met the particular needs of blind people (estimated full value: £40 million per year); it also provided the basis of RNIB's most successful cold mail appeals letter and its launch was included in five national TV news slots. What is also fascinating is that research among RNIB's stakeholders (representatives of organisations of blind and partially sighted people, major backers, government contacts and associated charities) as part of its strategic review showed that the needs survey was felt to be one of the three most important pieces of work that the organisation had undertaken over ten years. So marketing research can have wide range of benefits.

Structuring the information

Data can be gathered and structured in a number of ways.

Adapting Blyth's framework of questions, referred to in Chapter 2, for the charity sector, produces the following two questions:

- what do I know?
- what do I also need to know?

The first question is dealt with in the section on desk research, below. The second is one of the hardest to answer. Unless it is answered, the subsequent research will be much more expensive because more data than is necessary will be collected, and it may not answer the questions later identified as needing answers.

For example, RNIB wanted to know if age of onset of visual impairment was a critical factor in take-up of services and so asked the question 'At what age did you become visually impaired?' This allowed cross-tabulation of age of onset with a whole variety of products, such as Braille services. However, RNIB should also have asked how long after onset the respondent took up its various services. It did not do this, and only managed to calculate the time by undertaking complicated extra work.

So basic questions that need answers are:

Existing customers
- Who are you?
- What products have you taken up (if none, see 'potential customers', below)?

- How much product are you taking up?
- What is being paid and who is paying it?
- Where and how did you take up this product?
- When did you take it up?
- What else could you have taken up?
- Why?

Potential customers
- Who are you?
- Which products of ours do you know about?
- Which might you consider taking up and why?
- Which do you definitely not want and why?
- Which of those products you did not know about are the most attractive to you and why?

Personal marketing research/experience

Charities all too often use personal experience to collect data and draw conclusions, either on the basis of 'I have been through it and therefore know these things' or 'I have seen other people go through it'. This kind of data collection can be extraordinarily effective because it is based on first-hand experience and is totally absorbed into the mind of the committee members and managers concerned. It therefore avoids one of the problems of more rigorous market research, that of the findings being left to gather dust on the shelves. The findings of personal experience are very often rapidly absorbed into practice. However, the disadvantage is very clear, namely it is only *personal* experience and may not be typical. Even where it *is* typical of a large customer subgroup, it will most likely result in an over-dominance of services to this particular subgroup.

Representation and experience

Some charities are able to achieve formal representation on their committees from their customer groups, especially beneficiaries. This can have a number of advantages, including giving the charity's products an implicit seal of approval, but is particularly helpful in marketing research terms. Such representation gives a useful blend of the views of leaders and opinion formers, as well as those of the rank and file of the customer groups. In my experience charities outperform commercial companies in this respect.

Desk research

Another very useful and readily achievable form of marketing research is desk research of external and internal information.

There is almost always more market information available on an organisation's target groups than conventional wisdom suggests. If there is no appropriately qualified member of staff to undertake the desk marketing research, a modest outlay to a postgraduate student will gain the organisation an invaluable annotated bibliography of virtually everything relevant published. Many charities are luckier than commercial companies in that universities will have undertaken extensive research into at least their beneficiary target groups, the results of which are in the public domain. A review of this literature, indicating which documents are most valuable and drawing some of the most basic conclusions can be vital.

This desk research can be particularly crucial in taking the organisation a stage further in identifying the customers. In my experience, there is frequently a reaction along the lines of 'I didn't realise there were so many people in our potential as opposed to our actual customer groups' or 'we didn't realise how much our services were skewed towards a particular subgroup within our overall target market'. Assessing the size of the potential user group is not only crucial to giving a marketing perspective on existing services; it is also crucial because it will help with subsequent sampling for the organisation's own marketing research.

As for internal customer information, an undergraduate or MBA marketing student will leap at the chance to do an audit of existing customer information. There is often a wealth of customer data 'hidden away' in sales order processing, in the accounts department, at various distribution points or even in the post room. With luck the data will go back several years and trends will therefore become available.

Qualitative research

Qualitative marketing research at its simplest allows us to gain insights into our user group in some depth, but does not enable us to be sure how widely applicable these conclusions and insights might be. It can take the form of depth interviews with individual potential or actual customers who, you have predicted, have some of the attributes in which you are interested. For example, if a service charity is aware that the majority of its target group are older women, but it is not successfully reaching this group, then a dozen depth interviews with individual older women, both users and non-users, is likely to be very instructive. It is important to be aware that to be done well, qualitative research is both difficult and expensive. Good depth interviewers are hard to come by (for example, they have to be sympathetic and encouraging but not over-prescriptive) and the design of the interviews is at least as complicated as larger surveys. However, such a process has the immediate advantage that it can be tried out by service managers (assuming that they are not dominating by predisposition, or can at least control this in the interview) and thus draw the research directly in to the line manager.

Group interviews are a variation on individual interviews. Here between six and twelve individuals are brought together into a group discussion about a particular service or problem area. Obviously group dynamics are important; the group leader needs to have many of the attributes of the depth interviewer but must also be able to facilitate a group. With careful selection of group participants it is possible to introduce a semblance of a quantitative set of conclusions. Such groups can be useful to help assess products such as a new technical aid or charity logo at the pre-test stage.

Quantitative research

Provided that there is sufficient budget for a robust random sample, or that a representative sample can be drawn or later constructed, quantitative research is excellent for establishing the size of the market for your product or service and for measuring the extent of individual strengths or weaknesses. It is particularly good useful for measuring the physical, social and demographic characteristics of the target group – how many are over 65 years old, how many are men/women, how much money they have or do not have, their economic/class background, and so on.

In essence, in quantitative research one asks similar questions of hundreds of actual and potential customers through either a printed questionnaire or trained personal interviewers. The questions must always be tested out on a small subsample, and are often constructed on the basis of initial qualitative work.

The results and conclusions can come close to measuring hypotheses, attributes, attitudes and behaviour identified in preceding qualitative research.

Process

Many charities have experience of research, and so there will be some expertise to transpose into marketing research. It is vital to go through the stages of planning, execution, analysis and presentation of findings meticulously. As with any good marketing approach, it is vital that staff and committee members who are going to have to act on the research findings are involved from the earliest stages. It is too easy for conclusions to stay on the shelf. Where the market researcher involves managers and committee members before and especially after the research, the chances of the findings being acted upon increase enormously.

Impact

Marketing research can make discoveries of dramatic importance to a charity and its physical, service and idea products, but in the main they come up with evolutionary conclusions. For example, market research by Macmillan Cancer Relief discovered that professional support and advice was directed at people with cancer, with little support going to carers (Scott 1993, p. 2); as a result charity services were modified. An example of evolutionary impact is where charities have worked with the Department for Work and Pensions (DWP) on research into programmes to help unemployed disabled people acquire work. This research discovered which programmes were most successful, and in turn this information was related back to programme cost so that the DWP was able to focus its activities on the most cost-effective ways of bringing disabled people into the employment market.

Market segmentation and targeting

The process of dividing the organisation's total customer market into subgroups or 'market segments' is one of the most useful conceptual and practical tools in marketing. This then enables decisions about which segments to target with which products.

For example, RNID does not think of its target market as simply 'deaf people'. People with a hearing impairment have as many needs and wants as hearing people – arguably more. There are as many kinds of deaf people as there are hearing people. RNID thinks in terms of hearing-impaired people under 16, of working age, and over retirement age. Among hearing-impaired people under 16 it has to think of the needs of the singly impaired as being different from the multi-disabled hearing-impaired. It has to think of the different needs of those who can communicate through speech and those who can only communicate through sign language; of the different needs of people who have been hearing-impaired from birth from those who become so later in life.

Such segmentation allows a charity to construct products that take account of the particular needs of a more homogeneous group than 'deaf people'.

Why segment?

There are two fundamental pressures that should persuade a not-for-profit organisation to segment its market. The first is an apparently negative one, namely that the organisation cannot serve every need of its whole market simply because there are almost certainly not enough resources in the form of money or expertise. If the organisation does try to serve the whole market it will fail or, at the very best, provide a low-quality service not appreciated by many people in its market. The positive pressure for segmentation is that it allows, and indeed encourages, the development of products that are much more likely to be appreciated by the customers. The associated downside is that some consumer segments may be ignored by the organisation simply because, on the basis of institutional aims, they have been selected as lower priority or are judged to be relatively inaccessible.

Lovelock and Weinberg (1989, pp. 157-9) list seven reasons for segmentation, which are still valid; namely that it helps:

- spotlight relevant segments;
- develop responsive strategies;
- efficient allocation of resources;
- effectiveness in attracting funding;
- efficiency in media selection;
- reduce competitive impact (choosing an area where few others operate);
- focus organisational efforts.

In charities it also important because it helps us to identify under-served groups.

Stages

Kotler and Fox (1985) identify three progressive stages of market segmentation, leading to three more progressive stages of target marketing:

Market segmentation
1 Identify bases for segmenting the market.
2 Develop profiles of resulting segments.
3 Develop measure of segment attractiveness.

Target marketing
4 Select the target market(s).
5 Develop positioning for each target market.
6 Develop marketing mix for each target market.

Lovelock and Weinberg (1989) identify two previous stages, which are particularly important to the not-for-profit organisation:
1 Define institutional objectives and set priorities.
2 Identify which market(s) within overall population is/are key to successful achievement of objectives.

Stakeholder theorists Mitchell *et al.* (1997) have developed a model of predicting stakeholder/customer activity useful to non-profit marketers. They propose that it is based on the extent to which an individual or group has legitimacy, power and urgency. Possession of all three will propel a segment up the priority list for serious consideration as a target. The challenge for charity leaders is resisting the demands of customers who have power and urgency but no legitimacy.

Criteria

There are four traditional criteria for segmenting the markets:
- geographic (region, density, climate, etc);
- socio-demographic (age, sex, family size, income, occupation, social class, etc);
- psychographic (lifestyle, personality, attitudes, etc);
- behaviouristic (benefits being sought, purchasing rate, usage rate, etc).

In a charity setting, the behaviour basis of segmentation is likely to be highest priority for beneficiary customers. The only danger is doing the selection and then discovering that there is no way of implementing the segmentation in terms of reaching the target market.

CASE EXAMPLE: TALKING BOOK SERVICE

A talking book service is available to all blind and partially sighted people. However, within this market it is much more likely that the service will be taken up by people who used to read a lot before they lost their sight, and not by those who did not read much. Since it takes twelve hours to listen to a whole book (approximately three times longer than for a sighted person to read an equivalent book), the service is more likely to appeal to visually impaired people with a lot of leisure time, such as older and unemployed people. There is no reason for believing that the tastes in reading are any different than for sighted people. The market segments are divided primarily by age. Taste in reading is solved by recording the most popular books on the sighted market. Target markets are older, newly visually impaired people and unemployed people. A separate library is developed for the target market of students and working people, on the basis that their needs and time availability are different.

CASE EXAMPLE: SPECIAL SCHOOL

Another example of target marketing that indicates its extreme complexity in the charity world is that of a special school run by a charity. In this situation there are four quite distinct target markets

cont.

CASE EXAMPLE: SPECIAL SCHOOL continued

whose needs and wants have to be satisfied. First, there are the children attending the school who are the ultimate beneficiaries, in other words, education has to be designed to serve them best. However, as with any school, parent(s) may be involved and they will have views about the education their child might best receive. In addition, as parent(s) they have an important educational role with the child, because they are, in part, a provider. Third, there is the LEA, which will decide whether to pay for the (expensive) education and will have its own needs and wants. Fourth, there is the regulator, OFSTED (which inspects the school and has the power and authority to require the school to provide education in an appropriate manner).

Donor market segmentation and targeting often uses all the traditional criteria for segmenting. For example, many charities, when aiming fundraising at the general public, try to target couples and single women over fifty years from upper socio-economic groups (socio-demographic) who have a religious orientation (psychographic) and who have an established track record of giving to charity (behaviouristic). While all parts of the United Kingdom are targeted, the South East and South West are often most lucrative (geographic).

Market segmentation and target markets are some of the most useful tools available to the charity manager. They allow the prioritisation of different target markets according to the organisation's aims and objectives . However, they explicitly recognise that not everyone in the overall needs group (market) of the agency can be served, and so many charity managers initially feel uncomfortable with the concept. However, even if they ignore explicit target markets and market segmentation, they will be undertaking it implicitly, and will have little idea about which groups they are prioritising and which they are, in fact, ignoring.

Other-player analysis

As described in Chapter 2, competitor analysis is essential in the commercial world if a product, product line or even company is to survive and prosper.

In the charity sector the term 'competitor' can seem either inappropriate or unhelpful. The term 'other player' (Bruce 1994) is not only more acceptable, but is also more appropriate. Other players in the charity world include not only other charities in the subsector (such as other cancer charities), but also all other charities, in some instances statutory services (charity and statutory services to beneficiaries interact and intertwine in a complicated and interdependent manner) and other commercial organisations. For example, in the residential care field there are four kinds of providers: charities, statutory organisations, housing associations (which are not normally charities) and commercial organisations.

So other-player analysis, especially when it comes to beneficiary markets, has to be very broad if it is to be meaningful. For example, an other-player analysis of charity services to beneficiaries in 1945 would have come to some very strange conclusions if it had omitted the role of statutory provision, bearing in mind the rapid and widespread extension of the welfare state between 1945 and 1950. Indeed, as argued in Chapter 10, one of the most important aspects of other-player analysis in charities over the last fifty years has been the interactive but changing roles of the statutory, voluntary and commercial sectors as far as beneficiary provision is concerned. This interaction has also spilled over into supporter markets, with changing attitudes towards voluntary work (varying degrees of encouragement or discouragement) and donations (changing tax advantages/disadvantages), as well as changing attitudes towards the acceptability and legitimacy of pressure group work (changing views as to legitimacy).

Components

Other-player analysis is the closest that this book comes to strategic planning. The world of strategic planning in commerce has been increasingly colonised by strategic marketing (see Chapter 10). However, in the charity and statutory sector, strategic planning has, for a long time, had a powerful and legitimate role. It seems more helpful to subsume a marketing approach within more general models and applications of strategic planning, provided that the latter accept the dominant customer ethos. That is an important qualification because this has not always been the case. Strategic planning has, in many instances, appeared to be a tool for ensuring organisational survival rather than for developing the backcloth to the creation of products relevant to customers. For example, strategic planning abounded in the old nationalised industries such as gas and electricity, which were hardly renowned for their customer sensitivity!

This introduction indicates that other-player analysis, as alluded to in the previous section, requires components of broad environmental analysis – economic, political, social and technological. Unless charities analyse and understand what is happening in those important areas of the environment, particularly where they may impact on the charity, its fortunes and beneficiaries are likely to wane.

Leaving this broader environmental scan aside there are some generally recognised factors from the commercial world that need to be analysed in other players and that can be applied to any organisation, whether other charities or statutory or commercial players.

- What is the product (physical, service or idea)? How modern and up to date is it? What is the quality like? Does the organisation have a track record of product innovation?
- What are the organisation's marketing skills and capacity? What is its share of the market? How strong is its marketing mix? In particular, how are the services spread geographically and how good is the market penetration?
- What is its manufacturing strength? This is less relevant to most charities given their service base, but still needs considering.
- What resources does it have? How does the other player compare in terms of financial reserves, income, staff and volunteer capacity, land and buildings?
- What is its overall organisational effectiveness? How good are the managers, the directors and lay committees?
- What is its organisational structure? Can it deliver products effectively, directly and flexibly, or is it a sluggish organisation?

Strategies

In the commercial world (as mentioned in Chapter 2), Porter (1980) recommends adoption of one of three strategies to maintain success against competitors – *focus* (where the company focuses its product on a market niche of customers and becomes the market leader in that narrow area), *cost leadership* (where the dominant market leader establishes the price rules), or *differentiation* (where the company establishes a product that is so distinctive from its competitors' that it becomes difficult to challenge).

Many charities occupy market niche (*focus*) positions, for example Guide Dogs for the Blind in the field of blind welfare or the Donkey Sanctuary within the field of animal welfare. Charities are quite often rather poor at achieving differentiation between themselves, but they have a very strong *differentiation* from other players such as statutory and commercial organisations. However, even here resource shortages and the organisational mutations such as NHS hospitals into hospital trusts and LEA schools into academies are in some cases reducing this differentiation.

Cost leadership is difficult to translate into the charity sector. For this strategy to be effective the organisation has to be a dominant player in the consumer field, and very few charities achieve this (perhaps the one exception is the Royal National Lifeboat Institution).

Position

Kotler and Andreasen (1991, p. 206) describe four choices of position, two of which are close to those of Porter. The position of 'market leader' is very close to that of cost leadership, because only the market leader can establish cost leadership. The position of 'market nicher' is close to that of focus. However, they introduce two other strategic positions that have some relevance to the charity sector. The first is 'market challenger' – a strategy that can be adopted more easily against other players such as statutory and commercial organisations through the greater flexibility and volunteer involvement (one example is charity hospices expanding at the 'expense' of nursing homes). The second is that of 'market follower', where a charity can let some other organisation (often a commercial one) develop the expertise and/or practical capability and then follow. For many years RNIB held back on changing its talking book format from tape to an electronic form, until the commercial market decided between the competition of compact disc, digital audio tape and video disc. Saxton (1996a) proposes four strategies for competitive advantages in charities: externally driven, niche (which has two sub-categories – issue/emotional and geographic), differentiation (which has three sub-categories – by customer group, product and belief) and awareness. These strategies have been developed with charities in mind and deserve empirical testing.

Positioning

Positioning the charity's physical, service and idea products follows logically from segmentation, targeting and other-player analysis. Harrison (1987) defines the position of a product as:

> 'The sum of those attributes normally ascribed to it by the consumers – its standing, its quality, the type of people who use it, its strengths, its weaknesses, and any other unusual or memorable characteristics it may possess, its price and the value it represents.'
>
> (p. 7)

This definition makes it clear that, while the charity can have a major impact on how customers view the charity (the brand), and the position of its products, at the end of the day it is the customers, and not the charity, who position the charity and its products.

Branding

With charities the branding situation is more complex than with many commercial companies that avoid a creating a corporate brand, such as Unilever or RHM. This is because the charity itself is the brand, but it also has a large number of customer groups that may expect to receive different messages. The positioning challenge for charities is that they must have an openly recognisable and consistent position to beneficiaries and supporters, as well as to stakeholders and regulators – with such a consistent position being acceptable to all four groups.

Some charities have on occasions failed to achieve this, with difficult consequences. Examples include War on Want and SCOPE, when it was called the Spastics Society. War on Want attracts supporters because of its radical stance on social and political change necessary to improve the position of the developing world, but because of this stance it has attracted criticism from the regulator, namely the Charity Commission. Key stakeholders in the then Spastics Society were parents of beneficiaries; significant tension over policy arose between them and adult beneficiaries, which has made it difficult for the society to have a consistent approach.

Customer groups

Positioning a charity, with its variety of physical, service and idea products, to its various customer groups is undoubtedly an art rather than a science. In the vast majority of cases it is also done unconsciously rather than consciously. However, lack of attention to positioning in the charity sector generally, and within specific subsectors such as the various cancer charities, provides us with a developing, long-term problem. For example, the comparative positioning (consumer view) of Cancer Research UK, Marie Curie Cancer Care and Macmillan Cancer Relief is indistinct. As competition in the supporter market intensifies, charities with clearly identified positions, such as Save the Children and Red Cross, are bound to have a competitive advantage.

Intermediaries

Positioning is equally important in the constituency of beneficiaries and their intermediaries. Service-giving products in the field of child care are relatively indistinct and undifferentiated. For example, over fifty charities provide some form of support to children. NSPCC and Barnardo's occupy the dominant positions in the market, but differentiation confusion abounds. More distinctive positions would benefit not only the charities, but also the beneficiaries and their intermediaries. It is generally thought that, whatever the customer group, the market leader (at least in the customer's mind) benefits from indistinct positioning. So, for example, unbranded or weakly branded work by one of the smaller children's charities will often be attributed to Barnardo's or NSPCC.

Conclusion

In summary, a charity marketing approach requires analysis of other players in the market – both immediate and obvious competitors (as in the fundraising field) or other charities, statutory services and commercial organisations in the fields of offerings aimed at beneficiaries.

However, this is the natural interface with strategic planning which has long been strong in the statutory sector, and is growing fast in the voluntary sector. Provided that strategic planning has a strong customer focus, it is probably the best specialism to deal with the complexities of a charity operating in the rough seas of changing economic, political, social and technological environments.

Key points

- Identify the separate target groups or 'customers': beneficiaries, supporters (donors, volunteers and 'advocates'), stakeholders (including staff) and regulators.
- Understand the social and psychological factors that influence customer take-up behaviour in the context of charities and social marketing.
- Marketing research – collect data to understand customer and beneficiary need via personal experience, desk research, individual/ group interviews (for qualitative assessment) and large samples (quantitative research).
- Segmentation – segment the separate market groups to target specific products and services to particular need.
- Other-player analysis – analyse the activities, products and services of other players (other charities, statutory services or even commercial organisations) operating in the same sector. Consider their skills, resources and organisational effectiveness in comparison with yours (use a SWOT analysis - strengths, weaknesses, opportunities and threats).
- Positioning – how do customers view your products and how should you change the marketing mix in the light of these views and the position of other players?

4   The charity marketing mix

This chapter, like the previous one, introduces the concepts and terms of the commercial marketing world and puts them into a charity context. Chapters 6–10 apply them to voluntary and community sector work.

Construction

The marketing mix is what is required to bake a successful marketing cake. It has a more or less constant list of ingredients, which interact. Unlike making a cake, however, the marketer has to construct each of the ingredients as well as mix them together in known proportions. In short, the marketer has to ensure that the individual ingredients are valid in their own right as well as making sure the interaction between the ingredients is successful. The term 'marketing mix' is attributed to Borden (1964, pp. 2–7). It has also been encapsulated into the well-known dictum of the four 'Ps' (McCarthy 1981, pp. 42–3):

- product;
- price;
- promotion;
- place.

Doyle (2003) reframes McCarthy's elaboration of the four 'Ps':

- **product** (brand, quality, design, features, variety, packaging, service, support, guarantees);
- **price** (list price, discounts, allowances, trade margins, payment terms, credit, trade-in);
- **promotion** (advertising, personal selling, sales promotion, public relations, direct marketing, exhibitions, internet);
- **place** (distribution channels, coverage, assortments, locations, inventory (stock), transport).

It is clear that this commercial definition is heavily orientated towards physical goods rather than services and was constructed with no reference to voluntary organisations' pressure group work or fundraising activity.

As we shall see later in this chapter, and in Chapters 6–9, despite the initial unattractiveness of the language to the charity manager, the terms and the concepts behind them are useful and applicable in the voluntary sector. However, given the strong orientation of the list to physical products, other writers, in particular Booms and Bitner (1981), have argued that it needs adaptation to be useful to service managers. This is useful, given the preponderance of services in the charity sector.

Booms and Bitner (pp. 47–51) argued that three extra 'Ps' should be added to the list where services are concerned – people, physical evidence and process of service assembly:

- **people**: personnel and their training, discretion, commitment, incentives, appearance, interpersonal behaviour and attitudes; but also *other customers* and their behaviour, degree of involvement and customer-to-customer interaction;
- **physical evidence**: environmental factors such as furnishings, colour, layout and noise level; facilitating goods; tangible clues;
- **process**: policies, procedures, mechanisation, employee discretion, customer involvement, customer direction and flow of activities.

While we have discussed the four Ps in earlier chapters, this is the first introduction of the three service 'Ps'. Figure 4.1 (overleaf) gives a visual representation of the full charity marketing framework and tools.

People

The reason for including the two groups under people is straightforward. Unlike physical goods, the *personnel* of services are crucial in customer assessment and will have a major impact on whether customers will recommend the service or use it again. This is particularly true for charity products. The attitudes, behaviour and commitment of charity staff are crucial in retaining and developing donors and, in particular, fundraising volunteers. These factors are similarly crucial in service provision to beneficiaries, who can be active promoters or detractors of charity services, depending on the quality of staff providers.

In the fundraising context *other customers* make the difference to the success or failure of an event and whether the volunteer organisers will remain involved. Other customers are also important in services

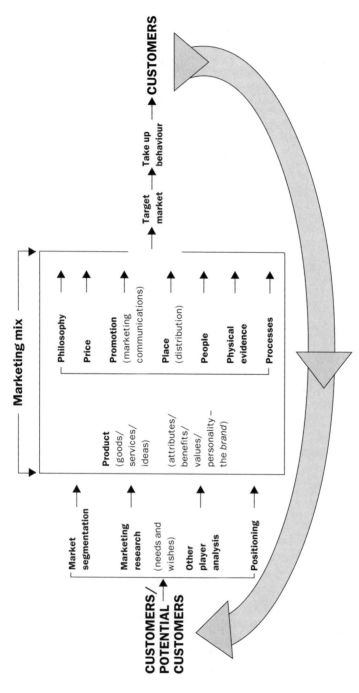

Figure 4.1 Charity marketing framework and tools (*Source*: Bruce 2005, reframing Borden 1964, and Booms and Bitner 1981)
© Ian Bruce

delivered to beneficiaries. For example, charity beneficiaries are not naturally homogeneous groups and peer group interaction can make or break some charity service offerings. If empathy develops between clients say, on a rehabilitation course, then peer group support after, as well as during, the service experience can provide very positive benefits. If the service clients are poorly or unimaginatively grouped, then peer group antagonisms can easily develop, which will be destructive in themselves and will undermine the value of the service provided.

Physical evidence

The argument for including physical evidence is that so much of a service is intangible, at least before it is experienced. Physical evidence, such as the cleanliness and modernity of a building, can have a triggering effect on a decision whether to take part in the service.

Process

The rather esoteric list under this heading includes activities that are fundamental to successful service products, for example how easy is it to access or pay for the service. Chapter 7 looks at these and builds, in particular, on the important contributions of Len Berry, A. Parasuraman and Valerie Zeithaml.

The mix for the sector

Do the seven 'Ps' – product, price, promotion, place, people, physical evidence and process – provide a satisfactory marketing mix for charities? I would say yes, except for one important omission – *philosophy* (which I would also add for the public sector) (Bruce 1994). A charity's philosophy in delivering goods, services or ideas is absolutely fundamental to a good marketing approach. Is the philosophy of the charity one of empowering beneficiaries to become as independent as possible? Or is it one of trying to change the beneficiaries' environment with less emphasis on personal empowerment, or one of caring for and segregating the beneficiary, with little emphasis on empowerment and environmental change? The philosophy that a charity (and, I would argue, a statutory or public organisation) adopts will have a fundamental effect on the organisation's offerings. Lack of clarity about the organisation's guiding philosophy will result in an inconsistency among its services, ideas and even physical goods, depending on the managers' individual philosophies.

Relevance

Some people have questioned whether the marketing mix as it is currently interpreted is relevant to not-for-profit organisations. Blois (1987, pp. 386–97) argues that Borden (1964, pp. 2–7) did not have a rigid list of what must be part of the marketing mix but provided illustrative lists, stressing that other people and other situations will require different ingredients. This is helpful and will be taken up later. Blois argues that over-concentration on the four 'Ps' distracts from the essential task of not-for-profit managers, which is to identify:

- the organisation's product features and controllable variables and, separately, those features that they can alter;
- those market forces that influence demand and, separately, those forces that they can modify.

Clearly both factors are crucial but do not detract from the usefulness of a charity marketing mix.

Checklist

The (now) eight 'Ps' of philosophy, product, price, promotion, place, people, physical evidence and process provide a useful checklist of all the factors a charity manager needs to consider in constructing and delivering an effective physical, service or idea product. Three additional sub-elements (Bruce 1994) have been added and are shown in italics.

- **Philosophy**: of the charity as a whole, and philosophy to be applied to the specific product.
- **Product** (goods, services or ideas): brand, quality, design features, variety, packaging, support, guarantees.
- **Price**: list price, discounts, allowances, trade margins, payment terms, credit, trade in.
- **Promotion**: advertising, personal selling, sales promotion, public relations, direct marketing, exhibitions, internet, *coalition building, intermediary referral, customer referral.*

- **Place**: distributors, retailers, locations, inventory, transport.
- **People**: personnel (training, discretion, commitment, incentives, appearance, interpersonal behaviour and attitudes) and other customers (including behaviour, degree of involvement and customer-to-customer interaction).
- **Physical evidence**: environmental factors such as furnishings, colour, layout and noise level; facilitating goods; tangible clues.
- **Process**: policies, procedures, mechanisation, employee discretion, customer involvement, customer direction and flow of activities.

The following sections look in more detail at the different elements of the marketing mix as applied to charities.

Philosophy

By philosophy I mean an explicit recognition of the value-laden approach to be taken or encouraged in the product, be it a physical good, a service or an idea aimed at the beneficiary, supporter, stakeholder or regulator markets. For example, part of RNIB's organisational philosophy is to empower blind and partially sighted people to be more independent, not inadvertently to make them more dependent on someone else. Therefore each RNIB product has to be judged in this light and there needs to be an explicit part of the marketing mix that looks at this issue. Is the educational content and curriculum of an RNIB school such that it helps the child become more autonomous? Does the promotional activity, including the prospectus, give a dignified image of the multi-disabled child? Do the people (staff) involved in the school treat the children with respect and encourage maximum independence? In other words, the philosophy to be used in the marketing mix has to be explicit, and understood and applied to all the other seven elements. This philosophical consistency is particularly important to ensure an integrated approach between service and fundraising messages.

The purpose of this section is not to say what the philosophy of any charity, or its individual offerings, should be. That has to be a decision of the individual charity. What is being proposed is that voluntary organisations should be explicit about their values and philosophy, and ensure that these are integrated firmly into the marketing mix in an explicit and understood fashion. If the philosophy is not explicit, it will still surely exist. However, it will probably be more apparent to the customers than to the organisation; it may vary from one unit of the organisation to another; the variance may be contradictory; and the philosophy applied to any individual product or product line may change as staff change. If the philosophy is explicit and is made a clear part of the marketing mix, everyone will know where they are and what is expected of them. Its very explicitness will allow this element of the marketing mix to be reviewed from time to time.

Developing the philosophy

So how does a charity go about creating a philosophical position for incorporation into the marketing mix, and on what should it be based? The most obvious answer is that the philosophy should be based on the needs and wants of the beneficiary customers. It is beneficiary customers' interests that should be paramount in a charity (subject to the legal expression of its charitable purposes, although even these can be changed). However, this immediately prompts a distinction between needs and wants. The term 'needs' implies some objective assessment of the end beneficiary's situation. The term 'wants' implies pre-eminence to the views of the end beneficiary. These views and objective assessments may or may not be identical. Another problem is how to balance the needs and wants of the present generation of beneficiaries with those of future generations (or even non-generations in the case of a charity undertaking research to prevent a medical condition such as cancer). Third, is it possible to adopt the same philosophical or value position for all beneficiaries? In other words, the development of a philosophical position for the organisation and its offerings is extremely challenging.

To a large extent the responsibility for developing this position is outside the prime responsibility of charity marketing and is within the purview of charity strategic planning. Indeed it is within a charity's vision and/or mission and/or value statement that we can look for evidence as to the required content of the philosophy element of the marketing mix. Increasing numbers of charities are creating mission statements and a fair proportion of these have vision and value statements. For example, Shelter's vision and value statement (McKechnie 1993,) says:

'A home is somewhere affordable, of adequate size and design, in good repair, safe, secure and with support when required. To be without a home is unacceptable. It is degrading and damaging to individuals and the community and has enormous social and economic costs for us all . . .'

It goes on to say:

'As an organisation we recognise that we can only achieve our aims through effective management and promoting equality of opportunity in the widest sense. Shelter's integrity and independence will be safe-guarded by its Trustees.'

(p. 47)

It will quickly be seen that, while significant parts of the above statement are to do with aims and objectives, there is a strong value-laden philosophy. This is shown in words like 'unacceptable', 'degrading' and 'damaging'. By implication it follows that any provision or proposals that Shelter makes must give dignity to the individuals and must not inadvertently give support to certain forms of homelessness.

Save the Children Fund's mission statement includes the sentence:

'In all its work Save the Children endeavours to make a reality of children's rights.'

(Hinton 1993, p. 11)

The rights referred to are those adopted by the United Nations in 1989 and include the following:

'The child must be protected beyond and above all considerations of race, nationality or creed. The child must be cared for with due respect for the family as an entity. The child must be brought up in the consciousness that its talents must be devoted to the services of its fellow men . . .'

Once again the philosophical position that needs to be adopted in the marketing mix of any Save the Children offering is to ensure that, at least, it does not inadvertently damage the implementation of the rights of children, and at best enhances them.

Are charities different?

Does this eighth 'P' make charities different from commercial organisations? It is certainly true that the commercial marketing texts seldom, if ever, make reference to the philosophical or value-laden position of a product as a separate section of the marketing mix. It is interesting to question why this has not occurred. However, things may be changing. Embley (1993) has titled his book *Doing Well While Doing Good: The marketing link between business and non-profit causes.* He lists over fifty examples of mainly American commercial companies that have developed their business platform on the basis of 'doing good'. One of the companies he quotes is The Body Shop, which will be familiar to UK readers. He describes seven principles under which the company operates, which include the following:

> 'All the products do is cleanse, polish, and protect the skin and hair. The Body Shop makes no promises about rejuvenation; it promotes health rather than beauty. Ingredients and products are obtained in an unpatronising, non-exploitative manner . . .'
>
> (p. 100)

These statements, along with The Body Shop's position on product testing on animals, give a very clear philosophic position for the organisation's various marketing mixes. So The Body Shop certainly has an eighth 'P' for philosophy. Embley (1993, p. 2) argues that companies with a social mission as well as a business mission will become the models of the future.

Product

It is vital in charity marketing to emphasise that the term 'product' covers not only physical goods, but also services and ideas. At one level it would seem unnecessary to emphasise this because, in theory, all are covered by the term. It is simply that, in lay person's language, the word 'product' is associated almost entirely with physical goods. Further, marketing arose out of the FMCG world and all the academic and practical literature is dominated by physical goods. While the American Marketing Association includes equal emphasis on physical goods, services and ideas, this latter area hardly ever gets a mention except in the more thoughtful academic texts, where such consideration is consciously excluded as requiring more attention than a general book can give (Cowell 1984, p. 36). In the charity, and indeed statutory sector, ideas as products are very important and come in three main guises: pressure group work, public education activity and fundraising.

Kotler and Fox (1985, p. 221) suggest 'offer, value packages or benefit bundles' as alternative names for product in the not-for-profit organisations. Kotler and Andreasen (1991, p. 389) use the term 'offering' as an alternative to product. The term is used from now on in this text as being synonymous with 'product'.

Physical goods

Little elaboration of this heading is given here, first because overwhelming attention is given to this area in the literature and, second, such differences as there are between charity goods marketing and commercial goods marketing are covered in Chapter 6.

Lovelock and Weinberg (1984, p. 285; 1989, p. 202) argue that physical goods represent a relatively small area of output for not-for-profit organisations. This is true but it is still a valid and significant output for a number of voluntary organisations (such as disability organisations selling or giving their beneficiaries technical aids). Physical goods sold by charities to realise income for their primary mission (such as direct mail catalogue activities) also appear to be on the increase. Charities are putting greater emphasis on trading, particularly in the area of physical goods, but also services. Palmer *et al.* (1999) report that 67 per cent of the largest (over £10 million total income) British charities have trading subsidiaries with an average of 40 per cent for the whole sector.

Services

What is overwhelmingly clear is the dominance of services in the public and charitable sectors. This means that the relative lack of writing and research on commercial services marketing is a real problem. For every one book on services marketing, there are between ten and twenty on marketing in which the dominant concern is physical goods, and a chapter or two at most will be devoted to services marketing. This is ironic given the fundamental tenet of a marketing approach, which is to be customer focused. Manufacturing industry as a proportion of GDP has been in decline for some while. The EC reports that in Europe as a whole, nearly 60 per cent of the workforce is in services, around 30 per cent is in industry and a little less than 10 per cent is in agriculture (Eurostat 1988). In the United Kingdom the figures are approximately 67 per cent, 30 per cent and 3 per cent. So it is not only the charity sector that needs more marketing writing and research on services!

What is so different about services in comparison with physical goods, and what does the literature on commercial marketing say about them? Building on the earlier work of Eiglier and Langeard (1977), Gronroos (1980) and Shostack (1977), and on their own original research, Zeithaml *et al.* (1985, pp. 33–46) conclude that the unique features of services are as follows:

- *intangibility* – a service cannot be stored, protected through patents, readily displayed or communicated, and prices are difficult to set;
- *inseparability* – the consumer is involved in production; other consumers are involved in production; centralised mass production is difficult;
- *perishability* services cannot be inventoried (stored);
- *heterogeneity*: standardisation and quality are difficult to control.

These unique service features and their resulting marketing problems help us to understand the nature of a service and the marketing approach required. These ideas fit well into a charity service context. Take the service examples from Chapter 1. The special school is intangible (prior to experiencing it); customers (children) are inseparably involved in the education; an empty place for a term cannot be recovered (perishability) and standardisation of the service is difficult and not necessarily desirable.

Shostack (1977, p. 77) proposed a continuum, ranging from a pure tangible good, through a tangible good with accompanying services and a service with accompanying goods and service through to a pure service (see Figure 4.2).

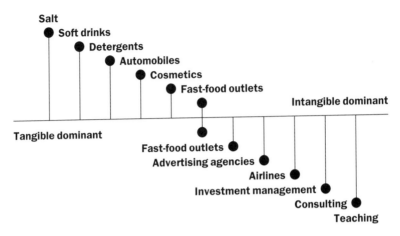

Figure 4.2 A goods–service continuum (source: Shostack 1997, p. 77)

A. Wilson (1984, p. 10) adjusted his model of practice development from its concentration on consumer/commercial subjects to include professional services and extended Shostack's continuum further right to include medicine, architecture and the law.

Quality
Berry and Parasuraman (1991, pp. 15–21) argue that in services marketing, quality is of paramount importance – indeed they go as far as arguing that in the traditional product marketing mix of the four 'Ps', there should be a fifth 'P', only this time it would be a 'Q' for quality. They have conducted extensive research among customers of service companies which suggests five dimensions that influence customers' assessment of service quality, namely:

- *reliability*: the ability to perform the promised service dependably and accurately;
- *responsiveness*: the willingness to help customers and provide prompt service;
- *assurance*: employees' knowledge and courtesy and their ability to convey trust and confidence;
- *empathy*: the provision of caring, individualised attention to customers;
- *tangibles*: the appearance of the physical facilities, equipment, personnel and communications material.

They argue that all these factors are crucial in the quality assessment a customer inevitably undertakes when receiving a service, rated in that order of priority, so for example, reliability is the most important factor.

This quality, they argue, can be delivered first through top managers, who believe that high quality, reliable services are always essential, providing service leadership; second, through thoroughly testing and retesting services in relation to customer expectations; and third, through building and nurturing an organisational infrastructure that delivers error-free services.

My experience of service delivery to both beneficiaries and supporters suggests that this list and its application make a lot of sense for charity services managers. Parasuraman *et al.* (1988) have encapsulated their dimensions into an evaluation tool, SERVQUAL. As a tool it has been criticised by Teas (1994), and Cronin and Taylor (1994) have developed an alternative tool based primarily on performance. Other important contributions on delivering quality in the voluntary and community sector have been made by NCVO's Quality Standards Task Group.

Shostack (1982) argues that one method of ensuring quality is through 'blueprinting'. Physical goods can be specified minutely so that substandard variations are reduced to a minimum. She argues that 'services are very often defined in terms of poorly articulated oral and written abstractions' (Shostack 1982, p. 55). She argues, rightly in my view, that service marketers should make much more effort in directly and indirectly specifying the service blueprint, concentrating particularly on those parts of the service process that seem to cause problems.

Several writers (including Lovelock and Weinberg 1989; Zeithaml and Bitner 2003) support a definition of services marketing as being 'deeds, processes and performances'. Vargo and Lusch (2004) introduce the necessity for the application of specialised competences (knowledge and skills) in delivering these services.

Ideas

The third product area, ideas, needs greater explanation. Products composed exclusively of ideas are seldom found in the commercial world except perhaps in trade associations (which in themselves are voluntary organisations) promulgating positive ideas about their membership and business concerns. However, ideas as products gained full legitimacy when the American Marketing Association (1985) announced its revised definition of marketing as:

> 'the process of planning and executing the conception, pricing, promotion, and distribution of ideas, goods and services to create exchanges that satisfy individual and organisational objectives'.
>
> (p. 1)

However, as long ago as 1969, Kotler and Levy were proposing ideas as a category of product. Voluntary organisations spend a significant amount of their time on ideas activity outside the context of a physical good or service.

Ideas as products in charities are normally exemplified in three ways: within pressure group and campaign work, public education and fundraising.

Pressure group work and campaigns

Pressure group work tends to be aimed primarily at organisations/institutions such as legislatures, the civil service and established/establishment organisations. There are numerous examples of pressure group work. These include trying to change Sunday trading laws; campaigning for better treatment of prisoners; pressuring for an increase in foreign aid; demanding a higher value social security benefit. Pressure group campaigns may be focused on the broader public, but nearly always as a means to an end – build broad-based sympathy in the public in order to influence decision-makers in, say, legislatures.

Public education

Public education tends to be the aiming of ideas at larger swathes of people to try to change their behaviour as an end in itself, for example energy conservation, smoking reduction, keeping the countryside tidy, health education. While there are important exceptions, very few charities engage in significant public education campaigns to change mass behaviour, as they need extensive resources usually only available to governments and their agents. Where charities do claim to be implementing public education campaigns, they are often superficial 'nine-day wonders' that do more for charity awareness than they achieve in changed general public behaviour. Even heavily resourced government campaigns can make little impression on behaviour. For more detailed consideration of public education initiatives (in the US called social marketing) see Kotler *et al.* (2002) and MacFadyen *et al.* (2003)

Fundraising

At first sight, fundraising seems too practical and down to earth to be thought of as an idea product. However, it is seldom a physical good (except when charities market goods for profit), and it cannot easily be described as a service; it fits primarily as an idea. Charities raise money for a product that, for the donor, is essentially an intangible idea. Funds are raised by response to a direct mail letter, a collection tin or a written proposal or brochure. Even where the prospective donor visits a charity building or a service to which they will contribute, there is little concrete connection between the donor and the building or service. The donation goes into the charity coffers and the donor trusts the organisation to make sure that the money gets converted into the chosen building or service. In other words, the donor is contributing to a distant idea, which they cannot experience in the way they could a physical good or a service aimed at them.

It is useful to note that the fundraising idea product aimed at a donor is only an interpretation or partial representation of a charity's physical or service product aimed at beneficiaries. Unique selling propositions (USPs) for products aimed at beneficiaries may not be those that readily appeal to potential donors. In my view it is legitimate to propose re-ordered benefits to donors. However, two things are essential. First, the beneficiary product must not be modified in order to attract supporters. Second, the tone and content of messages being relayed to potential supporters must be acceptable to beneficiaries. For example, it is not unusual for a talking book direct mail appeal letter from RNIB to land on the doormat of a visually impaired talking book member. A key criterion in the final clearance of RNIB direct mail letters is that that talking book members should find the tone and content of the letter acceptable if by chance they receive one. Nevertheless the points in the letter, promoting the idea product, may not be those at the top of the beneficiary's list of product features. For example, two key features to a visually impaired member is that the book arrives by post and that listening to the book is a stimulating experience which relieves boredom and loneliness. The appeal letter will prioritise the latter attribute because it is more likely to prompt a potential donor into action, but the postal feature will not, because experience shows that it does not have 'pulling power' with donors.

This complexity is dealt with in more detail in Chapter 9.

Action arising from idea products

There is an important difference, at least in degree, between action arising out of a pressure group/public education idea product and a fundraising idea product. In the former the 'seller' (the charity) has virtually no control over how the idea is actioned. Indeed the idea could be actioned in a way that the charity regards as totally unsatisfactory (see below). With a fundraising idea product the charity can institute much more control over the immediate action of the target customer, and responsibility for actioning this idea is with the seller or charity.

For example, we shall see in Chapter 8 how the Disability Benefits Consortium was proposing both a fundamental review of the UK benefits system for disabled people and its modification to adopt a disability income and costs allowance scheme. The pressure group was successful in getting the first idea adopted, but only partially successful in persuading the government (the target customer) to adopt the second, at least in the form that the pressure group wanted. In short, the Conservative government of the early 1990s adopted the second idea, but implemented it on its own terms, with far less money than the pressure group was seeking.

Customer behaviour arising out of fundraising products is easier to control, in part because the behaviour response required is more modest, and in part because promotion and distribution mechanisms can be put in place more firmly. Raising money via a direct mail letter to an individual potential donor (for example asking for £25 to purify an existing water well in a developing country) allows the fundraising idea to be set out clearly. The response mechanism – a reply slip and envelope addressed to the charity – is there in the letter. So in this way the customer take-up behaviour arising out of the idea product is simple and reasonably well controlled. However, even here things are not straightforward. The letter recipient may be convinced about the proposal but before they have time to act in the way requested, they may have passed a competitor overseas aid charity collecting box in the street and, prompted by the direct mail letter, decided to contribute to that instead because it is easier and more direct. But the marketing twist in the tail of the fundraising idea product is that, although the customer (donor) pays for the idea product, it is the seller (charity) who implements it, normally without any involvement of this purchaser (donor). In a sense the donor is paying 'something for nothing'.

Implementation of idea products

A successful approach to ideas marketing requires the voluntary organisation to develop ways in which it can be involved in implementation, rather than to feel that its job has been done once the idea has been 'sold'; for example, by being invited to join the civil service implementation group for the new benefit, or by gaining a ministerial commitment that the charity will be consulted at each stage of implementation. In the case of action by a mass of individuals, this can be through down-to-earth practical advice on the detailed steps that need to be taken via public relations and promotional material. Table 4.1 shows who does and does not control implementation in the case of three common categories of charity idea products.

Table 4.1 Implementation of idea products (Bruce 1994)

Idea product	Who controls implementation	Who does not control implementation
Pressure group idea product (e.g. new social security benefit)	Decision-makers	Pressure group/charity
Public education idea product (e.g. anti-smoking)	Individual members of the public	Promoting agency/charity
Fund-raising idea product (e.g. to build a new rehabilitation centre)	Charity	Donor

Features

Ideas have to be developed (manufactured) and put across (sold), and then implemented (acted upon). Ideas are all of the following (Bruce 1994):

- *Intangible*: idea products are the ultimate in intangibility.

- *Separable*: voluntary organisation idea products are almost always developed separately, by people other than those to whom the idea product is 'sold' and those who implement it.
- *Durable*: idea products are highly durable – some have been around for thousands of years.
- *Precise*: in description they can be precise (carefully and accurately designed and promoted).
- *Heterogeneous*: in application and implementation there will be almost as many versions as there are individuals or units implementing them.

Comparison of goods, service and idea products

Using the features of ideas above and the service features presented by Zeithaml *et al* (1985, pp. 33–46), an interesting grid emerges in which the service features have been modified and the ideas column added (Bruce 1994) (see Table 4.2).

Table 4.2 Comparative features of goods, services and ideas

Goods	Services	Ideas
Tangible	Part tangible	Intangible
Separable	Inseparable	Separable
Relatively durable	Perishable	Highly durable
Homogeneous	Heterogeneous	Homogeneous in presentation, heterogeneous in implementation

As described above (see Figure 4.2), Shostack proposed a continuum ranging from a pure tangible good (salt comes near to this), through a tangible good with accompanying services (such as cosmetics) and a service with accompanying goods (such as investment management) to a pure service (teaching could approach this). In other words, most products have both a goods and a service element. But Shostack does not place the idea element in the frame. The place of idea products would seem to be further along the continuum to the right, past 'intangible dominant'. This leads to the additional idea that the continuum is not from goods to services only but from goods to services to ideas. Just as services enter into the continuum shortly after goods, so do ideas.

However, let us take this much-favoured example of Shostack and subsequent writers – salt (close to a pure physical good). The customer has more opportunities to engage with the product in addition to its use as an additive to make food salty. For example, the customer may be buying it to pour into hot water to soothe tired feet. There again the potential customer may be refusing to buy salt at all because of the *idea* that salt is bad for blood pressure. In short, there are traces of ideas and services lurking around what one might think of as pure physical goods. At the other end of the continuum, approaching pure ideas, we shall find traces of goods as well as services.

Pursuing these ideas with a variety of products, it is possible to construct the following models.

Salt (Figure 4.3): unbranded, bulk-purchase cooking salt is virtually 100 per cent pure physical good (no service elements, and virtually no idea element).

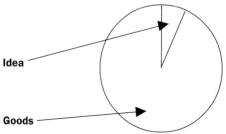

Figure 4.3 Salt

Fast-food (Figure 4.4): from a highly regarded fast-food chain has strong physical goods, service and ideas components (by buying here I know I shall get good food cooked how I like it; served by people who are quick

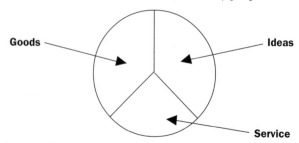

Figure 4.4 Fast-food

and friendly; and eating fast food confirms to me and my friends that I am so busy, I don't have time to cook and can afford to pay someone else to do it).

Liquid level indicator (Figure 4.5): sold at subsidised prices to (mainly) newly blind people, it hooks over the rim of the cup and makes a buzzing noise when the beverage reaches 1 cm below the rim. This is mainly a physical good, and there is no service element, but there is a significant ideas element of empowerment in that use of the device encourages/ empowers the newly blind person to entertain sighted friends once again.

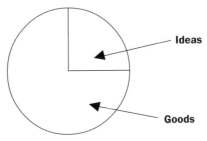

Figure 4.5 Liquid level indicator

Talking books (Figure 4.6): complete books are recorded onto disc and posted to a blind person's home on request, backed up by volunteer service engineers who visit to explain how to use the player and give useful information on other services available.

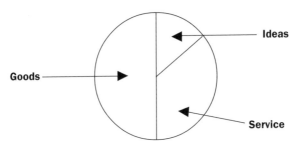

Figure 4.6 Talking books

The books relieve boredom and loneliness (especially among newly blind people) and are a source of pride and accomplishment to friends and family in that the majority of older users have never used a disc player before. Without the sense of pride in using the machine and, more importantly, without the service back-up, many newly blind older members would not have taken up or sustained the activity. The books have a high physical goods component, with significant service and ideas elements.

Empowerment (Figure 4.7): the idea of empowerment of disadvantaged groups is fundamental to many charities. However, without supplying some resources (goods such as wheelchairs for disabled people, and food and shelter for homeless people) and services (such as self-help/mutual aid organisations), disadvantaged groups will not take up the idea of empowerment.

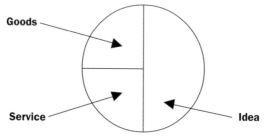

Figure 4.7 Empowerment

As an aside, devising structures to deliver the goods and services in a way that empowers, rather than encourages dependency, is problematic.

Religion (Figure 4.8): in organised religion, ideas and service components dominate and physical goods feature less (depending on the religion and the particular subdivision). In other words, the essence of religion is belief in certain ideas which are supported and developed through services such as regular communal worship, where physical items such as an altar may play a role but only as part of the service.

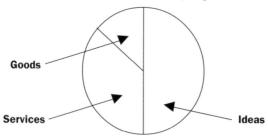

Figure 4.8 Religion

Politics (Figure 4.9): the (ideal) essence of politics is in its ideas. The individual 'buys into' a set of beliefs which others will put into practice (if elected). Because of their extreme intangibility, these ideas need to be supported by service organisations (political parties) which run a whole range of activities to recruit and sustain supporters (ranging from recruitment events and leafleting to social occasions, etc.).

Physical goods are seldom involved except at the periphery, for example sale of T-shirts indicating support for a candidate.

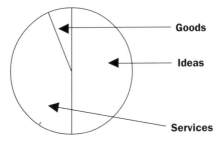

Figure 4.9 Politics

All the above products, indeed in theory all products, can be placed in a three-dimensional model, in relationship to each other (see Figure 4.10)

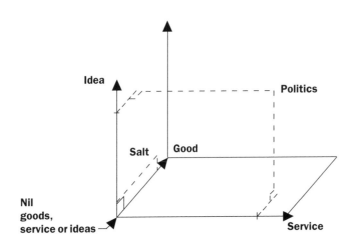

Figure 4.10 Comprehensive product model, positioning products according to the relative weighting of their constituent elements of goods, services and ideas (plotting two examples – salt and politics) (Bruce 1994)

There are three axes at right angles: degree of idea element, service element and goods element.

Conclusion

There are two simple, but fundamental conclusions on product composition and marketing (Bruce 1994):

- All products have actual or latent physical goods, service and ideas components.
- Successful marketing requires that all three components are attended to if the maximum number of customers is to be recruited and retained.

So, for example, organisations will sell more cooking salt if they brand it, offer guarantees and give advice on usage. At the other extreme, political parties will gain and retain more supporters if they not only put forward ideas, but also increase the penetration and effectiveness of services such as regular party meetings, social and community events, advice to and representation of individuals with problems and, albeit less importantly, and within the limits of the law, if they sell and distribute branded physical goods such as badges, pendants, pens and T-shirts. Empowerment of disadvantaged individuals and groups will not just happen. It also requires significant goods and services to be delivered, albeit within the enabling structure of rights, not largesse.

New product development

Development of new products (physical goods, services or ideas) or modification of the existing ones depends fundamentally on relating the charity's aims to the target markets selected. The kinds of issues that need considering in new product (good, services, ideas) decisions are:

- What is the intensity of unmet need?
- How many people in the target market are so affected?
- Do we have or can we develop a product that can wholly meet those needs?
- Do we have necessary resources – money and expertise – to deliver?
- Are there other providers?

The answers to these questions do not give the final answer, which requires an overall judgement from management (and sometimes committees). But they do provide a framework of evidence. Ansoff (1965, pp. 109–10) proposed a useful model for considering market development (which he called 'product-market posture'), which has been widely used and adapted over the years (see Figure 4.11).

Growth through:

A	B
existing products in existing target markets (market penetration)	existing products in new target markets (market development)
C	D
new products in existing target markets (product development)	new products in new target markets (diversification)

Figure 4.11

Increased market penetration gives growth through market share of the present product markets. An example from quadrant A would be to increase the number of existing Braille readers purchasing RNIB's Braille magazines and/or increase the number of magazines taken. In B, it might be to increase the numbers of Braille readers through education programmes (a new market) and sell existing magazines into this market. In quadrant C it might be to introduce new Braille magazines into the range to promote to existing purchasers. In quadrant D it might be to introduce new magazines on subjects designed to appeal to newly Braille-literate people.

The above examples are ones of evolutionary growth. However, more revolutionary ones can also be adopted. For example, in quadrant D the logic could be as follows. Only 20,000 out of 1 million blind and partially sighted people read Braille. This is because most of the 1 million are relatively newly visually impaired in older age and so reduced finger sensitivity makes learning Braille very difficult. One of the products they miss is being able to read national newspapers in full on the day they are published, rather than 20 per cent on an audio tape version arriving three days later. Electronic technology in the 1980s had advanced to such an extent that a computerised newspaper in voice output form could be beamed direct from the editorial offices of a national newspaper overnight via a television aerial into a home computer, ready for listening to in audio or reading in Braille form by 6 am – the same time as a printed newspaper falls on the mat. This was attractive to newly blind people of 40–60 years of age who previously could type or were familiar with personal computers. RNIB launched such a scheme, which has been superseded by newspaper websites.

Ansoff's growth framework is equally useful for other markets such as the environment and the arts. Rodger (1987, pp. 40–52) provides interesting examples from the visual arts. While the above model provides a framework for a strategic analysis of development, how does new product development happen in practice? This is discussed in more detail in Chapter 7. However, in short, the process consists of developing proposals, giving them preliminary analysis in relation to target markets and the resources of the charity and relating the proposal to the objective of the charity. If the product gets through this stage, one then undertakes more sophisticated business analysis and development of the product in some detail (this needs to occur more or less simultaneously because one feeds on the other), takes the product in the form of physical goods, services or even ideas out to an actual or simulated test market situation and, if the pilot is successful, launches the new physical good, service or idea.

New product development is crucial to charities and voluntary and community groups, not least because it is an area of major claim of superior performance of our sector in comparison with the public sector (normally referred to as the ability to innovate). The commercial sector has a reputation for innovation. An excellent review and ready reference of new service development in that sector is provided by Johne and Storey (1998).

Phasing out products

Deleting a product in whatever form is very difficult in any organisation, but especially in a charity where commitment to beneficiary groups, however few, is very high, and the straightforward pressures of profitability do not often apply. To avoid snap deletion decisions being made because of a funding crisis or customer complaints, all charity offerings should be reviewed on a regular basis. Ideally the review should not be simply on the basis of whether to remove a product. It would obviously be much more broadly based and would be part of regular effectiveness reviews. However, the basic question 'do we need this product any more?' should always be asked in such reviews. Some of the questions to ask in reaching a decision are:

- Is it central to our mission?
- How do our customers regard its quality?
- How many customers does it reach?
- What is the subsidy in total and the subsidy per customer?
- Are there other providers of better or comparable quality?

If there are other providers and the other answers are negative, this offering is a candidate for closure. In the case of closure, taking account of and managing the expectations of existing and past customers, especially beneficiaries, is crucial. Closures in our sector are usually far more complicated and problematic than ones in the commercial sector and so need careful planning.

Handling deletions or closures needs to be very carefully thought through. It is fairly easy for Unilever to cope with complaints about the deletion of a soap powder. It is much harder for a charity to deal with (especially organised) complaints by beneficiaries about the removal of a product, for example closure of a care home, particularly when the closure has the effect of dramatically disrupting the lives of existing residents by placing them in other homes away from the staff and fellow residents whom they have come to know and love.

Conclusion

The field of charity products or offerings is extraordinarily complex, involving not only physical goods and services, but also ideas. Successful product design requires attention to the eight 'Ps' of philosophy, product, price, promotion, place, people, physical evidence and process. Next we turn to one of the most challenging elements of the charity marketing mix, namely price.

Price

As has been noted above, this has traditionally been one of the most difficult of the 'Ps' to use in not-for-profit marketing. There are areas where it is readily, and normally, well applied, such as the pricing of fundraising catalogue items, or giving donors target response levels in direct mail letters. However, outside the field of fundraising, and within the product areas of services and ideas, the charity track record is generally very poor. Even the most fundamental information for considering price, namely cost of producing product, normally a service, is more often than not missing. Even accepting that setting a price greater than cost is normally inappropriate for activities associated with core charity aims, failing to understand the true relativity of price and cost is amateurish.

For example, it was only in the 1980s that the RNIB properly costed all the items within its sixty or so product lines (comprising physical goods, services and ideas); and 20 per cent proved particularly intransigent. Hardest to cost are those products that are part of a multiple product line, handled by several parts of an organisation. The field of costing of services in the charity sector has much to learn from other professional service providers such as lawyers or management consultants, who charge out every working moment in time chunks of fifteen minutes (or even five minutes). Going this far will seldom be necessary when profit is not the bottom line, but charities should have a better idea of the subsidy going into products as well as product lines.

Having costed our charity offerings, is it worthwhile or even appropriate to price them? It is worthwhile in many more cases than at present. Every product has to be resourced – something that properly idealistic service managers often forget! If the customer (whether end beneficiary, intermediary or supporter) is contributing nothing to this, a number of dangers emerge, such as:

- the intermediary or beneficiary customer not valuing the product;
- the beneficiary feeling patronised as a recipient of charity rather than a customer with consumer rights;
- relative over-usage by some customers (because price is no brake) which blocks off access to non-users.

If this seems like an esoteric argument we only have to look at the contribution of income from priced products (goods, services and ideas) to get a shock of realism. Earned income provides charities with well over one third of their income (43 per cent – see Table 4.3). For charities whose income lies between £1 million and £10 million, earned income contributes nearly a half of all income (47 per cent). Even for the smallest general charities with income below £10,000 pa it contributes 30 per cent.

Table 4.3 Income types by size of organisation (%)

	Under £10k	£10k– £100k	£100k– £1m	£1m– £10m	Over £10m	All
Earned income	30.2	40.2	38.0	47.4	43.5	42.9
Voluntary income	43.7	45.3	52.0	44.5	46.6	47.1
Investment returns	26.2	14.4	10.0	8.2	9.9	10.0
Total	**100.0**	**100.0**	**100.0**	**100.0**	**100.0**	**100.0**

Source: Wilding *et al.* 2004, p. 87

When it is realised that sales of general charity goods and services (earned income) provide over one third of charity income, the importance of appropriate pricing is very clear (see Table 4.3). However, the importance of pricing is even further underlined by the dramatic growth of earned income over the last few years. It is almost certain that sales growth is being fuelled by contracting, especially for medium-sized charities.

So a key conclusion is that sales income and pricing are crucial to general charities and are growing in importance. Charities ignore this trend at their peril.

Impact price

So much for goods, services and ideas that can be priced, but what about others that, superficially, cannot be? A good example here might be pressure group proposals, trying to persuade the government to increase social security benefit or introduce a new one. The charity can hardly charge the civil servants for battering them with ideas they do not really want to hear! However, here and in relation to many services and some physical goods as well as ideas, I suggest using the term 'impact price'. The price is obscured to the seller but not the buyer. This concept is widely applicable to idea products, partially applicable to service products and marginally applicable to physical goods products. These impact prices are often ignored by the seller, but readily appreciated by the consumer.

Returning to the example of the pressure group proposal, many charity pressure groups come up with calls for immediate changes that are very difficult for politicians and civil servants to implement. This is for a variety of reasons, including the fact that the resources are simply not available and/or the procedural changes involved are very significant and would create opposition from other government departments, let alone the fact that other pressure groups might lose out as a consequence. In short, the impact price that the politicians and civil servants would have to pay is too high, even if they think that the pressure group idea is a good one. When challenged on this impact price, campaigners will offer a variety of justifications for not having thought the issue through. One is that they are trying to establish a bargaining position which can later be reduced; another is that it is not up to them to become involved in resource and procedural deliberations, as that is the role of government; and another is that it would be letting down the interest they represent to demand anything other than the full proposal. In their way, all of these points have some validity, but on many occasions they are simply excuses for the pressure group not having thought carefully enough about the full price their customers are going to have to pay.

Marketing approach

A marketing approach would be to think about the impact price from the point of view of the potential implementers of the proposal. It may be that while the full demand is retained, suggestions can be put forward as to how the change could be introduced incrementally. The first increment would take account of resources likely to become available and would be in a form that is less likely to encourage opposition from other interest groups both within and without government. Such a pricing process is not dissimilar to a commercial company offering significant discounts to customers in the early stages in order to get them 'hooked'.

Chapter 3 described the application of exchange theory to understand customer take-up behaviour, listing costs and benefits to the target groups of taking up the offering. Such an approach helps us to assess the impact price.

Conclusion

In short, the 'P' of price is undervalued by the public and not-for-profit sectors in two main ways. Overt pricing is often not considered in relation to true costs, and under-pricing is too readily accepted. Second, impact prices, especially of ideas and to a lesser extent services, and also occasionally of goods, are seldom considered by charities, which accounts for many important 'sales' not being made. Charities need to use the concepts behind such commercial terms as price discounts, allowances and credit. These ideas are explored further in Chapters 6–10.

Promotion

If pricing is an element of the marketing mix where many not-for-profit organisations are weak, promotion of offerings (marketing communications) is an area where they are strong and frequently outperform their commercial counterparts. The traditional list of the promotion mix is advertising, personal selling, sales promotion and public relations. Three important additional areas, relevant to services in general and to charity service and idea products in particular, need to be considered, namely coalition building, intermediary referral and customer referral (Bruce 1994).

Advertising

Within the limits of relatively low spending levels, charity advertising can be among the best, giving high impact, high memorability and significant awareness. Among the classics are the Salvation Army's 'For God's sake care', Christian Aid's 'Give a man a fish and you feed him for a day. Teach him to fish and you feed him for life', and Barnardo's linking babies with subsequent drug taking and prostitution.

Personal selling

Personal selling, where it happens, can also be highly effective and professional. The volunteer fundraising forces of charities such as Save the Children, Oxfam and NSPCC make commercial sales directors green with envy. Personal selling of ideas (particularly in pressure group work and fundraising) by middle and senior management is also widespread and effective. This assessment is based on informal feedback from civil servants, politicians and senior business leaders who have been on the receiving end of such initiatives. However, personal selling of services – especially beneficiary services – by middle managers to intermediaries such as local authorities can be problematic. There is a widespread feeling among charity service middle managers that selling, self-publicity and even publicising the organisation is 'not why we are here'. Rather they feel that constructing and delivering the service is the key task. This fails to recognise the fact that without very active promotion, including personal selling, no one is going to want the services.

A good example of the benefit of effective personal selling can be seen among special schools run by charities. Here it is usually the responsibility of the head or a senior staff member to travel to interested local authorities and prospective parents. When prospective parents visit the school, this is not seen as an unwelcome intrusion, but is valued by all staff as an opportunity to meet prospective parents and to form a view as to whether the child will benefit from the school's education. Schools like this are full. NCH Action for Children is very effective at personal selling, as is shown by its greatly increased contract income.

Sales promotion

Sales promotion is probably one of the less useful methods and is certainly not widely utilised in the charity sector. An important exception would be in fundraising, where giving gifts to donors is becoming more widespread; also special opportunities for major valued donors are becoming increasingly the norm, such as meeting aristocratic and royal patrons and attendance at prestigious first nights.

Stripping back the purpose of sales promotion to its very core – promoting sales of a particular offering – one can see far wider applic-ability in the charity sector. All voluntary organisations have services and ideas that are reasonably well known and well regarded but are not expanding as fast as the agency would wish. A greater concentration on trying to create events, either in isolation or as part of third-party activity with a specific objective of clinching a sale, could reap rewards: for example, a disability charity providing 50 per cent of the costs of the extra equipment a mainstream school needs to integrate a disabled child, provided that the LEA will provide the extra professional staff support.

Public relations

Public relations is another area where charities are among the market leaders. They have products that are intrinsically interesting and newsworthy, and they achieve massive TV, radio and newspaper coverage of their interests through the editorial rather than the paid advertising channels. Charities have made a fine art of promoting their interests to journalists and researchers in all media. They treat these groups as the intermediary customers they really are. Indeed, charities are so good at communications that some people have argued that this emphasis is disproportionate and that charities need to adopt a more strategic or long-term marketing perspective (Conway 1997).

Pharoah and Welchman (1997) surveyed public communication methods and development in 1,000 charities showing a very wide range of techniques and strategy contributing to effectiveness. Deacon *et al* (1995) interviewed media professionals and concluded that they were most receptive to topical issues (pertinent to broader issues current at the time) or those demonstrably of general interest. This bears out two important media relations rules: (a) try and ride on the back of bigger stories and (b) establish your story's relevance to as wide a group of people as possible.

Coalition building

The promotion of services and, in particular, ideas can be greatly enhanced by building coalitions between statutory, voluntary and, in some cases, even commercial organisations with a common interest (see Chapter 8). Because of the superficially altruistic basis of the work, quite surprising coalitions can be achieved, which greatly enhance their power. It is not unusual for a variety of charities to join together with representatives from local government to promote a particular cause area such as child protection. Employers supported by disability charities have built a coalition to promote the recruitment of disabled people into employers' workforces, and as a side-effect this coalition has had a strong influence on disability policy. In 1987 a consortium of 250 charities in Britain concerned with disability (Disability Benefits Consortium) gathered together to present one voice during a period when it was known that the government was prepared to amend existing benefits and introduce new benefits for disabled people. Such coalitions significantly increase the impact of charity proposals.

Intermediary referral

Another area absent from traditional elaborations of the marketing mix relates to services and ideas. A. Wilson (1984, p. 161) points out the importance of professional referral for professional services and, along with Berry and Parasuraman (1991, p. 7), emphasises the importance of the word-of-mouth recommendation – especially from customers – as being that much more critical for a service, which can only be experienced, as opposed to a physical good, which can be inspected.

These forms of promotion are of critical importance to charity services and idea products and also to physical goods aimed at beneficiaries. Up to 100 per cent of new beneficiary customers to education and social service charities will come from professional referrals from social workers, doctors, teachers, lawyers, etc. The relative take-up of physical goods aimed at beneficiaries may also be strongly related to the degree and nature of referrals from professionals. In Chapter 8, which covers pressure group work, the importance of professional referral, commendation and advocacy is discussed. The obvious conclusion is that professional worker intermediaries are an important customer group, which needs to be identified for each charity offering, be it goods, services or ideas. They need to be developed, even nurtured, if the charity products are to penetrate their end customer market significantly.

Customer referral

Satisfied (or dissatisfied) customers of charity offerings are also potent promotional forces. This area is covered in Chapters 6–10. It is sufficient to say here that satisfied and loyal beneficiary and supporter customers will spread the word and bring in many more beneficiaries and supporters. Strongly dissatisfied ones will do the opposite. Again, existing customers need to be well served and nurtured in their own right, particularly if customer word-of-mouth recommendations are to increase target market penetration.

Conclusion

Promotion in the charity field is rather like the curate's egg, good and bad in different parts. Even where it is good, however, there is room for drawing promotion in as part of the marketing mix and involving line managers in the promotional work. Promotion is often undertaken by staff separate from the product line and the promotion is not integrated into the marketing mix, but stands alone, losing effectiveness.

Place

Place, or distribution, is the activity that ensures that products get to customers when and where they want to buy them. Doyle (1991 and 2003 p. 287) reframes McCarthy's '4Ps' of place as distribution channels, coverage, locations, inventory and transport.

Distributors and retailers

Public and charitable organisations often assume that they have a much harder task in reaching their end customer than the commercial world. In fact the list above shows that the commercial marketing organisation has many intermediary target groups to work through before it reaches its end customer, in the same way as a not-for-profit organisation does. Doyle (1991, p. 282, and 2003) argues that distribution intermediaries have 'goals that are at least partially conflicting with those of the manufacturer'. This produces many of the difficulties experienced by charities in the area of 'place'. The key difference is that commercial organisations are much more prepared to bolster the common interest between the marketing organisation and its distribution channels through the provision of financial incentives. Charities seldom provide financial incentives to intermediaries and have to rely much more heavily on common goals in relation to the end consumer. For example, charities running home visiting services rely heavily on referrals from social workers. Social workers and social services departments receive no financial incentive or 'percentage' of the subsequent fee (if any). They introduce the service because they feel it will help the wellbeing of their client – they have common cause with the supply organisation.

Wholesalers

Dibb *et al.* (1991, p. 698 and 2001), in their brief discussion of voluntary organisation marketing, point out that an important element of the distribution mix (place) – that of independent wholesalers – does not exist in the charity sector. In the sense of wholesaler services that can be purchased, they are right. However, charities have a plethora of distributors that they can and do use to reach their end clients. (For example, national charities may use local charities for stock-holding, with even more localised older people's clubs or local churches drawing down stock for onward distribution to end beneficiaries.) The difference is that these distributor channels cannot normally be bought in the way that commercial wholesalers and other onward distributors can. Thus these intermediary distribution channels assume the characteristics of an intermediary target group or intermediary customer group whose needs and wants must be addressed in a fundamental way if the charity is to be successful in reaching its end clients. Provided that this broader understanding of the terms 'distributors' and 'retailers' is understood, then Doyle's list is adequate.

As a generalisation, charities pay insufficient attention to this fourth 'P' of place. They tend to assume that because (in their view) their product, be it a physical good, service or idea, is intrinsically good, somehow everyone else will take up common cause and help to make it accessible and available to the potential end customer. This is not necessarily the case; greater study of the aims of intermediaries, and adjusting the product or the way it is designed, can increase its attractiveness to intermediaries and thus increase its chances of reaching the end customer.

Locations

'Locations' is a crucial checkpoint for developing new offerings and assessing existing ones. Locations where charity offerings are delivered to customers can change quite dramatically over a number of years; or if they do not change, can result in the demise of the product. As shown in the special school case example in Chapter 1, changes in social policy dictated that the delivery of education and rehabilitation to young visually impaired children should change from sending them to a distant residential home towards concentrating on delivery at the local level. If the Sunshine organisation had not changed its point of delivery, it would have gone out of existence. Similar changes are now taking place in relation to rehabilitating newly disabled adults into employment. Previously this was provided regionally, but now the purchasing authority in the form of the government is insisting that this should be provided locally.

The headings 'inventory' (stocks) and 'transport' are relevant to charities when dealing with physical goods but make less sense when considering services and ideas.

People

Booms and Bitner (1981, pp. 47–51) break down this area of the marketing mix, as applied to services, into personnel and other customers.

Personnel

Elements relating to personnel include training, discretion, commitment, incentives, appearance, interpersonal behaviour and attitudes. Looking at this list, charity marketing managers might feel they are being asked to take on responsibility for managing the whole organisation; and general charity managers must be either feeling threatened or becoming exasperated at the cheek of these marketing people who think that such aspects as staff behaviour and attitudes have anything to do with marketing staff. Chapter 5 will deal with this in more detail. However, in essence, the responsibility of the marketing function is to persuade line management of the importance of these elements if the service or idea product is to be attractive to customers and recommended by them.

Some line managers would argue that they already have all the above elements well under control. This may be true, but in my experience they are primarily under control in relation to other staff, their managers and the organisation in general. They are not always appropriately directed towards customers. Chapter 3 discussed the various reasons that charities, in particular, do not always think along the philosophical lines of 'the customer is always right'. Too often they appear to think and behave along the lines of 'the customers are lucky to have our help'.

For me, one of the most exciting bridges from marketing into service and idea delivery is a book by Berry and Parasuraman (1991). The reason for calling this book a 'bridge' is that they focus very heavily on quality as the way through to successful service (and, by implication, idea) products. However, their application of quality is intensely directed towards the customer. They argue that there is nothing better than quality to retain customers, gain new customers through word-of-mouth recommendation, and establish product differentiation.

At this point it is worth introducing the idea of high and low staff/customer contact; a distinction developed by Chase (1978, pp. 137–42). In short, the greater the contact between customers and (charity) service staff, the more important it is to get the staff personnel aspects up to a very high standard. At its most superficial, a charity can get away with grumpy but efficient staff provided they are not in contact with the customer. For charity service products such as schools, colleges, hotels, training centres and day centres, contact with staff is lengthy and intensive. The value that beneficiaries put on these services will almost entirely be the result of their interaction with staff.

Looking at the list of elements, it is immediately clear that charities should have a significant advantage over commercial companies under the headings of commitment, attitude and interpersonal behaviour. In my experience of working in both the commercial and voluntary sectors, charities do have the edge in these areas, but only just. A commercial organisation that involves its staff, praises them for good work and has good staff development programmes will almost certainly have better staff attitudes and commitment than the charity that does none of these things.

Discretion is a particularly interesting element. Berry and Parasuraman (1991, p. 49) make a very strong case for giving those service staff in direct touch with customers significant discretion to satisfy them, especially if they are dissatisfied. They quote Federal Express where, even though the average transaction costs only $16, front-line company service representatives are empowered to spend up to $100 to resolve a customer problem. That principle translates well into the charity sector.

Other customers

The impact that other customers have on customer take-up is a fascinating one, and is clearly also crucial to charity services to beneficiaries and supporters. If the offering involves a number of beneficiaries or supporters being in one place for some time, it is vital that they get on with each other. If they do not, then the offering will be much less well appreciated, they might not come back, and they will almost certainly not recommend it.

To some extent, good marketing analysis beforehand should overcome many of the potential dangers, because the customer group should be relatively homogeneous. However, there will inevitably be problems or dislikes between contemporaneous customers, and it is therefore vital for staff to be trained and skilled in resolving such issues. For example, a number of disability charities run holiday schemes. These are normally fairly well targeted, either to involve younger people or older people. In theory there is no reason that the scheme could not involve both, but the chances of negative customer interaction increase, for example younger people staying up late and wanting loud music, and older guests not appreciating this. Similarly, the fundraising case example in Chapter 1 showed that one reason for the success of the fundraising dinner was that it involved people with a common interest – horseracing – and the event was planned around this.

Physical evidence

Physical evidence of, and surrounding the product, can be very influential in establishing customer expectations before take-up, and can continue to be influential during take-up. While it is relevant to physical goods, it is particularly vital in the field of charity services and ideas because these are, in themselves, so much less tangible. In other words, the customer may place particular reliance, especially before take-up, on the physical evidence simply because the experience is not yet there. Even while the experience is taking place, the tangible aspects may set a very strong backcloth for judgement of the intangibles. For example, the quality of tea, coffee and other food on a rehabilitation course may be a strong influencer as to the clients' judgement of the effectiveness of the course. It is hard to be positive about any kind of course where the food is delivered late and is cold and poor quality.

Charity services

Whether a charity's services are aimed at beneficiaries or supporters, the design of the service environment needs to be thought through well. Factors such as physical layout, quality of furnishings and noise levels, can quickly set an atmosphere, either good or bad. A charity nature reserve, hotel, college or rehabilitation centre needs to be laid out as well as possible in relation to its function and its beneficiaries' expectations. For example, even if the hotel is old the lighting levels and furnishings can be improved.

There are similar considerations for services aimed at donors. The atmosphere of the fundraising dinner would be quite different if held in the (aristocratic) president's own home as opposed to the Hilton. The sponsored swim is likely to be much more effective in both attracting swimmers and encouraging them to offer their support again, if it is held in a modern swimming bath with clean changing facilities.

Once stated, these points are obvious. But it is surprising how many charities either ignore them, or take the view that there is nothing they can do to improve matters substantially. There are always relatively low-cost initiatives that can be improve the physical environment and so increase take-up.

Encouraging take-up of services relies heavily on adroit use of tangible clues in both advertising and promotion, and in responding to enquiries. Once again, if a charity responds to enquiries about its hotels, schools or rehabilitation centres promptly with an attractive brochure and informative covering letter, the intermediary or potential beneficiary is going to be much more certain about the quality of the service. Two colleges may provide comparable education, but if one has a poor brochure and responds late to enquiries, the enquirer is far more likely to go to the college with the prompt response and the well thought-out brochure.

Ideas

It is even more important to manage the physical evidence of ideas in a proactive way, simply because they are intangible. Take-up of fund-raising ideas can be much higher when tangible clues are offered. Direct mail letters get much better responses if, for example, a small sample of dehydration salts are included in an overseas aid appeal, a piece of Braille is included in a letter asking for support for services to blind people or, at a most basic level, if a photograph of the school for which the appeal is being made is included.

At first sight one might think that tangible clues about pressure group ideas are either impossible or inconsequential. Surely it is the quality of ideas that counts, rather than any kind of physical evidence. In my experience physical evidence can be absolutely crucial in an idea gaining ground. Even something as simple as using a flip chart with computer-generated large print headings will help nudge ministers out of their post-prandial doze. Drawing other knowledgeable or experienced people into the presentation, either in person or through video, adds to the credibility of the idea. Leaving well-printed and designed (but not expensive) proposal papers makes everything much more concrete.

This is not to dismiss the role of the informal discussion at a government reception, or over a private lunch, where not even papers change hands. However, when one has got through the door to the stage of formal presentation, physical evidence of pressure group ideas needs to be implemented very thoughtfully.

In summary, in order to encourage take-up, especially of services and ideas, a charity needs to look at the best possible physical evidence that it can present to potential customers before take-up. It also needs to look carefully at the physical evidence of services during their consumption.

Process

The subheads under this element of the marketing mix proposed by Booms and Bitner (1981, pp. 47–51) are policies, procedures, mechanisation, employee discretion, customer involvement, customer direction and flow of activities. Once again, reading such a list may prompt the charity manager reading this text to wonder if the marketing manager is trying to take over the world! However, what is actually being proposed is that operations managers have to 'think' marketing or, to put it another way, marketing has to go into the management line. All the elements initially look like straight operations responsibilities, where the purpose is to undertake all activities as efficiently, effectively and cheaply as possible. But these processes must be customer-friendly. If not, customers will either walk away or stay and feel dissatisfied.

Beneficiaries and supporters

When stated, it is obvious that beneficiaries and supporters are crucial. Their satisfaction must dictate the changes and the rate of change of operational activities. For example, too many charities have seized the advantage of computer systems to introduce much more 'efficient' invoicing and fee collection systems. Invoices are issued much more promptly and accurately, and non-paying customers are identified automatically and regularly. However, more often than not, these new efficient billing systems have been introduced with little thought to the paying customer. The invoices are full of number codes that cannot easily be related to purchases, the financial systems do not allow many words to be included, and they are difficult for the customer to understand. RNIB's original invoices were so customer unfriendly that some people stopped buying because they got so confused and upset by what they saw as the gobbledegook being thrown at them. RNIB now issues invoices in large print, Braille and electronically, to take account of beneficiary customers' needs.

Employee discretion

Another example of the need for operational managers to 'think' marketing and customers is in the field of employee discretion for those staff who work at the front line. Superficial operational efficiency would suggest that the most junior employees need have little discretion. However, customer contact personnel (however junior) are the first people to learn that a customer has received a substandard physical good, or an unsatisfactory service. Berry and Parasuraman (1991, pp. 47–50) describe four crucial requirements for resolving customer problems effectively. They argue that, first, employees must be prepared/ trained in recovering the situation; second they have to be empowered to undertake corrective action (the example was given above of Federal Express front-line employees being empowered to spend up to six times the average order cost to correct a problem); third, employees must be facilitated to correct problems (perhaps by allowing them to access information urgently from other, often more senior, staff and/or giving them the most expensive high-tech equipment in order to access other parts of the organisation); and fourth, employees must be rewarded for early and satisfactory customer complaints resolution and reporting them to senior staff so that problems can be grouped and solved as part of the system. To me this description seems an excellent example of how the common interests of operational and marketing trains of thought can be brought together to the benefit of both the organisation and customers.

Customer involvement

Customer involvement and customer direction are areas of particular interest to charity goods, services and ideas as applied to beneficiaries, and also make good sense in services aimed at supporters. We can learn a lot from the educational philosophy that people develop far more effectively if they are 'active in their own learning'. Charity customers, whether they be beneficiaries, supporters, intermediaries or staff, are not there to be 'done unto'. As a general rule they need to be involved, and certainly in the area of services they have to be involved whether the charity likes it or not (and obviously the charity should 'like it').

In conclusion, this element of the marketing mix is not an attempt by marketing managers to take over operational management. It is simply a proposal that marketing has a lot to offer to operations at the customer interface, especially in the areas of service and idea products, where the charity's processes are inextricably interwoven with the offering.

Conclusion

Charities and public organisations' products (goods, services and ideas) have a marketing mix whether or not the organisation recognises it as such. Adapting the commercial listings can help charities and not-for-profit organisations make sure that their offerings or products are more in line with customers' needs and wants. However, defining a marketing mix for a product or product line is one thing; implementing it in the services-dominant environment of charities is another, The next chapter suggests how we can do this, by looking at a charity's culture, resources, activities, processes and structure.

Key points

The charity marketing mix – the eight 'Ps':

Philosophy

- Voluntary organisations should be explicit about their values and philosophy and ensure that these are integrated into the marketing mix. Failure to do so will lead to tensions and contradictions between different physical products, services and ideas.

Product (or offering)

- Charity products can be physical goods, services or ideas.
- Successful product design requires attention to all eight 'Ps'.
- Develop new products or adapt existing ones to the selected target markets.
- In marketing services, quality is key – achieved by reliability, ensuring that the service continues to meet customer expectation and constructing an organisation that delivers the service without errors.

Price

- Charities are often weak on this element of the marketing mix .
- Know the cost of each offering or product and be aware of the dangers of under-pricing and over-subsidy.
- Understand the impact price of the ideas or services you are proposing.

Promotion

- Charity promotion is often very effective, but for best results make sure it is integrated into the marketing mix.
- Be aware of the importance of word-of-mouth recommendation and referral.

Place

- Charities have a variety of distributors and potential distributors. Because they are often not paid in the conventional commercial sense, they need to be treated as intermediary customers, with their needs addressed in much the same way as any other intermediary target group.
- Check the locations (the points of delivery) of new and existing products.

People

- Charities do not always have the advantage over commercial companies in terms of staff commitment and attitude, and the voluntary sector can learn useful lessons from the commercial sector.
- Service customers often interact with each other. Segmentation will help ensure this is positive.

Physical evidence

- Remember that the service customer may be relying on the tangible evidence of an experience as a way of interpreting it, whether the service is aimed at beneficiaries or supporters.
- Give potential donors or supporters tangible evidence to help them understand and remember your appeal or proposal.

Process

- Think how your usual administrative procedures could become more customer oriented.

5 How to introduce a marketing approach and a marketing reality

Virtually all marketing books, whether aimed at not-for-profit organisations or the commercial world, devote relatively little space to introducing marketing into an organisation. My experience, in three charities and one public body, is that this is a major challenge, which is not at all easy to accomplish.

Reasons for resistance

In the charity world of the early 1970s, marketing was not a word to be loved or hated; it was simply unknown. However, as advertising agencies became influential with more charities, the term began to be acknowledged. Yet the heavy involvement of the advertising agencies only tended to encourage the view that marketing was simply advertising and selling. The growth, first of fundraising advertisements (as opposed to awareness-raising ones) and then of direct mail, steadily introduced the term and its techniques into charity fundraising.

By the early 1980s the more successful charities were using marketing methods in fundraising in considerable and sophisticated ways. However, the term 'marketing manager' was seldom, if ever, seen. If a post did have this title it was attached to the post of the manager in charge of some combination of charity shops, Christmas cards and catalogues. In 1986 RNIB introduced four posts with the title 'marketing manager', three of which were wholly orientated towards physical goods and services aimed at beneficiaries (in education, employment and social services, and Braille and technical aid products). Fairly extensive enquiries at that time did not turn up any other charity marketing posts aimed exclusively at physical goods or services directed at beneficiaries. In the 1990s, it was still very unusual to find marketing managers in charge of offerings to beneficiaries. However, it was commonplace to find them in the fields of fundraising and public relations. In the 21st century there is increasing evidence of a more widespread adoption of a market orientation, but researchers such as Leighton Jones (Jones 2000) and Liao *et al.* (2001) are still cautious about the degree of penetration. I would agree. My experience of lecturing on charity marketing is that, typically, half the audience is surprised at how applicable marketing is to charity activities.

The basic tenets of marketing crystallised in the commercial world in the 1950s. As long ago as 1969 Kotler and Levy, in a seminal article, explicitly expanded the marketing concept for application in the non-profit world. So why did it take until the 1990s before charities began to apply the discipline to provision for beneficiaries? Even in direct marketing to supporters it was not until the 1970s that marketing tools were commonplace and in fundraising generally it took until the 1980s. This remarkably slow penetration should warn us that resistance is fundamental, not superficial; also that its introduction needs to be carefully planned and undertaken. Such an introduction requires us to understand in some detail why meeting customer needs is, surprisingly, quite an alien concept in charities (Bruce 1995).

Undervaluing needs

The following sections explore why we often do not fully meet beneficiaries', supporters' and stakeholders' needs; and why we often do not value them sufficiently.

Beneficiaries

1   Many not-for-profit organisations are in a *monopolistic situation* in relation to beneficiaries. This gives beneficiaries little or no choice and can allow, if not encourage, a 'take it or leave it' attitude in the not-for-profit provider. If unchecked, this situation can lead to neglect and even, on occasions, arrogance towards, and contempt for, beneficiaries. Critical views expressed by beneficiaries, especially if they are organised or semi-organised, are dismissed as the work of trouble makers.

2   A related reason for beneficiary neglect is that in many situations, even if there is competition between not-for-profits, *demand far exceeds supply*. In theory, two organisations serving older people, or two providing low-cost housing may appear to be competing for

beneficiary customers and offering choice. However, the reality is that the combined provision is still totally inadequate in terms of the number of potential beneficiaries and their needs. Indeed, some commercial marketers (see Baker 1987, p. 7) have argued that commercial marketing only flourished when basic needs had been met and supply had outstripped demand. In the not-for-profit world this seldom happens, except in the arts field (Hill *et al.* 1995). This view, coming from such an eminent commercial marketer, needs careful consideration, and I return to it later in this chapter. Ali (2001), Paton (1996) and Lindsay and Murphy (1996) also explore when and under what conditions marketing can be applied in the not-for-profit sector. O'Sullivan and O'Sullivan (1996) argue that marketing in our sector can best be described as 'naïve', bringing a fresh and more individualistic approach than 'orthodox' commercial marketing.

Where demand outstrips supply, not-for-profits can adopt a range of coping strategies, nearly all of which result in an undervaluing of the beneficiary customer. One strategy is to try and improve productivity through mass production of goods and services that help everyone to a basic level – 'you can have your individual needs met provided it is through our standard product' (goods or services). Another is to build in restraints on demand. The most customer-friendly restraint is not to make the product very widely known; this is a widespread technique in our sector. Less customer-friendly restraints are those that reduce demand by deterring beneficiary customers, such as means tests, complicated forms, lengthy queuing systems or poor or patronising customer care.

3   Paradoxically, some not-for-profit workers' predilection for *concentrated attention on too few beneficiaries* (which looks like a pure marketing or meeting needs approach) can militate against an effective customer attentive approach. One regularly comes across situations where an organisation has spent an inordinate amount of time on a product (be it a good or a service) for one beneficiary. This can occur for several reasons, such as compassion for a beneficiary in a desperate situation, or because an influential stakeholder (often a trustee) insists on an individual's needs being met. At the same time, the organisation often runs standardised, undifferentiated products to its whole beneficiary group, which

means that no one is particularly well satisfied. A marketing approach, which groups beneficiaries with similar needs, can avoid both the one-off help that ignores the silent majority of need, and the undifferentiated mass-production, which is sub-standard for everyone.

4   Many not-for-profits are trying to meet fundamental and basic needs, often in the bottom half of Maslow's (1943) Hierarchy of Needs, such as food, shelter and security. Thus, many not-for-profit beneficiaries are economically, politically, socially and, sometimes, even physically weak. As a consequence they are *too weak to make their voice heard* effectively. Organising themselves into representative groups is problematic.

5   Furthermore, it is difficult to prevent *'haves' who run the not-for-profit from developing a patronising attitude towards 'have nots'* on the basis that the organisation, rather than the customer, is always right. For example, if a charity has been providing a service in a given way for years, it is hard for it to accept the views of what it may see as a small, unrepresentative group of beneficiaries asking for change. 'Haves' serving 'have nots' are used to overwhelming gratitude, not criticism.

6   Many not-for-profits have significant numbers of professionals, including social workers, teachers, architects, accountants, lawyers and planners, on the staff and/or their volunteer boards. Professional training, by its very nature in passing on an exclusive body of knowledge, can encourage professionals into *'I know what is best for you'* attitude.

7   Related to the previous point is the practice of *professional distance*, which can protect the professional from pressure but is not always conducive to meeting the needs of beneficiary customers.

8   Voluntary organisations that have been set up on the basis of *belief* can be particularly antipathetic to customer needs (Blois 1987, p. 408). The most obvious ones are religious, but there are many others, such as those promoting vegetarianism or opposing blood sports. Blois argues that the effect of belief, in 'knowing you are right' can be two-fold. First, an organisation whose primary goal is based upon certainty (such as absolute belief in a deity with highly specific attributes) is much less likely to listen to the concerns and views of actual and potential customers. Second, even when these

views are noted they are less likely to result in a change of the product, service or message because such changes are likely to be interpreted as a challenge to the fundamental precepts of the organisation.

9   Not-for-profits have an action orientated approach – 'let's roll up our sleeves and get on with it'. This approach, linked with a desire to direct as much resource as possible toward the direct services, means that *consumer research (especially independent consumer research) is not widespread*. Consequently not-for-profits are less knowledgeable about the real needs and desires of their beneficiary customers than might be expected.

10   Consumer sovereignty or *consumer rights may be seen as alien* to the fulfilment of the institutional mission. Lovelock and Weinberg (1989) give examples from social cause activity such as trying to stop people drinking or eating too much.

11   Organisations involved in amelioration of disadvantage rather than removing its causes can easily slip into an underlying assumption that it is the *'beneficiary customers' fault'* simply through accepting the status quo of the socio-economic environment.

12   Finally, there are all the reasons associated with marketing's business connotations and language, such as being linked to profit making, hype and, at the most extreme, to economy with the truth and downright fraud.

I am not arguing that all the above conditions occur in all not-for-profit organisations. However, even when only two or three exist, it is clear that the needs and desires of beneficiary customers may be undervalued and the, often unexpressed, perceptions of the beneficiary customers will be at variance with those of the not-for-profit supplier.

Supporter customers

One might expect that charities would value supporters and respect their needs to a greater extent than beneficiary customers. First, the supply of supporter opportunities far outstrips demand from potential supporters. Second, the competition in the market place for donors and volunteer service workers is intense and therefore potential supporters have a wide variety of choice. Lastly, a marketing approach, which values customer needs and desires, has penetrated much further into the fundraising, if not the volunteer service, side of not-for-profit activity. So, ironically, given that supporters are not normally regarded as the prime customer group for charities, supporters are probably more highly valued and respected than beneficiaries.

Nevertheless, there is still cause for concern at the way donor supporters and volunteer worker supporters are valued. The over-riding reason for this is that many charities still operate in what marketers would call a production mode. The concentration is on processes and making these apparently more efficient, with far less concentration on the needs of supporters. In the most extreme cases supporters are seen as a necessary evil, simply required to get the job done.

1   Donor supporters often claim to being bled dry by strident, too frequent demands, which treat them as impersonal groups to be 'milked' of their money.

2   Donors frequently complain about not being sufficiently appreciated and thanked, or at least thanked in a way that recognises them as individuals rather than a class (donors). Direct mail is probably the worst offender of the fundraising methods, despite the supposed ability of sophisticated computer programs to help build up a 'relationship' between the not-for-profit organisation and the supporter. The mail donor complains about the frequency of approaches, the lack of recognition of previous donating actions, and the not infrequent double and triple mailings caused by transcribing errors in the address or, even worse, the donor's name.

3   Volunteer service workers can also feel undervalued and undersupported. Mass volunteer recruitment campaigns can leave volunteers lost or stranded because of the inefficiency of the recruiting process leading to, for example, too many volunteers being recruited in communities with fewer needs.

4   Charities can treat volunteer service workers like 'cannon fodder': being marched forward to be overwhelmed by many beneficiaries' massive needs, which they simply cannot meet.

5   In many situations the volunteer service workers can feel sustained more by the relationship they have with beneficiaries than through any relationship with or appreciation from the charity. In the worst of situations volunteer service workers can be inexorably

tied to one or more beneficiaries, knowing deep down that they are not really able to help substantially. However, they feel they would be letting people down if they withdrew.

(Shenfield and Allen 1972)

Stakeholder customers

Structural conditions can also lead to an undervaluing, or at least a perception of being undervalued, of two of the main stakeholder groups, namely staff and committee members.

1 On a job-by-job comparison with the commercial and sometimes the government sector charity staff can often be underpaid. When things are going well this is not normally a problem. However, when other hidden additions to the pay packet (such as job satisfaction) are undermined, this structural weakness is, in effect, undervaluing the staff stakeholder customers.

2 With the rapidly changing boundaries between the not-for-profit, government and commercial sectors so typical of the 1990s, security of job role has reduced. Pressure on voluntary income as well as demands from statutory purchasers for more value for money have led to growing uncertainty among charities' paid staff. One hears more frequently the cry 'if they cannot look after us, how can we look after the beneficiaries?'.

3 Often all is not well with committee member stakeholders. As charities have become increasingly professional and sophisticated, then unpaid committee members with too little time to devote to the increasing complexity and with insufficient relevant knowledge and skills, feel unwanted and powerless in relation to the professional management team.

Interactive reasons for undervaluing customers

The very fact that not-for-profits have multiple constituencies or customer groups militates against valuing each constituent to the full. For example, when one charity customer is paying (and has needs) and another is receiving (and has different needs) it is unlikely that both sets of needs and desires will be fully met. Add in stakeholder and regulator needs and the situation becomes even more problematic.

An example of this *inter-customer group tension* might be an avant-garde theatre where there is a tension between the need to keep audiences (beneficiaries) coming, bringing on new avant-garde writers (additional beneficiaries), satisfying the grant makers (supporters), the board (stakeholders) and the regulators (health and safety, obscenity, etc.). If the product is too avant-garde it will drive away audiences and upset the board. If the product is watered down to please the audience the avant-garde writer will be upset and may walk out. The grant maker may want avant-garde performances but dislike low audiences. The regulators may try and close the performance because it offends the public or close the theatre because cost cutting is threatening safety. Such inter-customer group tensions pose major challenges to the not-for-profit marketers.

It can be seen that valuing customers and meeting their needs (a marketing approach) is very challenging in a charity context.

Support for adopting a marketing approach

Paradoxically, all the opposition outlined above only confirms the need for charity marketing if one believes charities exist to help people, primarily beneficiaries. So marketing – meeting customer need within the objectives of the organisation – provides a philosophy, management approach and a set of operational tools that can address the anti-customer tendencies of charities.

However, there is the important technical challenge introduced by Baker (1987, p. 7) which says that marketing can only flourish and is only useful when supply outstrips demand. He argues that marketing as a discipline only received a huge push into prominence as the world's commercial ability to over-supply its marketplaces became the norm. It is therefore natural that marketing should find a secure and growing base in the charity fundraising field, where supply of fundraising products vastly outstrips the amount of money that supporter customers are prepared or able to pay.

Meeting needs

Applying Baker's commercial logic to offerings to beneficiary customers would suggest that, as the demand from actual and potential beneficiaries far outstrips the supply capability of charities, the ground would not be fertile for a marketing approach – a straightforward production approach should be sufficient. However, it is not possible to apply this commercial logic to the charity sector. Charities are committed to, and locked into, their beneficiary customers in a way that commercial organisations are not. At its crudest, if a commercial organisation found out that a particular customer group could no longer afford its products, an option would be for the company to walk away. That option is not open to charities, which may be legally as well as morally committed to certain beneficiary groups. Again, a commercial company that suddenly found a business activity was no longer profitable, and was unlikely to become so, would almost certainly close down that part of the business. Those charities that are not committed by their legal purposes to beneficiary groups will be committed to an area of charitable activity such as education or religion. They cannot simply transfer their charitable activity into a totally different area. It is this legal requirement, which is essentially based on a moral imperative such as the relief of poverty, that makes marketing so useful to charity work among beneficiaries. Charities are committed to their beneficiary customers in such a way and with an intensity that commercial marketing companies are not. Therefore a management approach, which has at its heart a commitment to meeting customer needs and wants, should have a welcome home in the charity sector.

Improving quality

Other reasons have been given as to why a marketing approach suits charities (Bruce 1993, p. 94). In particular it helps charities to act more responsibly and effectively in meeting the needs of beneficiaries in a market situation where the brutal reality is that beneficiary customers often cannot easily choose between a number of alternatives, either because these alternatives simply do not exist or because low incomes among beneficiaries mean that they cannot be afforded. Therefore a marketing approach can help charities to improve the quality of their offerings to beneficiaries in situations where, because demand massively outstrips supply and there are few competitors, it would be easy to get away with delivering substandard offerings. Charities normally operate with a good deal of resource constraint, and so operational efficiency and cost saving is given a high priority. But operational efficiency can also easily lead to products being not very 'customer-friendly'. Conversely, changes that may make the products more customer-friendly will often add costs and are not therefore readily acceptable. Marketing can help us find a way through these two challenges. Last, given the dominance of professionals in charities, it helps the organisation to guard against the syndrome of 'professionals knowing best'.

Staff attitudes

However, this last point gives an indication of some staff attitudes that have to be addressed, especially among professional charity workers on the beneficiary side. A. Wilson (1984, p. 19) argues that groups of professionals such as lawyers, accountants and architects have a 'trained-in' antipathy to commerce in general and marketing in particular because of the way their professionalism has been established over the centuries and their training delivered. This point is relevant to professionals in charities. But there is an additional attitude cluster that has to be addressed and which is particularly relevant to professionals such as social workers, teachers, doctors and nurses, all of whom are readily found in the charity sector. These professional groups, while having complete sympathy with the concept of 'meeting need', also associate marketing with commerce. For them marketing has the overtones of a 'hard sell', which they rightly feel is inappropriate for their vulnerable clients. Second, marketing can have the implication of payment with which they have not traditionally been involved (and are therefore not confident about) and they know that many of their clients cannot afford to pay. So introducing a marketing approach into a charity needs to take account of, and meet, these objections.

Spillard (1987) gives an additional reason for the problems of introducing a marketing approach:

> 'Because marketing so often acts at the boundaries of other groups' activities and achieves what success it does through pursuing its objectives effectively by a process of negotiation, most of what it claims to influence is subject to dispute by other groups. These groups are put on the defensive by the very act of marketing trying

to influence the outcome of decisions which they traditionally have regarded as their own.'

(p. 54)

Conclusion

So, in summary, the reasons for introducing marketing are that as a philosophy, management approach and set of operational tools it will help ensure that charities, in meeting the needs and wants of beneficiaries:

- do not act as (arrogant) monopolies;
- operate services sensitive to real needs;
- do not concentrate on too few beneficiaries;
- recognise beneficiaries' needs and desires, even if they are weak;
- do not develop patronising attitudes of 'haves' towards 'have nots';
- do not adopt 'professional' attitudes of 'knowing best';
- do not keep professional distance in the overall delivery of service;
- are sensitive to the tension between belief and customer need;
- use customer research and customer representation to understand and meet needs and desires;
- recognise that beneficiaries have rights;
- do not become institutionalised into the status quo, thinking it is their (the beneficiaries) fault.

Introducing a marketing approach

Here the obvious needs to be stated, namely that the introduction of marketing requires a marketing approach. People in the organisation need to be treated as customers. For example, firm decision-making by top managers to introduce a marketing structure, without cultural acceptance by staff, is bound to fail. But sensitive development of the cultural acceptance of a marketing-orientated approach, without introducing new structures and processes, will also fail. Although it sounds challenging, what is required is concerted and coordinated action in the following areas:

- organisation culture;
- resources (both expertise and money);
- activities, processes and marketing plans;
- structure.

It is difficult to work in all areas at once, and the areas of activities and structure can come after the injection of work in the areas of culture and resources. The next four sections deal with these areas in turn.

A needs-led marketing culture

If a marketing approach is to be introduced successfully it has to permeate the whole organisation. People's attitudes have, ideally, to be welcoming, preferably accepting and at least acquiescent. So here is a major challenge to a marketing approach because of the widespread antipathy to the term 'marketing' and what many people believe it stands for.

The key axiom, as in all marketing, is 'start from where your customer is, not from where you would like them to be'.

Encouraging cultural change

So how does one encourage a cultural change towards being receptive to a marketing approach? An important starting point is to recognise how cynical charity staff are about commercial marketing, not least because of the behaviour of some marketers, for example apparently marketing alcohol and cigarettes to young teenagers. Nevertheless the strongest weapon is one of logic. Whatever the implicit assumptions and attitudes, it is probably more true for charities than for any other kind of organisation that the reason for it existing is to serve its beneficiary customers. Charities must be needs-led. This gives marketing the moral and logical high ground. If this high ground is further promoted and defended by the chief executive and senior management and committees, this begins to set explicit standards for public opinions and actions inside the organisation, whatever some people's private opinion may still be. In short, the chief executive and the senior staff can give a strong lead on 'how we do it round here'.

Other actions, such as awareness-raising activities, role play within and outside training activities, and marketing training will have important impacts. Also, the appointment and promotion of staff with a strong customer orientation will send out strong messages to staff that listening to customers, especially beneficiary customers, and acting on their needs and wishes is important and the 'way we do things round here'. Concentrating initially on particular sub-activities of marketing which one has assessed as being of interest to line managers, such as service promotion, market research or customer care, can change views. Holwegger (1996) describes how introducing a customer care orientation and programme into RNID led to the adoption of a broader marketing approach.

Apart from gaining knowledge of marketing it is crucial to encourage all staff whose work impacts on customers to feel that marketing is part of their job, not something the marketing experts do.

Marketing resources

Resources in this situation come in two ways – people's expertise, and money and what it can buy.

Expertise

Increasing the quality and quantity of marketing expertise inside the charity is crucial to its success. In the early stages it may be the most important factor. Organisation culture, activities and structures all require the time of knowledgeable and experienced marketing people to talk through, promote, design and implement. If this is left to hard-pressed existing staff, the introduction of marketing will at best be delayed and at worst will fail. A useful way of injecting expertise rapidly is to combine the early appointment of a very limited marketing staff resource with the use of external marketing advisers through a consultancy. The consultancy will bring in a breadth of knowledge and experience that will be impossible, and unwise, to install at such an early stage. But the weakness of the consultancy – not being regarded as one of the staff – can be overcome in part by the internal appointment(s). Any medium-sized charity will need one person. A small charity is unlikely to need or be able to afford a separate marketing person. However, just one champion of marketing in a small charity, especially at senior level, is likely to achieve more, and more quickly, than in a large charity.

RNIB, as a large charity, appointed four people to cover the main operating divisions (then totalling 2,000 staff). In a medium-size charity the appointee will need to be accountable to the chief executive. In a large charity this may not be possible, but they should report to the second tier. Even though these posts will be staff, rather than line management, their importance will be signalled by their accountability and access to the chief executive and senior manager. They will need the authority to call people together in meetings and make firm proposals for action. If these proposals are likely to be challenged they will do well to get their manager's backing first.

However, after a fairly short phase, say six months to a year, there will have been enough initial work on cultural change and discussion of possible structural change to enable a more significant build-up of expertise. This next phase can be achieved through the training and subsequent promotion of internal staff as well as the recruitment of external staff.

Training

The role of marketing training is absolutely crucial here and can easily be underestimated. Marketing training for charity personnel is not widespread. The marketing consultancy that has become familiar with the charity can be extremely useful in either modifying external training packages or developing in-house ones, which can make the training more user-friendly. Simply sending charity personnel onto commercial marketing training courses can be a disaster if the trainee is unenthusiastic about the concept to start with. Even if they are enthusiastic about the external, commercially orientated training, it is quite difficult to translate what has been learned back into the charity. However, organisations such as the Directory of Social Change and the Centre for Charity Effectiveness at London's Cass Business School have developed charity-specific marketing training, and this can be a cost-effective way for charities of all sizes to achieve positive change.

Finance

It is clear that the initial staff recruitment and consultancy involvement will require money. Money will also be needed for additional short-term work such as market research and training. If possible, money for this phase should be 'new' rather than budget substitution from operational activity because the expenditure will bring no immediate and tangible gain to operational managers, and the budget transfer will antagonise them. The sums can be quite modest, especially for small organisations.

However, the budget for subsequent marketing activity should ideally be a mix of new money and budget transfers from existing spending heads. Such financial resource is likely to be spent on activities such as, once again, market research, but also promotional activity, which ought to show short-term benefits to operational managers. The transfer of budget responsibility begins to show the iron fist in the velvet glove. Nevertheless, whatever the source, money for the marketing function will be required. Marketing personnel without spending power simply become friendly, advisory appendages.

Marketing activities, processes and plans

In this context activities refer to what the appointed marketing staff are likely to do, especially in the early stages. Processes refer to what needs to be done as a matter of course, primarily by the existing operational staff in order to lock them and their work into a marketing framework. Marketing plans are particularly important to this last area.

Activities

In the short and medium term the marketing champions will be wise to concentrate on activities such as market research, targeting and elements of marketing mix, rather than strategic marketing planning – this latter produces no short-term gains and can, quite reasonably, follow on later. The activities to be worked on should depend on the wants/needs of the operational managers (the internal customers). Interviews with these internal customers will reveal which operational managers are most open to additional help and what kind of help they need. The two activities most likely to be welcome early on are those of *promotion* and *marketing research*. Operational managers (such as heads of schools, theatre directors, social work managers, field fundraising managers) often feel that 'people' do not really appreciate or even know what their service does. But they also have little expertise in and are personally less comfortable with the active promotion of their work in order to gain additional customers. Therefore a marketing champion with suggestions as to how their goods, services or ideas can be more actively promoted is likely to gain a warm welcome. Further, the production of even fairly basic tools in a professional manner, such as leaflets, articles placed in external magazines and newspapers, advertisements, specially convened promotional meetings and professional conferences can be achieved fairly quickly and at relatively low cost. They are also very tangible to the internal customer.

Marketing research is also a potentially sympathetic intervention tool for the short or medium term that will give the marketer more locus in the medium term. It obviously must be designed in conjunction with the operational manager in order to ensure that the results are sufficiently service-specific and usable. The very process of deciding what to ask of whom for what purpose helps to educate the operational manager about marketing. The research data will also be a major resource to the marketer, who can introduce the results into their work on the marketing mix. If it can be achieved with the goodwill of the operational manager, marketing research among the intermediary customer groups can be particularly important in providing the marketing person with new ideas and suggestions for operational improvement.

In the medium term the marketing champion will need to intervene in all areas of marketing mix as well as be active in the area of marketing research and promotion.

Processes and plans

Marketing processes mean those activities of a bureaucratic (using the word neutrally) nature that need to be built in to what is likely to be an operationally dominated organisation. Every organisation will need to develop its own tailor-made marketing processes that need to be followed. However, a good starting point is the annual plan for each of the major goods/service/idea areas. More often than charities would care to admit, service areas have only very patchy plans, which are normally dominated by budgets and have little narrative. Nevertheless they are a starting point for a *marketing plan*, which could be called a *service plan* if this would help acceptability. The plan needs to be timed to fit in with the budget/financial planning cycle as this tends to be the major fixed point in any charity's planning cycle. If from the marketing point of view this is subsequently felt to be bad in terms of timing it can be changed, but it is an optimistic marketer who tries to cross the finance function in the early stages.

Marketing plans can be very sophisticated or very basic. One way of introducing them is to produce sophisticated plans for a minority of products (services or goods), and use their success to roll the idea out to the full range of the organisation's offerings. However, this method can easily get elongated and bogged down, and may never get rolled out across the charity. This is because a sophisticated marketing plan requires much fundamental thinking about the market-place of the whole organisation and its strategic plan – which may not have been developed at all, let alone from a marketing orientation.

The alternative, which I have found to be more successful, is to produce basic marketing plans for a wider range of the organisation's goods/services/ideas. These need to be produced with the close involvement of the operational manger and the finance representative. They should concentrate on the absolute core of the generic marketing plan. They should include the basic *marketing mix* (product, price, promotion and place); *target market; target take-up* in terms of quantity and quality; *unique selling points; marketing resources* to be applied; all the financial *budget information* that has traditionally been required; and an *action plan* of who is going to do what by when and what results are expected. If quantified targets for the product area have been set and measured in previous years, then it would be sensible and reasonable to include these in the marketing plan. However, if they have not, it would be unwise to insert these in year one, but a good marketing discipline would require them in year two. If this approach to applying basic marketing plans is to be followed quite widely, it is unwise to include too many, or any, strategic marketing elements, such as proposals for *marketing research*, a broad situation analysis including *other players* or a *SWOT* analysis because of the 'slowing-down factor'. The remaining elements of the marketing mix, *people, physical evidence, process* and *philosophy*, could be included first time, but might be problematic for two reasons. First, they intervene quite heavily in operations, which the line managers will rightly regard as their territory. Second, they make the process that much more difficult, and risk the plan not being completed in time. The one exception might be philosophy, as the operational manager may find this attractive as it could buttress the manager's activity from what he or she feels may become too commercial an approach.

If the resulting marketing plan is more than five pages long, there should be a one-page summary capable of standing alone. Service managers will hate doing this, preferring other readers to have no choice but to read the whole plan; but senior managers and committees may have dozens of papers to read, and will skip-read if there is no summary.

Basic marketing/service plan

A suggested structure of a marketing (or service) plan is given below. Where relevant the measures should describe the last two years' *actual*, this year's *forecast*, and next year's *target*.

- Name and very short description of the product (goods/service/idea).
- Key volume data, numbers of units (of activity) incoming, expenditures and subsidy.
- Existing customers: who are they, how many, what characteristics, how segmented?
- Total market size: who are they, how many?
- Key customer needs and how the product meets them.
- Philosophy underpinning the product.
- Price.
- Promotion (plans including expenditure plans).
- Distribution (how is the product delivered?).
- People involved.
- Key physical evidence.
- Key aspect of processes to ensure take-up.
- Marketing and market research (include evidence of unmet need).
- Other players.
- Appendix of other/additional relevant data.

A one-page summary of key facts and figures is essential.

Structure

A marketing organisation structure is simple to draw on a chart, but complicated to implement. Whatever structure is implemented in the early stages, it is likely to require revision after a few years, as the organisation comes to understand, accept and implement a marketing approach. It is to be hoped that the processes and activities described above, and the first structure, will have encouraged marketing to permeate the organisation, to be built 'into the management line'. Indeed Baker (1987, p. 9) says: 'in a truly marketing orientated organisation the need for a specialised marketing function is probably far less than it is in a sales or production dominated company'. Even where the conscious attempt needs to be made to insert a formal marketing unit, Spillard (1987) argues that it should be a 'soft form of organisation' which recognises that the:

> 'boundaries are loose, constantly shifting and frequently ill defined and open to debate ... the responsibility and area of influence of marketing tend to be both diffuse and lacking in structural integrity, at least in the sense of possessing a well bounded and undisputed sphere of influence.'
>
> (p. 54)

Many writers on marketing emphasise that it is possible to implement a variety of marketing organisation structures, depending on factors such as the size of the organisation, the variety of products (goods/service/ideas) on offer, and the degree to which the products are in the same or different market areas. However, what appears to be much more problematic is relating the particular situation in any one organisation to the particular form of marketing organisation that would suit it best.

For medium-sized and large charities the choices of organisation structure, crudely described, put the marketing function in one or more of the following locations:

- at the corporate centre;
- at each main operating area (containing several products);
- at the product level.

Corporate centre

Where the function is at the corporate centre it may have effective line authority for strategic marketing, but it can only be advisory in relation to product lines and product groups. Andreasen and Kotler (2003) give sample job titles of marketing posts in the corporate centre of various non-profits. Among other things, the 'marketing director' contributes a marketing perspective to the planning deliberations of the top administration; prepares data on market size, segment, trends and behaviour dynamics; conducts studies of the needs, perceptions, preferences and satisfaction of particular markets; assists in the planning, promotion and launching of new programmes; assists in the development of communications and promotion campaigns and materials; and analyses and advises on pricing questions. So it can be seen that this is very much an advisory function.

Operating area

If the marketing function is located halfway down the organisation, at the level of a major operating division, it can either be at the advisory end or more towards the line management end of the continuum. If the operating division has a large number of service products going across several markets or if it runs services managed by technical professions such as teachers, social workers or doctors, the function is more likely to be at the advisory end. If the products are in a fairly homogeneous market, and especially if they are physical goods, then it is possible for the marketing function to have strong authority over the marketing mix.

Product level

Where the marketing function is located at the individual product (goods/services/ideas) level, then the marketing manager is either appointed as operational manger, is in charge of the operational manager, or the operational manager is trained in marketing. The choice normally depends on staff turnover, availability of staff with the right qualifications, the complexity of the operational side, and whether the product is physical goods or services. For example, a marketing manager can call the shots if the product is a straightforward physical good. But if it is complex or the product is a service, especially a professional service such as a school or rehabilitation centre, then the marketing manager can only be advisory, and it will normally be better to train the operational manager in marketing.

CASE EXAMPLE: RNIB INTRODUCING A MARKETING APPROACH

RNIB activities

In the mid-1980s RNIB drew up a corporate strategy, involving committees, staff and beneficiaries. This strategy identified, among many other things, a need for the charity to undertake more market research among beneficiary customers, more promotion and more target segmentation. These became the starting point for introducing a marketing approach, which was formally stated in the strategy.

At that time RNIB involved over 25,000 volunteers and 2,000 paid staff and ran provided 60 direct services to end beneficiaries and indirect ones to intermediary customer groups. The *direct* services included:

- schools and colleges – some for able youngsters who went to college and university, but most for multi-disabled blind and partially sighted people;
- a wide range of educational support services for visually impaired young people in mainstream education;
- a Scottish and English national residential rehabilitation centre for newly blinded adults;
- two vocational training colleges, which ran a wide variety of courses such as telephony, office skills, computer programming and physiotherapy;
- an employment service to support people getting into work;
- three hotels catering for about 7,000 blind people each year;
- the RNIB talking books service which lent over 3.5 million books a year to 65,000 members;
- a weekly large-print national newspaper;
- an electronically delivered daily newspaper;
- the largest Braille publishing house in Europe;
- a large factory and distribution centre which sold over 600 technical aids;
- a benefits rights office handling over 6,000 cases a year.

RNIB also ran a wide range of *indirect* services aimed at other people who impact on the lives of blind and partially sighted people. These included consultancy and training services aimed at social services departments, health authorities, local education authorities and even commercial producers and service providers. These services included campaigning and pressure group activity, with eight staff, including parliamentary officers covering Westminster and Brussels/Strasbourg.

cont.

CASE EXAMPLE: RNIB INTRODUCING A MARKETING APPROACH
continued

At the time, 7 per cent of paid staff were blind, spread across all levels, including top management. The majority of the RNIB executive council and its main standing committees comprised blind and partially sighted people, who held the leadership positions; and the majority of these were elected representatives of organisations of blind and partially sighted people. In other words RNIB's end beneficiaries decided who represented them, and they helped to propose policy and monitor implementation.

The organisation's structure at that time is laid out in Figure 5.1 (overleaf).

Placing marketing management

The structural question was where to insert the marketing management. Each of the main service division directors had between five and seven managers accountable to them, and RNIB created a marketing manager post at this divisional second-tier level (M). It also created a marketing manager post in the second tier of the External Relations Division (CM), together with support, with the aim of facing in two directions: one facing inward, into the division providing marketing for external relations, and the other facing the marketing managers in the three other service divisions to give them support and advice. A crude comparison would be to regard the three main service divisions as being separate companies, and the marketing manager at divisional second tier being the equivalent of a marketing director. RNIB considered placing all these marketing posts in the corporate division, the External Relations Division, but on balance concluded that there would be greater ownership of marketing if it was located in the individual functional divisions.

The Technical and Consumer Services Division (with 500 staff and 600 (mainly) physical goods products) had three product managers, (operational marketing managers) – for talking books, Braille magazines and technical equipment. At the divisional level there was also the marketing 'director' (M) responsible for line-managing these product managers, but also responsible for the actual and potential product areas for technical and communication products. Thus the divisional marketing 'director' not only had responsibility for delivering targets on the existing product lines, they were also responsible for

cont.

CASE EXAMPLE: RNIB INTRODUCING A MARKETING APPROACH
continued

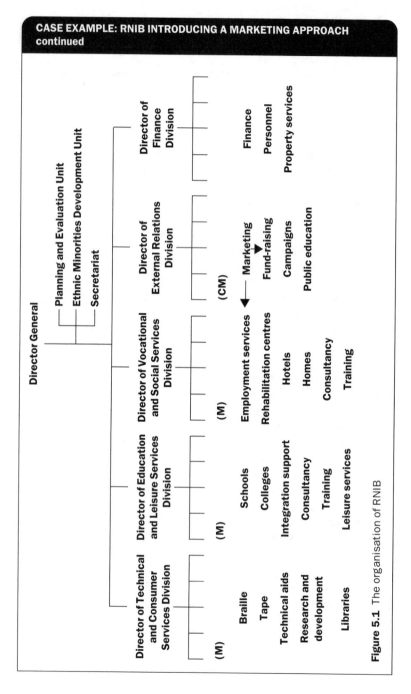

Figure 5.1 The organisation of RNIB

CASE EXAMPLE: RNIB INTRODUCING A MARKETING APPROACH
continued

identifying any gaps in the market in the technical and communications products area which RNIB should fill. The division also had a market research manager who commissioned market research and wrote interpretations of the results to make them particularly relevant to technical and communication products.

RNIB also had marketing managers in its two other divisions (Education and Leisure with 550 staff, and Vocational and Social Services with 450 staff) both located at the divisional centre (M). In both divisions the marketing manager was at head office level and had an advisory rather than a line management function. One division had two other marketing staff associated with operational services. In all cases the marketing function at the operational service level was accountable to the operational manager who, in each case, was a technical professional.

The intention was that the marketing function in the External Relations Division (CM), as well as providing marketing direction for that division, would provide marketing planning support and marketing services to the other divisions. In particular, a publications unit provided large numbers of professionally produced leaflets, brochures and prospectuses for the other divisions. It is interesting to note that this corporate advice and service role only worked to a degree. In common with other large devolved organisations, the functional divisions were loath to accept the advice and services of the corporate centre.

While this pattern may not have been ideal, it showed that the three structural possibilities described at the beginning of this section – the corporate centre, main functional operational areas and product level – could coexist in one organisation. The description also shows how the marketing structure developed on the basis of specific characteristics of the organisation or parts of the organisation. For example, the reason that the marketing managers in the Technical and Consumer Services Division were line managers of the communication products was that, by and large, these products had many of the attributes of physical goods, whereas the marketing managers in the other two divisions were advisory, in part because they were dealing with services and ideas rather than physical goods. As we saw earlier in this

cont.

CASE EXAMPLE: RNIB INTRODUCING A MARKETING APPROACH
continued

chapter, having marketing line management responsible for operations is easier to implement for physical goods than it is for services and ideas.

It is important to emphasise that these structural changes did not take place until there was a cultural commitment among staff, supported by senior management and committees.

Effectiveness

How successful was the introduction of a marketing approach? After five years RNIB brought in an external consultant to evaluate its marketing effectiveness across the agency. Although his evaluation was largely qualitative, the subsequent description detailed percentages because it gave a simple, clear picture. The consultant crudely estimated that RNIB was about 60 per cent of the way towards becoming a truly marketing-orientated organisation. However, this was an average that masked differential rates of implementation in the four divisions.

In the External Relations Division, comprising fundraising, publicity and campaigning, it was judged that RNIB was almost completely marketing orientated. In the Technical and Consumer Services Division the estimate was put at around 75 per cent. The marketing 'director' had a staff of around 40 people – the combined total of customer services and customer sales staff. The majority of the products and product groupings such as Braille magazines, talking books and technical aids had marketing managers or product managers line-managing them, and these staff, rather than those in production, were in the driving seat. However, marketing plans and their implementation were still problematic. There was also a market research officer who undertook considerable research for various product managers.

In the Education and Leisure Division and the Vocational Social Services Division the picture was less advanced – only about 40 per cent effective. These divisions made extensive use of market research, promotion and segmentation but marketing plans were not well developed and implemented, and in many cases did not even exist. Pricing policies that took full account of the external market were only being implemented at the time of the review. The divisional second-tier

cont.

CASE EXAMPLE: RNIB INTRODUCING A MARKETING APPROACH continued

marketing managers' posts were problematic. In one of the divisions the post-holder stayed for four years but had an uphill struggle. In the other division the post was empty for half of the four-year period.

Different levels of success

So why were two divisions more successful in implementation than the others? First, the overall heads of these two divisions had a professional marketing background. Second, both divisions had, in the main, products that were either physical goods, non-professional services (in a sense of not employing social professionals) or ideas, for either fundraising or campaigning. Third, the divisional second-tier marketing managers had line management control over reasonable staff numbers, and had either direct control or a controlling interest over the production side of their business.

The heads of the two divisions where a marketing approach had not come as far were professionally qualified in non-marketing fields and therefore had much less experience of marketing. Second, the majority of output activities of these two divisions were professional services (such as education and social work) and, as in the commercial world of professional services, marketing was harder to apply. Third, the divisional second-tier marketing managers had advisory posts, rather than line management posts, with relatively little budget and staff support.

These two divisions had also suffered because the corporate marketing planning support anticipated from the External Relations Division had not been given the necessary resources or authority to do this work. Rather, this post had been responsible for encouraging the External Relations Division to be the most marketing-orientated division in RNIB. The originally allocated resources for corporate marketing had quite understandably been drawn into supporting the fundraising, publicity and campaigning requirements within that division. There was also some thought that the corporate marketing planning coming out of one of the five operating divisions was not regarded as 'neutral' (and should be a staff function responsible to the chief executive). The exception to this lack of outreach into other divisions was that of certain marketing services such as public

cont.

relations, corporate identity, publicity, publication and advertising material, which came from the External Relations Division and were widespread across the whole of RNIB.

Developments

There were further developments arising out of the review. First, a senior corporate marketing manager with direct access to the chief executive was appointed in the Planning and Evaluation Unit. This, it was argued, had two advantages. The marketing function and marketing planning could be integrated into the wider RNIB planning process, so that each strengthened the other. Also, the new senior strategic post was not to be located in any one of the five operational divisions, and had more direct backing from the chief executive. This senior corporate marketing manager, with senior management support, introduced a structure for a marketing plan – service plans – which were utilised in all 120 service delivery units (SDUs). These SDUs were also all budget centres, which meant that financial and marketing planning could be integrated. In order to take account of different divisional needs there were some differences in terminology in the plans, but their structures were similar.

Second, a process of core competency analysis involving representative groups of staff identified marketing as one of four core management competencies required of all RNIB managers. This was the jumping-off point for comprehensive marketing training as part of managerial development and put marketing 'in the management line'. The training involved half-a-dozen modules developed jointly between RNIB and the Open College and, completed in full, led to a Certificate in Marketing. However, most managers and customer-facing staff only needed two or three modules to gain a firm understanding of the marketing approach.

Third, the two second-tier advisory marketing management posts in the two professional service divisions were abolished and more marketing support and responsibility was pushed down to the level of operational management in the education, employment and social services parts of the agency. A marketing approach was fully adopted in the Technical and Consumer Services Division and the External

cont.

CASE EXAMPLE: RNIB INTRODUCING A MARKETING APPROACH
continued

Relations Division and more brand or product managers were appointed.

Finally, a second strategic review of the whole organisation and its services fed into a new corporate strategy which, like its predecessor, confirmed a marketing approach as 'the way we do it round here'. There was greater emphasis in this new strategy on improving the quality of services to beneficiary customers and the need to be more customer focused. In other words, rather than fall back on imperatives couched in marketing jargon, the strategy went to the core of marketing, namely customer-focused, quality products.

The third stage of implementation during the third strategy period, which began in the early part of the new millennium, had a further evolution. This was the first strategy in which senior management champions did not need to encourage a marketing/needs-led approach. Instead, the push came up from third-tier managers. Indeed there was an exhilarating period where third-tier managers regularly told the chief executive that the organisation needed to be more customer focused. This bottom up pressure came just in time, because the wave of interest in performance management, which originated in the private and public sectors, was just hitting the charity sector. Interest in this from the Board, promotion of the corporate marketing manager and a lack of budget coincided, with the result that the corporate marketing manager was not replaced.

However, with middle management naturally thinking 'customer focus', this was not the catastrophe it would have been five years previously. Arguably RNIB had reached the ideal for a service organisation, with a customer focused/needs-led approach being the new organisational paradygm. That cemented the continuing culture and ensured the commitment to action that is likely to survive staff turnover. However it remains to be seen whether new staff can gain the necessary technical expertise they need to complement 'the way we do it round here'.

This case example shows that in a large charity where the senior management and committees are committed to a needs-led culture a marketing approach can be implemented effectively over a relatively short timespan (three years) in those parts of the charity delivering physical goods, high turnover non-professional services, and fundraising and campaigning ideas. But it also shows how difficult it is to implement fully a marketing approach in the area of professional services even when the senior management and committees are committed, and even when many of the operational managers (such as heads of schools) are also committed and are natural marketers. While the external environment in which such professional services operate remains stable, the marketing approach has been successfully embedded in the management line. This cultural absorption is critical and can even overcome loss of expertise however undesirable that is. However technical experts without cultural support will not succeed.

Conclusion

Most medium-size and larger British charities now have a reasonable marketing approach installed in their fundraising and publicity functions aimed at supporter customers. However, very few have a formalised marketing process installed for the offerings they deliver to their beneficiary customers.

Those charities that are experimenting with introducing a marketing approach can make fairly rapid headway where the products are physical goods and fundraising or campaigning ideas. There has been less development of formal marketing approaches in the field of services in general and professional services in particular.

This pattern reflects the commercial world, although developments are almost certainly less well advanced, except perhaps in certain areas of fundraising.

There are a number of reasons for the relative lack of progress in instituting a marketing approach in the field of services to beneficiaries, which have been identified in the preceding pages. The main reasons are that charity services to beneficiaries still operate in an environment where demand massively outstrips supply; the multiple customer groups are extremely complicated to deal with; and professional services and associated professional workers play a leading operational management role.

Factors likely to propel charities further into a formalised marketing approach are:

- their normally very different and quasi-legal commitment to their beneficiary customers (in comparison with commercial marketing organisations);

- the fact that the majority of charity chief executives recognise the importance of understanding the needs of customers as part of a managerial structure;
- because the charity market is becoming increasingly competitive both on the fundraising side and on the service-giving side through statutory organisations' competitive tendering procedures for contracting out services.

Charities would benefit from more research and writing on the successful and unsuccessful attempts to introduce marketing into commercial professional services and similar work in their own sector.

Key points

- A marketing approach must permeate the whole organisation if it is to succeed.
- Encourage acceptance by showing that marketing has the needs of beneficiary customers as its raison d'être.
- Appoint a limited marketing resource, supplemented by external marketing advisers if necessary, pro bono in the case of small organisations
- Train internal staff.
- Make sure that money is available for marketing and/or promotional activity; this can be quite modest where the organisation is small.
- Encourage communication between the marketing person and his or her internal customers.
- Establish marketing plans, keeping them simple at first.
- Establish where the marketing function fits into the organisation structure.

PART II

Applied Charity Marketing

6   Physical goods

While services dominate voluntary organisation activity, physical goods are much more widespread than might at first be thought. The provision of information products is probably the most ubiquitous role of voluntary organisations, with printed and e-publications in particular providing a massive output. The development and provision of physical goods aimed at disadvantaged groups is much more widespread than casual observation would suggest: for example, technical aids for different groups of people with disabilities; medically orientated aids; appropriate technology goods for the developing world; environmentally friendly products. Selling profitable goods in order to raise funds occupies a significant part of many charities' fundraising and social entrepreneurial activity. All of these areas need a marketing approach if they are to be effective.

Goods for main beneficiaries

Some marketing texts suggest that marketing is only applicable in situations where supply exceeds demand (see Chapter 5). But I would argue that it is more important to adopt a marketing approach with disadvantaged customers. Voluntary organisations might get away with less marketing expenditure, especially in the area of promotion, but they still need a marketing philosophy and a marketing approach. Perhaps the most dramatic illustration of the negative consequences of a non-marketing approach is where inappropriate food provided by aid agencies to people in famine areas is rejected by the indigenous people because of cultural or religious traditions.

Offerings of physical goods to beneficiaries play an important role among charities. A significant part of the output of overseas agencies is still the provision of food and equipment, although technical advice has rapidly grown in importance. Among home charities, many working in disability and health fields provide physical goods to their primary beneficiaries. For example, 15 per cent of RNIB's expenditure is on such products for blind and partially sighted people; the Scout Association has a major trading subsidiary selling equipment, clothing, publications and other articles to people in scouting; some sports voluntary organisations sell equipment to members; and voluntary organisations in the broad environment field sell environment related products to their members, although these have some of the attributes of physical goods sold for profit, which are considered in the next section.

Price

It is the pricing of physical goods that provides the most striking comparison of commercial and voluntary organisations' roles. Where the target market has enough potential for profit, commercial companies will be dominant. MacDonald's serves burgers to people with cash and the Salvation Army serves soup to homeless people. The waters get very muddy in niche markets where charities providing free or subsidised goods cannot satisfy consumer demand, but subsidisation has driven out commercial suppliers; or where commercial suppliers, normally of high-tech equipment to disadvantaged groups, have very high, perhaps unreasonable, mark-ups. An example of the latter has been the hearing-aid market where the high prices and profit margin of commercial suppliers encouraged the RNID to move into the market in its own right. However, it has suffered all the difficulties of the new, late market entrant and is dependent on government patronage.

Niche markets

It is quite difficult to understand the impact of charities providing free or subsidised physical goods in what commercial operators might regard as potential niche markets. At its simplest, if a charity is meeting the vast majority of demand for a particular product or product grouping with subsidised prices, then there is no dilemma. However, if the charity is not meeting market needs, especially in volume terms, but through its subsidised pricing is squeezing out commercial competitors, then there is a moral and practical conundrum. To allow commercial providers in, the price of products must go up, to the detriment of existing purchasers who are already disadvantaged. However, if the charity prices are heavily subsidised on each unit sold (offerings are sold at a loss) and there is low market penetration, then there is a huge disincentive to the charity to increase its volume output and market penetration even though there are potential beneficiaries going without help. At its simplest, the more it sells, the more it drains limited charitable income.

This pricing dilemma becomes even more complex in markets where the statutory authority purchases on behalf of the charity beneficiary. This can distort the market in two ways. If the charity is selling goods at a subsidised rate and the state is purchasing on behalf of a charity beneficiary at the subsidised rate, then effectively the charity is subsidising the state, which is hardly what donors had in mind. Where the state is purchasing on behalf of disadvantaged individuals and from commercial suppliers, this can easily lead to distortion in the other direction – unreasonable profit margins. However, this situation is outside the primary purpose of this book.

CASE EXAMPLE: RNIB

An example of this complex interaction around price is the RNIB Talking Books service. Until 1985 the subscription rates were very heavily subsidised, which inevitably inhibited the charity's ability to expand the service without undue drain on its charity money. Further, local government paid the vast majority of the subscriptions on behalf of individual blind people. So in effect the RNIB low price was subsidising local government in its responsibilities to provide a library service to the wider community. Research showed that many more blind people wanted the service and so expansion was planned. In order to avoid the financial 'losses' (through the subsidy) of a major expansion and to stop subsidising local government, RNIB raised its prices quite significantly on memberships paid for by local authorities. But it kept an artificially low rate for individual subscribers. Until 1990 this pricing policy worked like a dream. Membership, previously static, almost doubled. But the amount of donor income RNIB had to put into this service expansion remained relatively constant at just over £1 million.

By 1990 things began to change dramatically. Because of the

cont.

CASE EXAMPLE: RNIB continued

recession and central government policy, local government had less to spend. More and more local authorities began to cash limit the budget head for talking books memberships and only raised them year on year at a nominal inflation rate. Thus membership expansion from this source ceased. Even worse, the difference between the individual blind person purchase rate and the local government purchase rate was sufficiently large to encourage some local authorities to manipulate the system by giving grants to individuals to purchase at the individual rate – something which was formally forbidden by RNIB rules, but was very difficult for the charity to police. RNIB's response in April 1993 was to raise the individual subscription rate to equal that for local government, but only for new individual members.

Conclusions

I suggest that the following conclusions can be drawn on pricing policy for physical goods provided by voluntary organisations:

- If a charity is aiming to be a high-volume supplier of physical goods then a necessary, but not sufficient, condition is to have a price that covers or is close to costs.
- The greater the subsidy a charity puts into physical goods, the greater the disincentive to expand the volume of output. The only exception would be where the charity has a very restricted brief and a very high voluntary income.
- Where a charity is heavily subsidising goods, it should satisfy itself that this action is not inadvertently depressing supply and preventing other players coming in to meet unmet need.
- Charities need long-term pricing strategies that take account of the social and economic policies of governments as well as their responsibilities to their beneficiaries.

Subsidised pricing of physical goods provided by charities is an under-acknowledged and extremely complicated area. Pricing and subsidy policies have traditionally developed in a very haphazard way. Decisions are sometimes made by committees, or sometimes evolve from decisions made decades previously. In fact pricing decisions have to be taken from

a strategic (long-term and taking account of social poli
tactical (short-term) viewpoint.

Distribution (place)

After price, distribution is probably the least carefully thought-out area
of the marketing mix in the voluntary sector. Elation at having developed
a new product, or having obtained substantial goods as in-kind
donations, is often rapidly followed by depression about how to get
these items through to the beneficiaries. In the early stages of the Balkan
crisis, charities trying to help in Yugoslavia rapidly had warehouses in
Britain filling up with goods they could not deliver. Free gifts of
computers to charities often stick at head office for far too long before
being distributed. Geographic patterns of homelessness are created by
the fixed location of soup kitchens. Technical aids for disabled people
have a low turnover because the centres where people can try them out
are few and far between; perhaps fifty or more miles away from the
potential beneficiaries.

Intermediaries

Of course, it is not always like this, but it can be initially because the
charity normally gets much more enthusiastic about the physical goods
themselves rather than thinking about the nuts and bolts of how they are
going to be delivered to the customer. Many charities have a complicated
set of intermediaries between them and their beneficiaries. As with
intermediaries in the commercial supply chain, they can have subtly or
substantially different objectives that can undermine or even destroy the
distribution process. To be effective, it is necessary to regard these
intermediaries as customers in their own right, identifying their needs
and wants. Getting the support of intermediary distributors is arguably
more difficult in the voluntary sector than in the commercial sector. In
the latter, financial incentives by way of margins and fees are universally
applied. In the voluntary sector this is far less usual or acceptable, or in
some cases even illegal.

All too often we assume that intermediaries will at best have common
objectives with us to help the customers, and at worst will do it out of the
'kindness of their hearts'. But intermediaries are equally as busy as the

ipplying voluntary organisations. Distributing charitably donated food gifts by a community worker on a high-tension estate may be desirable, but may be of much lower priority than their other work, leaving aside the difficulty of deciding who gets what and whether these decisions may actually hinder or undermine the community worker's role. The last thing the local fundraising group might want will be 500 newsletters for onward distribution arriving from head office two weeks before it organises a local house-to-house collection.

Summary

In summary, charities delivering physical goods to beneficiaries need to think very carefully about distribution. There are a number of methods that can be used to help recognise and meet the wants of intermediary distributors, so that they will help the charity deliver its offerings. These can range from fees or percentages such as those used in the commercial sector, through to personalised thank-you letters. What is certain is that if voluntary organisation providers do not systematically plan and monitor their distribution networks, the number of beneficiary recipients will be well below target, and significant amounts of physical goods will simply 'rot' somewhere in the supply chain.

Promotion

At first glance, voluntary organisations would appear to be very effective at promoting their physical goods. Regular news items appear in the press, on radio and even on television covering a genuinely revolutionary new charity product, or featuring the departure of a convoy of food lorries, or describing extra feeding arrangements for homeless people at Christmas. In their ability to gain editorial coverage, voluntary organisations are the envy of their commercial counterparts.

However, closer inspection from a marketing standpoint often reveals that these promotional activities are often towards the general public rather than to potential beneficiaries. How many homeless people just before Christmas are watching television? How many deaf people will absorb media coverage about a new hearing aid? These promotional efforts have a valid role in creating a greater public awareness, understanding and donations, but they need a lot more thought and

planning if they are to be effective in reaching potential b
Effective voluntary organisations plan their promotions a
professionally as a commercial company, first considering
questions. How best can one reach the beneficiary target gɪ ⌄an
one reach more people through specialist or mainstream radio
programmes? Given that most blind people in this country are over
retirement age and simply regard themselves as having 'weak eyesight',
is it better to try to reach them via on a mainstream radio programme
such as 'You and Yours', rather than 'In Touch', aimed at visually
impaired people? Or do you go for both with different content
approaches? What are the take-up rates for different forms of media
exposure?

CASE EXAMPLE: LARGE-PRINT NEWSPAPER

Promoting a new large-print newspaper for visually impaired people on
the Jimmy Young show produced 700 requests for sample copies,
whereas a similar piece on the 'In Touch' programme (aimed at visually
impaired listeners) only resulted in 110 requests. But the conversion
rate from enquiries into subscribers was only one in four for the
mainstream programme and one in two for 'In Touch'. In terms of
numbers of new subscribers, advertising in a magazine aimed at older
people gave far better results, but whereas the cost per new subscriber
via the two radio programmes was £1.50, the cost per new subscriber
via the magazine advertisement was over £10. Now that the large-print
newspaper has a more substantial subscription base, the latest
promotional activity is peer group recruitment. The newspaper is aimed
primarily at older people – as many as one in four people over 80 years
old, and many people over 70 years old find large print much easier to
read. Therefore encouraging people to recruit friends is clearly a
potentially effective way forward.

This section on the promotion of voluntary organisation goods has
attempted to show that, while the high-profile, one-off editorial splash
coverage can be useful for general public awareness, promotion to
beneficiaries needs a well-thought-out plan and promotional mix. Unless
beneficiary target groups are extremely large, there is often nothing to
beat steady, relatively low-volumed methods of promotion.

Target markets

As we saw in Chapter 4, the attributes of a physical goods product are features (and more importantly the benefits they give to purchasers), quality, name, services and associated guarantees.

Each attribute needs to be planned. For example, a production-led rather than a marketing approach can easily result in a product being given more features than the customer either wants or can use. Deciding on the brand name looks straightforward but can be problematic, especially for new products. In development they tend to be given tag names which stick, and which may be far easier for scientists than the end beneficiary to understand. The area of associated services and guarantees can also be problematic for a charity. Supporting services for high-turnover, widely distributed products can be difficult to arrange even when there is the potential to use volunteers. Guarantees are an important area of development, especially with increasing legal requirements. It is helpful to divide physical products into two categories: existing and new. Long-established physical products in charities often do not get enough attention. The excitement and concentration is instead on new physical products. Good marketing requires a concentration on both.

As we have seen, it is all too easy for very useful charity physical goods to have a very low market penetration. In other words, the products can be very useful to a small percentage of the potential beneficiaries, leaving the vast majority of beneficiaries without the help of the product. It is therefore very important to assess the potential size of the target market and to measure what percentage the product is covering. If the market penetration is small, it is important to find out why. Is it because of promotion or distribution problems? Or is it because the product itself still is not quite right? This can be found out through marketing research among purchasers and potential purchasers.

New products

The area of new physical products provided by voluntary organisations has become a very exciting one over the last fifteen years or so. This is primarily because of the increasing expansion and accessibility of high technology, especially computer-based technology. Charities are almost in the position of having too many new physical products from which to choose. In a situation where disadvantaged people have too few choices, these statements need explaining.

Commercial companies have known for decades that for every twenty interesting new product developments, only about five will get tried out, and only one will succeed. Even these figures may be optimistic. In the commercial sector, at its crudest, the question is quite simply 'Are enough people going to buy this new product to make it viable and profitable?'.

However, in the voluntary sector 'success' is defined much more broadly and is more difficult to judge. For example, if resources are not a problem, then developing a new product for just one person in difficulties is justifiable. Of course resources are constrained, but in charities there is enormous pressure to develop more new products than can be promoted, distributed or, even more importantly, piloted and market evaluated. Consequently there is more danger than in the commercial sector of new physical products being developed, put in the sales catalogue and then left to languish. The best interpretation that can be put on this process is that it means that the product is available for those few beneficiaries who want it. However, the worst interpretation is that many people who want or need the product are not getting it. Without piloting and marketing research, the product, while good in many ways, may be significantly flawed. For want of minor adaptation the majority of the target market does not want it. This latter situation is by far the most insidious, because it provides incorrect evidence that a particular product line is not wanted, when in fact, given minor but significant changes to the product features, it might be invaluable.

Balance

There are no easy answers to deciding the balance between new product development, new product launch and existing product expansion. It is important that the charity discusses the balance in its own setting and circumstances, and with an understanding of the target beneficiary markets. For example, it is not uncommon for a voluntary organisation gradually to realise that it is not serving a major segment of its population – the very elderly or the very young, women as opposed to men, urban rather than rural, newly disabled as opposed to congenitally

r under-attended segment is discovered, and no other
ving it, then that obviously has important pointers for
opment. The Ansoff Matrix (see Chapter 4 and
_____)4) can be helpful in establishing a balance of new
product launch and existing product expansion.

If a particular product line has become relatively high volume (in the
charity's terms) but is still only serving 10 per cent of the potential
market, then this product line deserves much closer attention. If it has
gained 10 per cent of the market despite being under-promoted and with
serious distribution problems, could it be that investment in these areas
would lead to a doubling or trebling of volume?

If the charity has an active research and development arm and is
producing a fair number of new products which may be gaining high
media attention but do not seem to be of much interest to the end
beneficiaries, then the research and development processes need closer
examination. Is there over-investment in this area? Or is there under-
involvement of the ultimate beneficiaries in new product selection and
too little pilot testing with marketing research?

Purchasing power

Another crucial area for attention is the purchasing power of the target
market. If it wants the goods but cannot afford them, the charity can
consider two disparate solutions. One that can be implemented quickly
but may have very difficult consequences is to increase subsidy. The
other, which takes much longer, is to use argument and persuasion for
some or all of the costs to be borne by the state, or for additional state
cost allowances to be distributed to the disadvantaged purchasers.

Conclusion

This section has looked at the marketing of physical goods from the
point of view of price, place, promotion, product and target market.
Philosophy, even for goods, is an important part of the mix, but will be
dealt with in more depth in the next chapter; as will people, physical
evidence and processes, which are less important here. However, most
charity physical goods, such as bicycles for health auxiliaries in
Mozambique, or wheelchairs for physically disabled people, have a

significant service component. So people, physical evidence and processes should not be ignored.

Print and e-publications

Voluntary sector publications are a nightmare to the marketer. Voluntary organisations produce far more publications than equivalently sized organisations in the statutory and commercial sectors. Several large charities produce so many publications which change so frequently that they cannot even give a list of them, let alone produce a publications catalogue. For one large charity it took one person working full-time for six months to identify all its publications and produce a partial print catalogue containing over 250 items. Small charities can produce dozens of leaflets and fact sheets, many of which are hardly ever used – not only a waste in itself but also a misuse of staff creative time in writing them.

The more important charity publications are usually overseen or produced by a hard-pressed publications officer or department. This results in the larger, longer-run publications generally being of a high standard of design, print and content with well-thought-out target readerships. But distribution and promotion are too often ill-researched and carried out.

However, the majority of publications pop out of organisations with a good core purpose but often with little thought given to target group, language, design, distribution, promotion and price. These documents either languish in large piles on shelves or get scattered around like confetti with no one knowing whether they are read, let alone acted upon.

Questions

Six questions need to be answered before a charity publishes, whether in print or via the internet. These are: who? why? what? to whom? how? and how effective?

- *Who?* The commissioner of the communication is crucial, and should have the final authority for signing off on the message and its form. For example, leaflets promoting the charity's services may be written by an internal or freelance copywriter and be finally signed off by the senior manager of a large service group. But the head of the particular service about which the leaflet is written has to have ownership otherwise the service will not actively distribute it. In this situation the commissioner is effectively the individual service and service head. The role of the senior manager of the group of services or the corporate centre is to check for acceptability rather than be the real commissioning agent. This still allows for corporate requirements – on design, house style and families of publications. But the final signing-off/acceptance of the copy should take place where it really matters.

- *Why and what?* The why and what of a publication are inextricably linked. In essence, what do you want to say, and why does it need to be said? The objectives (why) of the communication exercise are of central importance, as is being absolutely clear about what (the product) needs to be communicated. For example, is the aim simply to help the recipient identify a problem area, and indicate where they can go for help? Or is the object of the publication to do that but also help people to help themselves more directly? Is the idea to create sympathy for the cause and recruit volunteers to help, or is it to elicit donations, or (with more difficulty) both? Answering these kinds of questions makes decisions on the actual content (the what) much easier to determine.

- *To whom?* Being clear about the target audience is a prime requirement because it will to a large extent predict the message in terms of particular content, language and style. If the target audience is too broad it will lead to the document having far too many objectives, and result in a style that will either appeal to one subgroup and not to another, or attempt to be acceptable to all and convince none.

- *How?* This deceptively simple question covers several very important parts of the marketing mix, namely distribution (place), promotion and price. The target audience and the budget will largely predict the medium through which to get the message across. It might be a leaflet, a more substantial pamphlet, a mass-mailed letter, a book or, increasingly, via e-mail or the internet. However, it could well be that a publication is not the right medium at all. These considerations are not the end of the matter. The distribution decisions are also of fundamental importance. For example, will the charity use inserts in newsletters or distribute multiple copies to local groups for onward distribution? If so, how will the charity encourage the groups to do this rather than leave them on the shelves? If they are to be distributed via doctors' practices, how will they get there and how will the practice manager be encouraged to display them? Good promotion is also critical. If the target market actually asks for the publication, this is halfway towards getting the recipient to act, rather than simply to be passive. Good promotion to the end receiver so that, for example, patients ask their general practice for a particular leaflet, can partially overcome poor distribution and reinforce good distribution.

Pricing publications is always a tricky issue and, not unreasonably, is related to costs and who pays them. If the costs are coming out of the central publications budget, then the service manager usually wants it to be free. If the document is free, how can the enthusiasm of intermediaries who ask for more copies than they can distribute be dampened? If the document is priced, will this stop it reaching its end recipient? Or could it be that for some customers having an affordable charge might enhance its value and encourage sales? 'Putting it on the internet' is increasingly seen as a panacea, an easy way out to escape costly print routes. But the internet route has hidden costs of creative production, promotion and keeping it up to date, even assuming your target group has easy access. So all the questions above still need answering.

- *How effective*? It is extremely difficult to assess the effectiveness of a publication. The most basic performance indicator of how many (relevant) hits have been achieved or copies have been sold or distributed is easy to track. If that can be combined with knowledge of which subgroups of the target audience are taking the publication up, then the information begins to have more evaluative use. If the purpose of a publication is to encourage action, then a prompt on the lines of 'for more information click on …/write to us at …' can be a partial indicator of how many recipients are actively taking up the ideas. These supportive calls for action can be constructed in such a way that audience response can be coded so as to learn more about the active responders. Where the publication is a regular one, such as a newsletter or magazine, or even on occasions for a one-off publication, an enclosed questionnaire can give useful information. Because the readers of charity publications are often highly motivated and committed, it is not unusual to be able to achieve anything up to a 30-40 per cent response rate, and exceptionally as high as 70-80 per cent. Completed questionnaires, suitably aggregated, can give a lot of information about the customer group and what it finds helpful and unhelpful about the publication. This attempt at quantification is more effective and reliable if it is combined with some form of depth discussion with a smaller number of assumed 'typical' readers.

Conclusion

Perhaps with the exception of organisations set up exclusively as publishers, charities are among the most prolific distributors of information, particularly in the form of printed documents. These types of products, where they are large or have a high circulation, tend to be well thought out and well produced, using professional publication staff input. Nevertheless, even in these instances it is quite normal for most attention to be devoted to the product and insufficient attention devoted to price, promotion and distribution.

However, except in the most professional and best-endowed charities, the majority of print and e-publication products such as information or advice sheets and guidelines are produced with far too little attention to the six important interrogatives of who? what? why? to whom? how? and how effective?.

For-profit fundraising goods

This section could just as easily sit in the chapter on fundraising. It is included here for two reasons. First, there are commonalities (as well as differences) in the marketing of physical goods, whether they be for profit (to supporters) or loss-making (to beneficiaries). Second, marketing approaches and techniques have become much more pervasive in the acquisition and selling of goods for profit than they have in the provision of physical goods to end beneficiaries. While this is ironic, juxtaposing the two areas in this chapter may provide additional lessons and comparisons for marketing of goods to end beneficiaries.

From a marketing perspective charity Christmas cards and charity shops are interesting examples of for-profit physical goods.

Christmas cards

Charity Christmas card activity exhibits some of the best and worst practice of charity marketing.

As a concept of added value, charity Christmas cards must be one of the neatest and most brilliant ideas ever developed. They combine to be simultaneously attractive to Christmas card senders, card manufacturers, retail distributors, the Post Office and obviously to charities themselves, both trustees and staff. People who send charity cards feel good about having done so; card manufacturers arguably gain increased sales or at least defend themselves against decline; retailers benefit; similarly the Post Office protects its volume; and charities feel it is good public relations and sometimes make a profit out of it. Everyone wins – or do they?

My guess is that the majority of charities with their own Christmas cards only make a profit through the associated donations that come with the card orders. If those donations could have been secured by other means, then the majority of charities are actually losing money on their card operations. So why do the smaller charities carry on with this activity? There is tremendous pressure on charities to be in this market. Charity trustees and senior staff somehow feel that they are not significant charity players if they do not have a card operation. Their family, friends and neighbours will continually be asking them why they do not do Christmas cards. In so far as the card operation is wobbling around the break-even point, or even making a loss, justifications (or rationalisations) about the importance of the public relations aspect of the Christmas cards will be trotted out.

So what distinguishes the more successful from the less successful? As one would expect, it is down to a good comprehensive marketing approach, once again concentrating particularly on the Cinderella areas of the charity marketing mix, namely distribution and promotion. The less successful charities are essentially production orientated and trustees and staff spend hours debating, or even arguing about whether the right designs were chosen. Then the vicious self-justification spiral starts to dominate – we are in the charity Christmas card market because it is good PR and the 'done thing'. In other words, narrow public relations objectives begin to dominate. Cards are chosen because the senior managers, trustees and sometimes their spouses like them, and consequently fewer and fewer other people buy them.

Promotion and place

It is probably not over-simplifying to say that the two 'Ps' of product and price are not the reason for success or failure. As far as product design goes, it would take a thick-skinned aesthete to distinguish between the myriad of charity card designs. There is little differentiation between charities on price – it is a highly price-competitive market even among the high-price business card end of the range. What makes all the difference are the two 'Ps' of promotion and place.

In essence, distribution and promotion get a charity the volume, and volume gets the cost price down, which gives the profit. This is achieved with a great deal of difficulty because the major charities have now commandeered an enormous volume in the market.

The key to successful promotion is the list. This involves the number of names and addresses the charity has of existing supporters who might be interested in purchasing cards. If there are 50,000 or more, then diligent marketing will bring success. If there are fewer than 10,000, success is possible but the risks are high. Such a loyal database of customers will give breathing space while the charity tests promotion elsewhere. Purchasing segments of lists from agencies, swapping them with other charities, putting inserts into regional sections of magazines, all allow test marketing to establish profitability. Coding leaflets and analysing subsequent sales can, in the space of one season, establish profitable areas for expansion. Timing of promotion is also critical. Small, relatively unknown charities are wise to promote their cards at the end of August or in early September.

The other key area of promotion is sales promotion. There is a whole range of possibilities. Are there any corporate donors who send a relatively high volume of business Christmas cards? If so, talking with them, arranging a special (but profitable) price and letting them choose their design can bring success. Does the charity have local groups that will sell actively, either for a share of the margin, or for a share of the public relations (which will involve overprinting the local group's name in high-volume situations or providing stickers in low-volume ones)? All

these and similar activities require assiduous atten
profitability and comparative donations, which in ι
coding of brochures and post-receipt analysis.

Distribution

Distribution is important, especially linked with sales ι   ⌐ıı. If it is
a popular cause, national and regional retailers are increasingly taking
on individual charities' cards. A charity's profit margins may be small,
but the volume is very large and so therefore is the public relations
benefit. While managerial responsibility of in-house volunteers may be
too much in the early stages, significant costs can be taken out by a
charity handling packaging and distribution itself rather than using a
company. Access to loyal and competent volunteers, providing there is
space, improves efficiency and cuts costs.

However, the real key to success in Christmas cards is 'shops'. If a
charity has its own shops, or can negotiate sales through national
retailers, then volume follows. A relationship with a national retailing
chain will add enormous card sales, but not a lot of profit. If a charity has
its own shops, then it can get both volume and profit.

Charity shops and trading

Since the late 1980s there has been a startling growth in the number and
net income of charity shops, approaching 6,000 in 2003/04 with a
combined net profit of £96 million, approximately 22 per cent of sales
income (Charity Finance 2004). Just twelve national charities have
consistently controlled around three-quarters of the shops and the net
profits. In the three years to 1992 the twelve largest charity operators
had added over 800 shops to their total (+ 23 per cent). In 1993 Marie
Curie was opening a shop a fortnight. However, by the late 1990s and
the early 2000s there was a slump in profitability and shop numbers
declined and did not start to rise again until 2004.

There are three main reasons for this sudden expansion: the search for
additional income; the publicity presence offered; and the market and
location opportunities offered by the recession in the early 1990s. Of
these three, new net income can be the most challenging. Harker (1993,
p. 9) reported the Cancer Research Campaign and British Heart
Foundation having net profit margins of 12 per cent and 14 per cent

ctively and around 2000, some chains were briefly losing money. The largest and most successful players include Oxfam, Cancer Research UK, British Heart Foundation, the British Red Cross and Scope.

Publicity and public presence provide a further push towards expansion. Voluntary fundraising of all types is heavily dependent upon, at least as a prerequisite, high public awareness. Charity shops, strategically located in high pedestrian volume areas, make a major contribution to public awareness. It is no coincidence that Oxfam and Cancer Research UK have some of the highest levels of unprompted awareness among the general public, and also have the largest networks of shops. The recession provided the conditions for a burst of expansion in at least two important respects. First, more shop sites became available either at no or low cost. Second, the majority of customers are less well-off and the low prices of second-hand goods are even more attractive in times of recession and increasing relative poverty.

But this does not account for some charities being so much more successful than others. The answer is quite simply a professional marketing approach. The product range is well thought out in relation to target markets. Pricing is effective. The various elements of promotion are very carefully attended to. Corporate style is particularly crucial.

Most important of all, place receives a great deal of attention. The operational nuts and bolts of distribution, location, inventory/stocks and transport assume a massive importance if profitability is to be maintained and extended.

Helping beneficiaries

Some charities, for example Age Concern and Oxfam, manage to achieve profitable trading activity that also helps beneficiaries.

CASE EXAMPLE: AGE CONCERN INSURANCE SERVICES

The trading division of Age Concern England exists for four reasons: to provide products and services relevant to older people; to enable the Age Concern network to provide 'commercial' services to older people, along with advice and practical services; to enable Age Concern groups to build up a source of independent income (social entrepreneurship); and to generate income for Age Concern England.

In Age Concern's case the product is largely a service rather than a physical good, but it is included in this chapter because of its profitable trading objective. Age Concern Insurance Services was started to help older people insure their homes at competitive premiums. In the early 1980s home contents insurance from the majority of companies had minimum sum-insured levels that were significantly higher than many older people wanted. For example, many older people only had £3,000 worth of contents to insure and the minimum sum that companies would insure was £6,000. This meant that, to be insured, older people were paying a higher premium than necessary. So Age Concern developed a product that was more in line with older people's needs. Initially the insurance brokerage activity was handled in-house; as it grew, it was contracted out to an external broker. Gradually the range of insurance products has increased both in range and quantity.

The products offered include pet insurance (covering the cost of veterinary treatment or kennel fees during an older person's hospitalisation), holiday travel, home and contents and private car insurance. Beneficiaries (older people) benefit by receiving a low-cost product specifically designed to meet older people's needs (low sums insured, payments by instalment at no extra cost, hospital cover under pet insurance policies). Local Age Concern groups that promote the policies benefit by receiving commission for the business they generate. For some of the more active groups this can result in significant annual sums. Age Concern England also benefits. As long as it continues to negotiate insurance packages that are relevant and represent value for money for older people, this form of practical marketing combines the best of all worlds for the national charity, its local groups and its beneficiaries.

> **CASE EXAMPLE: OXFAM AND PROGRESO**
>
> Oxfam undertakes profitable trading activities in a way that benefits beneficiaries, not as consumers but as producers. In late 2004 and early 2005 it launched a ground-breaking initiative, Progreso, opening its first two Progreso Fairtrade coffee bars in Covent Garden and Portobello Road in London. They showcase the quality of fairly traded coffee in a way that closes the gap between their beneficiaries (here the coffee growers in the developing world) and potential and actual Oxfam supporters and purchasers of fairly traded coffee.
>
> The producer cooperatives own 25 per cent of Progreso's shares and 25 per cent are being held in trust for projects in the wider grower community. Oxfam owns the remaining 50 per cent.

These case examples show the potential for charities to become involved in the marketing of products that benefit beneficiaries, provide the charity with 'profit' and also serve supporters. The sophistication of the marketing model developed would leave many FMCG brand managers gasping for air!

Conclusion

In this chapter we have looked at the application of marketing to charity publications, charity goods aimed at end beneficiaries, charity goods sold to the general public for a profit and charity goods sold at a profit but which aid beneficiaries.

The social entrepreneurship of providing physical goods (and services and ideas) to a voluntary organisation's end beneficiaries is more widespread than many commentators have presumed. In the main they are subsidised, which brings a complex series of interactions that are unique to the voluntary sector. To the libertarian right, this results in unhelpful distortions of the market. For those supporting a mixed economy of welfare, such an approach can make provision that would stimulate the commercial market or provide additional goods where the commercial market cannot operate. In general, marketing of physical goods to end beneficiaries is poorly developed and is more akin to a production-orientated approach to commerce in the 1950s without the benefits of mass production techniques. Voluntary organisations owe it to their end beneficiaries to become more effective in marketing their physical goods.

In each of these areas the more effective charities are increasingly applying a marketing approach. As a generalisation, however, marketing strategy is ignored. Target markets are not well thought out. Pricing is unsophisticated. Place is largely ignored.

For these reasons profitability, when it is sought, is low; market penetration, especially into beneficiary customer groups, is low; and publications are wasted and unread. Most charities have a lot to learn.

Key points

Physical goods

Voluntary organisations owe it to their end beneficiaries to become more effective in marketing their goods.

Price
- Be aware of the consequences of subsidising, or over-subsidising, goods. If the organisation is aiming to be a high-volume supplier, prices must cover, or almost cover, costs.
- Pricing strategy should take account of the social economic policies of government (which is often the purchaser) as well as responsibilities to the beneficiary.

Place
- It is essential to plan and monitor how physical goods are going to be delivered to the end customer.
- Get the support of intermediaries by understanding their needs and priorities.
- Consider using incentives, however small.

Promotion
- Promotion to beneficiaries needs to be carefully and regularly targeted in spite of the seeming attractiveness of obtaining high-profile coverage generating only general awareness.

Target market
- Assess the potential size of the market and measure how much is covered by the product.
- Do not let the organisation be distracted into developing new products that cannot be promoted properly.

Print and e-publications
- Who is responsible for the publication, its content, message and style?
- Why is it being produced, what is it going to say and to whom?
- How will it reach its target audience? Consider distribution, promotion and price.
- How will its effectiveness be measured?

For-profit fundraising goods

Common pitfalls
- Pressure to be seen to be trading in a particular market, such as Christmas cards, can cause smaller organisations to make bad decisions, as they may not have the resources to enter the market in sufficient volume.
- Promotion and distribution are often badly handled.
- Although the charity shops market is cyclical, the most successful chains still demonstrate that effective pricing, promotion and place are key.

7   Services to beneficiaries

Introduction

As we saw in Chapter 6, applying a marketing approach to charity goods, as with any physical goods in the commercial sector, is relatively straightforward. However, marketing of services, including in the charity sector is very challenging. Services are less tangible than goods; they have a complicated interface with beneficiaries and on many occasions have beneficiaries' active participation; production and consumption are often simultaneous; the service is an activity extending over some considerable time; and service providers' and users' attitudes and behaviour can make or break the quality of the service.

These differences between marketing services and goods are, arguably, different in kind, and are certainly different in extent. This has led some writers to modify the traditional marketing mix to make it easier to apply to services. Booms and Bitner (1981, pp. 47-51) have added three extra 'Ps' in the form of people, physical evidence and process (see Chapter 4) which are further elaborated in Zeithaml *et al.* (2006). I argue in Chapter 4 that a further 'P' – philosophy – is required for charity and public services. The explicit or implicit philosophy adopted by a charity has a significant impact on how a charity's services operate, especially in relation to customers.

Direct and indirect services

Direct

The vast majority of charities' service output is delivered direct to end beneficiaries. These direct services (which form the majority of voluntary and community sector activity) cover a huge range of areas, including self help schemes, pensioners' groups, play schemes, visiting schemes, social work in a variety of forms, museums, galleries, theatres, feeding programmes, education and development programmes, social and employment rehabilitation, employment training, wildlife sanctuaries, housing, financial aid and information services.

Indirect

Most charities have very broad-based objectives, which are far more interventionist in the external environment relating to their cause than might at first be expected. For example, Age Concern's mission is 'to promote the well-being of all older people and help make later life a fulfilling and enjoyable experience' (www.ageconcern.org.uk, 2005). Save the Children Fund makes it clear in its mission statement and history that, in order to achieve lasting benefits for children within the communities in which they live, it will attempt to influence policy as well as practice (www.savethechildren.org, 2005). These examples are typical of a vast range of charities in the United Kingdom, and almost certainly for not-for-profit organisations across the world.

These broad-based objectives mean that charities do not rely exclusively on direct services to their end beneficiaries. They also attempt to influence the policy and practice structures impacting on their end beneficiaries through indirect services aimed at intermediaries. For example, if the RSPB can encourage statutory authorities through advice and guidance to be more assiduous in their anti-pollution responsibilities, this might do more to protect birds than setting up several new bird sanctuaries.

The Wolfenden Report (Wolfenden 1977, pp. 22–7) usefully divided the world in which voluntary organisations operate into four sectors, which arguably cover all areas of human activity – the commercial sector, the statutory sector, the voluntary sector and the informal sector (of family, friends and neighbours). A moment's thought will establish that the end beneficiaries of any voluntary organisation are going to be affected considerably more by the combined attentions of these four sectors than they are through any direct services from charities. Charities and other voluntary organisations are therefore increasingly using the full interventionist potential of their broad-based objectives, by adding activities to their repertoire that can influence those parts of the statutory, commercial, voluntary and informal sectors that are important to their end beneficiaries.

For example, as early as the early 1970s Age Concern England started an active advisory service to the major retailers on the small package requirements of older beneficiaries. Oxfam has long given advisory support to government departments, voluntary and commercial organisations in other countries on a whole range of humanitarian issues and programmes. The Disability Alliance runs training courses for statutory authority social workers and others on the social security benefits available to disabled people so that these public sector workers can, in turn, give better information to the disabled people with whom they are in touch.

These indirect services form a very small proportion of financial turnover in comparison with the turnover of direct services but their impact can be considerable.

Structure and relationship of direct and indirect services

While the distinction between direct and indirect services is a helpful analytical tool to marketers and service providers, they may have some common attributes. For example, a school catering for disabled children is clearly a direct service. However, the placement process will involve the local education authority's professional expert visiting the school, where they might pick up ideas that can be applied in their own local education authority setting. Macmillan Cancer Relief provides and funds nurses to care for cancer patients in their own homes, which is clearly a direct service. But in many instances these nurses and other staff are outposted to the NHS and are funded for only the first three years, after which the NHS agrees to take the post on to the full-time establishment – a clear example of how a direct service can impact on and change the attitudes and behaviours of a statutory service provider.

This last example begins to reveal a direct/indirect service continuum (Bruce 1994, see Figure 7.1), with one end being the provision of direct services to end beneficiaries. Moving along the continuum, the proportion of direct service provision decreases and the significance of indirect service provision increases, to the point where indirect service provision shades into 'pure' indirect services or pressure group activity – working indirectly to achieve a policy change.

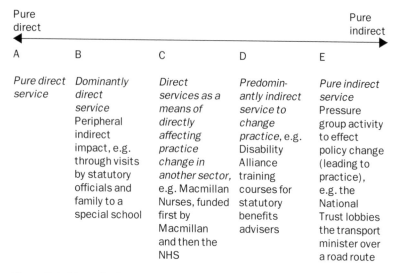

Figure 7.1 Direct/indirect service continuum

However, before reaching the pressure group end of the continuum, we find the location of the most common form of indirect service –activities such as advice, consultancy and training aimed at people who, in turn, impact on the charity's end beneficiaries. For example, Volunteering England provides advice, training and consultancy services to voluntary and statutory organisations that wish to involve (more) volunteers in their work. The Children's Society runs similar activities aimed at statutory health, social and education services, encouraging them to be more effective with children and families.

Running along the continuum in Figure 7.1 are four vital but changing attributes, as laid out in Figure 7.2.

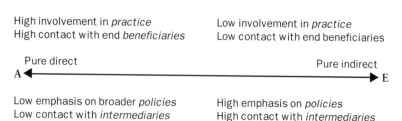

Figure 7.2 Changing attributes in the direct/indirect service continuum

So what does such a model contribute? For the marketing or charity manager, it can be a useful analytical tool in understanding and guiding the positioning of a service both within the charity and outside it in respect of other charities' services and other sectors' activity. For example, in the 1960s and early 1970s the legitimacy of charities (rather than the state) running so many direct services (positions A and B in Figure 7.1) was questioned. Charities continued to run them, but they tried to do so more from position C – to influence policy and practice in statutory services, for example by pioneering services (new product development) which would be taken on by the state (family planning, for example). At the same time position E became more attractive, as we shall see in Chapter 8. Government policies to encourage contracting-out have re-legitimised areas A and B (direct services in their own right).

Opportunities and challenges

The model also begins to help to predict the particular opportunities and challenges that will be met from any one position. It can also make the process of effective service development more conscious and logical. For example, in the school for disabled children which only provides direct services, it prompts the question, 'What about indirect services that could be added on?' Who are the other target groups that impact on the children in the school, and how can the school services be modified or added to in order to impact on these relevant indirect target groups? The answer to the question of 'who else' will almost certainly initially be parents/family and/or local authority professional workers in the child's home area. Where the disabled child has a close family, the family is likely to be extremely influential on the child's development. What can the school do to share and exchange with the parents, particularly in knowledge and skills? In the case of local authority professionals (who may not be familiar with the particular disability in which the school specialises), what can be shared with regard to knowledge and skills?

This discussion leads naturally into service positioning.

Positioning and other-player (competitor) analysis

Chapter 3 looked at the component parts of other-player analysis and positioning and some of the strategies charities can follow.

Throughout this book the term 'other-player analysis' (Bruce 1994) has been used rather than the normal commercial marketing term of 'competitor analysis', as the latter description sits uncomfortably in the charity market, especially when considering services to beneficiaries. I could not possibly count the number of times that people have said to me (particularly those from commerce and industry) 'Why don't you all get together and merge into one charity for such and such a cause?' While superficially sensible, such proposals, especially coming from commercial entrepreneurs bred on the merits of competition, always strike me as a bit rich! Nevertheless the arguments for cooperation between charities in the field of service provision seem invincible – in theory at least. In my experience charities do try quite hard to cooperate on such activity, either through formal processes such as cross-representation on each other's boards, or through informal groupings of service managers sharing information. In comparison with the commercial world, it probably has been quite cooperative and well ordered. For example, Age Concern and Help the Aged have an understanding as to who does what, albeit somewhat uneasy at times. The RNIB and Guide Dogs for the Blind have clear activity boundaries. Similarly the National Federation of Women's Institutes and the Townswomen's Guild have reasonably clear geographic, if not functional, boundaries.

Competition

If and when competition breaks out between two or more charities, it is important from a marketing point of view to have the affected services positioned properly. For example, Help the Aged services are largely positioned out of its high priority for fundraising, while Age Concern services are positioned largely on its strength of being able to gather together at national and local level all the parties interested in older people into a cooperative effort.

However, this can change, and there are some indications that there will be increasing competition between charities in the field of service provision over the next decade or so. While the arrival of new 'dynamic' service managers or chief executives can increase the amount of competition, in general growth or decline in competition occurs for broadly structural reasons. For example, declining numbers of disabled children going into residential schooling will up the competition stakes between such schools. Similarly, structural changes such as new commissioning policies by (usually) statutory funders bring change. While statutory authorities' introduction of a purchaser/provider split and the expansion of commissioning from charities and non-profits offer charities opportunities, the simultaneous introduction of competitive tendering for work has increased competition between charities. The statutory purchasers are actively encouraging competition to gain keener tender prices.

Certainly, with government, trust and company funders looking for value for money and maximum effectiveness, charities that provide services would be wise to undertake a careful other-player analysis, comparing strengths, weaknesses, opportunities and threats between themselves and significant other players. Such other players need to include not only other charities but also government and commercial providers as well as changing expectations and the reality of the role of the informal sector of family, friends and neighbours.

Needs research

Needs (or marketing) research has long had a legitimacy in the charity sector, although the quality and frequency leaves much to be desired. The insufficiency of research can be explained in a number of ways. First, as demand usually outstrips supply, there is no impelling business reason to understand the end beneficiaries' needs better. Second, even sensitive professional workers in charity services dealing with disadvantaged groups often develop the 'I know best' syndrome. This is not exactly akin to the 'production-orientated' approach in the 1950s manufacturing industry, because the charity service professional is much more closely in touch with the end beneficiaries, but it has some echoes of that way of thinking. Third, charities have a tradition of policy-making committees having fairly large numbers of 'the great and the good', who are somehow meant to know the answers. Fourth, the more progressive charities (such as UK Youth, Age Concern, SCOPE and RNIB) have been involving increasing numbers of their end beneficiaries, or organisations representing them, on their policy-making committees. Ironically such representation can lead the organisation to feel that it is taking on the beneficiary voice. In one sense it is, but these are not typical beneficiaries.

They are the ones who are confident enough, able enough and available enough to join committees. In other words, they are seldom typical. It is wholly good to have increased beneficiary representation, but not as a substitute for needs research. Indeed beneficiary representatives can often be the first people to acknowledge that they cannot know all the needs of their group and, for this reason, can be some of the strongest supporters of marketing research.

Impact

Needs research can have a significant impact on a charity's services. For example, RNIB spends more than of £200,000 per year on needs research among beneficiaries, a figure that would rise to nearer £500,000 if service take-up and quality monitoring were included. In particular, two major pieces of research among nearly 1,000 blind and partially sighted adults and young people have had a significant impact on the organisation's services. Interestingly they were also rated among the three most important RNIB initiatives by a clear majority of RNIB stakeholders – showing that policy-makers and other key external customer groups welcome marketing research as much as service managers. Macmillan Cancer Relief is another charity that spends considerable sums on marketing research among people with cancer, their carers and friends, relatives and colleagues. Its major 1992 MORI survey revealed needs not previously fully acknowledged, in particular difficulties with non-medical day-to-day tasks such as shopping and child care. As a result it amended its services. It continues to be committed to undertaking and acting upon customer research, especially among users.

Such needs research is particularly valuable to a charity's indirect services. Externally validated, quality research among existing and potential beneficiaries first, describes the situation of the client group, which can be compared with others; second, indicates the areas of priority need within the client group; and third, indicates what needs to be done from an evidence base. This information provides powerful and credible ammunition to the indirect services trying to make an impact on relevant intermediary groups of professionals and managers, such as social workers, doctors and environmental heath officers.

Market segmentation and target markets

Chapter 3 described the reasons for segmenting the charity market. These included to allow prioritisation of groups to be served, higher quality services to be delivered via homogeneity and to identify under-served groups. It describes in more detail the criteria that can be used for segmenting the market (including geographic, socio-demographic, psychographic and behavioural).

One of the key differences between professional companies and charities is that the market for the charity is more likely to be prescribed, even to the extent of being identified in the legal charity registration document. It could be argued that this gives charity service managers a flying start – we are here to serve deaf people/children/theatre-goers in Coventry or people/animals suffering pollution, etc. However, as Chapter 3 described, this is only the start if real need is to be met effectively when resources are in short supply. Unfortunately few charities analyse their market much further than that outlined in their charity registration document by asking and answering such questions as how many; what ages; where do they live; what characteristics are most relevant to our cause; which subgroups are we serving and which not; and among those we are serving, are we reaching a high percentage or a low percentage?

For example, a charity providing services for people with learning difficulties might segment its beneficiary market by age, severity of learning difficulty, and presence or absence of parental support under the age of 40 years. Following that segmentation, needs research and other-player analysis might indicate that children and young people up to the age of 25 across all severity groups are relatively well served and are likely to have younger parents. The charity may identify potential beneficiaries in middle to late middle age with ageing parents as a particularly vulnerable group, under-served by statutory services, which have for too long relied on parental support. Such targeting does not predict how this group might best be helped, and a final decision on whether to go ahead with this particular priority group would depend on further needs research, review of existing services capable of adaptation and potential new services, identification of additional or substitute resources, choice between direct and indirect service intervention, etc.

But because a group with some degree of common need has been identified, this will allow a *higher quality service* to be introduced in that the recipients have certain common characteristics, and will therefore be an object of *efficient allocation of resources*; and if the segmentation and needs research have been efficient, there should be a strong case for attracting funding. (The words emphasised repeat the list of reasons that segmentation can be helpful to decisions on service delivery, as outlined in Chapter 3.)

Service design and construction (product)

Under the first 'P' of the marketing mix, the list of elements to be considered consists of 'brand, quality, design, features, variety, name, packaging, service support and guarantees' (Doyle 2003).

Let us use the example of the voluntary visiting service quoted in Chapter 1. What is its quality – are the volunteers trained well enough to be sensitive to the needs of the older person to be visited? What are its features – can the older person decide in principle and in practice how often they would like a visit? Does the service have an attractive name? Does it have a good reputation locally? Is it generally believed to be provided only for people who are mentally confused, and if so, is it unlikely to be attractive to people who are simply lonely? Are the volunteers invariably polite, reliable and punctual? Do they seem able to refer effectively any problems the older person may have? Is there a clear procedure for the older person to indicate that they would like to try an alternative volunteer visitor? Is there a regular assessment meeting (every six to twelve months) with a social worker so that the visiting relationship can be reviewed, and a more fundamental but associated assessment offered? All these characteristics need to be thought through before the service is launched, and monitored throughout its existence, otherwise many of the failures enumerated by the pioneer research of Shenfield and Allen (1972, pp. 159-69) will become apparent.

Concepts

The service marketers Berry and Parasuraman (1991, pp. 15–76) elaborated by Zeitham and Bitner (2003) and Zeithaml, Bitner and Gremler (2006) introduce some very useful concepts in everyday language. They argue that delivering a top quality service presumes 'doing the service right the first time'. How much more true is this for a charity service? How many patrons of an orchestra will be lost if the first performance they hear is a bad one? If an older client has a bad or poor experience with their visitor or social work assessor, their confidence in the service will be shattered, far more than if the gasman turns up on the wrong day (to use a commercial service comparison). If the worst happens, Berry and Parasuraman then talk of 'doing the service very right the second time': in our case bringing in an alternative volunteer or assessor whom we know is one of our best and going to great lengths to listen and repair the damage as perceived from the client's point of view. They argue, and everyday experience would confirm, that taking a great deal of trouble to rectify a bad experience has a very convincing impact on an upset customer.

Chapter 4 introduced the five dimensions that influence a commercial service customer's view of the quality of a service which, in order of priority, are:

1　reliability (delivering the service dependably and accurately);
2　responsiveness;
3　assurance (confidence in the service);
4　empathy;
5　tangibles (physical clues to the service).

Except for 'tangibles', all these features were found by Shenfield and Allen's research to be critical and would seem to translate into almost any charity service to beneficiaries. The older people being visited want the visitor to be dependable. 'Assurance' is perhaps too narrow a term for many charity services, especially complex ones, but it conveys the necessity for a thoughtful, high quality professional service. Responsiveness and empathy are clearly vital service attributes.

New service development

Adding to or closing services in a charity's range of products is often given too little thought and analysis. For example, new services can be added into the portfolio almost unilaterally by an enthusiastic staff member or group of staff in response to needs they have identified from their beneficiary contact (for example, staff in a social work advice unit adding in advice on social security, which is very complicated and

individualised work – this results in the service not being done properly
and clients being turned away). In one sense this staff initiative is what
charities are famous for – quick, flexible, innovative responses to newly
identified need. But then demand becomes greater than existing staff
and/or volunteers can supply and more resources are requested. If these
are granted it is often outside a new product analysis (still not thought
through) and, hey presto, the service has grown like Topsy. If extra
resources are refused, either the new service has to be closed, resulting in
accusations of bad faith or, more likely, it stumbles on, making little
penetration into the market and providing poor quality through being
under-resourced and stretching staff and volunteers to breaking point.

While this 'try it and see' method can be akin to informal test
marketing, it needs to be more efficiently handled. Dibb *et al.* (2001, pp.
299–304) describe the process of new product development as idea
generation, followed by screening, concept testing, business analysis,
product development, test marketing and, lastly, commercialisation
(which is essentially planning the full launch and the first year's activity
plan). This process is probably not as linear as described, but it does
provide a rough and ready cross between a checklist and a process to be
followed. In the above social work advice example, idea generation was
good but there was virtually no screening or analysis of the resource/
business implications and the unit shifted from idea generation through
to service development and straight into the market-place in a form that
was halfway between a test market (without any evaluation built in) and
a full launch.

New product development can be a disorientating term, encouraging
a concentration on the product as opposed to the whole marketing mix.
Johne (1996) emphasises the importance of developing the whole
marketing mix. This is particularly useful with a mature product range.
For example, community service as an alternative to custodial sentencing
is well established, with several variants, many focusing on remotivating
disillusioned young offenders and trying to get them into jobs. Product
augmentation development (Johne 1996) as an approach concentrates
on which marketing mix changes can add value. In the community
service example several schemes have concentrated on the people
elements of the eight-point service marketing mix and introduced
volunteer 'buddies' to the young person – these buddies (or mentors)
being successful, employed people (rather than social workers) who can

help the young person through example, mentoring and introductions. The core community service product is retained but is augmented by attention to one or more of the marketing mix elements, in this case the 'P' for people.

Johne also argues that in the commercial world new product development is often simply incremental change that avoids failure but does not maximise potential. Not-for-profit organisations not required to achieve business success and often required by their funders to innovate can exhibit the opposite characteristics – innovating for the sake of it and dropping the new product the minute the (three-year) funding ends. Nevertheless the growth of contractually funded services (government as purchaser and charity as provider) may make the commercial comparison more apposite. Competitive bidding between charities, with the cheapest quote winning, may encourage a climate where genuine innovation is forced out by the requirement from the purchaser for the successful bid to be cost-effective, recognisable and low risk – 'more of the same'.

Service closure

Cutting out services can be even more rough and ready, verging on the amateurish. It is not uncommon for a service area of a charity to be effectively in terminal decline but largely ignored by charity decision-makers until the service becomes 'critical'. This can be triggered by an overall financial crisis in the charity that engenders analysis of major subsidy areas, and the realisation that the subsidy per client in service A has become untenable. Another trigger is when a major funder decides either to withdraw funding completely or cut it back to levels where charity subsidy is so high as to be judged unreasonable. A hasty decision to close a service is made, almost under panic conditions, with a lot of blame being spread around. Also unexpected opposition to closure can emerge.

CASE EXAMPLE: RNIB's RESIDENTIAL HOMES

An example, rather better thought out than the one outlined above, occurred in relation to residential homes provided by RNIB. RNIB's needs research revealed that the vast majority of older blind people were in ordinary residential homes. Market analysis showed that RNIB's four residential homes occupied less than 5 per cent of the charity market of specialised residential homes for older blind people. They were also heavily loss-making, with high subsidies per older person accommodated. This led to the proper question of 'why are we providing this service?' As a major provider of nationwide services, it was decided that there was no justification for such a small contribution to need in this area, as it was limited to four fairly narrow geographic locations and provided for only 140 blind people out of 150,000 blind and partially sighted people in other homes.

Closure plans were developed. However, this triggered an unexpected and vigorous campaign in the four localities against closure, led by relatives and engendering the support of local political and social services leaders. A mixture of sound argument and thinly veiled threats to develop a fairly major national publicity campaign (one of the relatives was a senior executive of a national PR agency!) persuaded RNIB to review the plans. The organisation had for some time been thinking of providing a national advisory service to integrated residential homes (where approximately 150,000 blind and partially sighted older people live with their sighted counterparts) to advise on the special needs arising from visual impairment. Two of the homes had developed special expertise in accommodating deaf-blind older people. Also, the Housing Corporation proved very sympathetic to requests for substantial investment of capital improvement monies and a Department of Health inspection had made a number of recommendations for improvement, which RNIB felt could be made. Consequently three of the four homes were upgraded and one (of two in the same region) closed. The remaining three were used as centres of excellence and as 'shop windows' for an RNIB national advisory service to mainstream residential homes on the care of blind and partially sighted residents, especially those (very many) who also have hearing impairments. Because physical and service facilities were improved it was possible to raise fees and occupancy, and subsidy was dramatically reduced.

Although the outcome was unexpected, this process showed the stages of idea generation, service and business analysis, proposal (to close), public announcement and consultation, review of decision, reformulation, testing, and final and full planning and implementation.

The difficulties of such an analytical approach, especially in a service as opposed to a physical product, are clear. The temptation is to make a snap decision ('we cannot keep shilly-shallying around') that avoids a lot of investment of staff time in the analysis of options. But the snap decision may not be in the best interests of the broader client group, let alone the narrower one directly affected.

Price – overt and hidden

Doyle's list of price elements (Doyle 2003, p. 287) is list price, discount, allowances, trade margins, payment terms, credit and trade-in. Even Booms and Bitner's list (1981, pp. 47–51) – level, discounts, payment terms, customers' perceived value, quality/price and differentiation – does not look much more encouraging for the charity service manager. However, charity service managers are learning fast. The swing away from grant aiding and simple fees paid to charities, towards charities having to tender against commercial companies as well as charities, has made the 'P' of price a major point of the charity service marketing mix.

Size and structure

Fees and charges (largely for services such as home care, technical aids or rehabilitation) are enormously important to charities, eclipsing even donations as a source of income – a position regularly reported but often forgotten (Posnett 1992; Hems and Passey 1996; Palmer *et al.* 1999; Wilding *et al.* 2004) The main purchasers are statutory bodies such as central and local government and the NHS (either directly or indirectly). In certain circumstances, individuals will be charged, almost always at heavily subsidised rates. Some of the fees will surprise the casual reader. For example £50,000 paid by a local education authority for a 32-week residential school year for a multi-disabled student (someone with severe learning difficulties, severe sensory impairment, unable to walk and doubly incontinent) or £120,000 for 52-week provision. The charity might also be adding a further £10,000 (or more) to top up to the full cost. At the other extreme, a charity might charge a nominal amount of 5p for pamphlets in order, simply, to control unusable over-ordering by local groups.

In the 1980s Gabor (1980, pp. 168–76) and Cowell (1984, p. 147) argued that the pricing of commercial services has received too little attention. This has not been rectified in the intervening years (Diamantopoulos 2003). Gabor divided pricing into either 'cost-based pricing' or 'market-orientated pricing'. In the former, services will be either profit orientated or government controlled. In the latter, services will be either competitive (the going rate) and/or customer orientated (set with regard to consumers' attitudes and behaviour).

Except in the minority of cases, none of these categories fits usual practice in the charity sector, where the most common pricing policy is last year's price plus inflation. Because services have a cost structure where salaries and wages form the largest component, this formula was a recipe for near disaster for several charities in the 1970s and early 1980s when wages rose faster than inflation. Although not so extreme we have over the last ten years had a return to this situation.

Price review

The resulting growing subsidy of many charity services during the 1970s and 1980s, combined with the recession of the early 1990s led a significant number of charities to review their pricing policies, especially where statutory bodies were paying. In short, this has meant increasing prices as much as the market will stand where there is a multiple purchaser base (such as national services paid for by local government social services departments, education authorities or health trusts). This policy has been remarkably effective where the local purchaser can see no obviously cheaper method of provision. However, increasing central government funding restraint of locally delivered statutory services has introduced a predictable but unhappy consequence.

It is now more usual that, if charities raise the price of services by more than inflation, the local statutory purchaser will pay but will reduce the number of individuals (or units of service) for which it is prepared to pay in order to stay within a cash-limited local budget. Some central government purchasers have been operating harsher cash-limited purchasing budgets for more than a decade. So attempts by charity services to reduce subsidy levels are meeting problems. The Deakin Report (Deakin 1996) recognised this problem and called for full cost recovery for commissioned services. The government accepted the argument in principle but in practice has huge ground to make up. This is a critical area for charity vigilance.

Statutory purchasers

Consequently the policy that most charities adopt is a fee of 'cost minus x per cent' where x is the percentage subsidy from its charitable donations that the charity can afford and judges right. In practice this policy is constrained by what (in the main) statutory purchasers will pay, and what sister charities with similar services are charging. Given that many contracting charities are not very good at costing their services fully, this approach is dangerous in the medium term. Charities under-price and over-subsidise, creating an unsustainable low market price. So, charities' most common policy can be stated as 'cost minus charity subsidy with a market eye on what other producers are charging', which amounts to three of the four methods quoted by Gabor (1980) above.

Particularly critical in charity service pricing is whether there are multiple purchasers or a single purchaser. Single purchasers such as the Department for Work and Pensions or a local authority are not dissimilar in their purchasing behaviour to supermarkets with their suppliers – tough, verging on unreasonable! Traditionally in these situations there have been detailed discussions between the statutory purchaser and the charity provider, with the provider declaring a detailed breakdown of costs for authorisation and clearance by the unitary, monopolistic purchaser.

Tendering

However, we are seeing a changing trend, which looks set to continue. This trend is being caused and encouraged by significant shifts towards competitive tendering, which charity service providers are finding very difficult, for a number of reasons. First, it forces them into a much more competitive stance with sister charity service providers with which they have been trying over the years to cooperate. Second, there are widely varying charity subsidies being put into bids that may or may not be declared to the purchaser. Third, as is not uncommon in the commercial service world, it is hard to cost individual units of service accurately – and given that purchasers are strongly pushed towards accepting the lowest bids, incompetent bid construction by charities can badly affect sub sectors of the charity services market. Fourth, there is an unclear interaction between lower priced bids and whether these are attempts to build volume savings.

While much of the charity service pricing is amateurish, some charities do give thoughtful discounts and/or use innovative sales promotion techniques. As with, say, contract catering in the commercial world, some charities enter into loss-leader contracts at both national and local levels, in the hope that after a set period a price rise will be in the interest of both purchaser and provider. An example would be a local charity setting up a voluntary visiting scheme for older people at a loss-making rate, but with a realistic price review built in after two years. It is unlikely that the local authority is going to want the major upheaval of re-letting the contract to another organisation, therefore the charity assumes/hopes that a more realistic price will be negotiated at the two-year break point. One the most creative discount/loss-leader schemes is undertaken by Macmillan Cancer Relief (see page 159).

Payments by beneficiaries

So far the discussion of service price has concentrated primarily on situations where a statutory body or some other third party is paying for a service to a beneficiary. This is the source of the majority of charity service income. However, there are two situations in which beneficiaries can be said to be paying. The first is in the non-monetary impact price the beneficiary pays by taking up the service (see Chapter 3) which he or she pays regardless of whether a third party pays the cash price. The second is those relatively few situations where the beneficiary pays the cash price.

Impact price

The non-monetary impact price can on occasions be critical. For example, certain forms of rehabilitation may require someone to go to a residential centre away from home. Even though a statutory body may be prepared to pay the fees, the impact price may be too high for the person or their family. The parents may not be prepared to 'lose' their child or the married couple may not be prepared to be separated for three months while the recently disabled spouse receives residential rehabilitation. In Andreason and Kotler's terms (2003 and Kotler and Andreason 1991, p. 477) the psychological price and the price of dislocation of social arrangements may be too high in relation to the potential beneficiary's perception of the benefits they will get from the rehabilitation. In their 2003 edition Kotler and Andreason used the term 'perceived cost' (p. 377). Therefore the charity has to try all avenues to reduce the impact price, for example by arranging transport home at weekends, having accommodation available for the family to visit at weekends or running part of the rehabilitation course at the beneficiary's home. Another complementary approach is to increase the perceived value of the rehabilitation course to the beneficiary and their family so that the impact price becomes worth paying. Methods include offering the potential beneficiary and the family a trial weekend to meet the staff and other previous beneficiaries.

Individual payments

Cash payments by individual beneficiaries are often a very small part of the charity service income. This is partly pragmatic and partly philosophical. Pragmatically, fees for services are usually high in relation to individual means. Philosophically, charging (high) fees to individuals goes against the charitable ethos. However, there are exceptions and there are some signs that things are changing. For example, most social services departments charge clients some or all of the costs of local authority care services in the person's own home. As the home care service becomes contracted out, charity bid winners will almost certainly also have to charge clients. Instances where service charges to beneficiaries might be made are where the service is relatively low cost and/or the service activity is something the beneficiary might have expected to pay for, such as a holiday. However, very often the service price will be subsidised by charity voluntary income and/or will provide benefits not available on the commercial market (see the Age Concern Insurance Service case example in Chapter 6).

Some charities operate variable discounts for their services, depending on who is paying – for example a higher rate for a statutory authority and a lower rate for an individual or family. However, this is open to abuse, in that some local authorities may develop complicated systems of giving grants to individuals for them to purchase at the lower rate. This has led some charities to withdraw these discounts. Variable discounts are common in arts charities, where they relate to the status of the customer (student, unemployed, retired), the volume of purchase and the popularity of the timing of the performance.

Conclusion

Service pricing in the commercial world is underdeveloped, and is in an even more embryonic state in the charity services sector. This is changing rapidly as both charitable income and statutory service fees have been squeezed, and central and local government have introduced competitive unit-price tendering. In the commercial world, losing a customer to a competitor is, at its worst, a loss of market share and potential profit. The moral tensions of losing a potential charity service beneficiary because of too high a price are significant. Charity services managers feel moral and personal tension when pricing policies result in them losing beneficiary 'custom'. This is because it is rare for their customers to be lost to a comparable 'competitor'. Instead, although the need of the beneficiary has been established, rejection on the basis of price results in no service being provided or, at best, a substandard alternative service having to be taken up (home care for only two hours a week for a 90-year-old housebound person as compared with a residential home place). Charity service pricing has moral and practical implications that are seldom, if ever, found in the commercial service world.

Marketing communications (promotion)

The commercial subheadings of promotion, namely advertising, public relations, personal selling and sales promotion and publicity all make immediate sense in the charity services market-place even if the words and concepts are not always attractive to professional service providers such as teachers, social workers and health workers. However, word-of-mouth recommendation and professional referral assume far greater importance and acceptability in the promotion of charity services, in the same way that they do in the promotion of commercial professional services (as opposed to non-professional services).

Advertising

This is important, especially against a background of difficult market conditions described in the previous section and generally low penetration levels of charity services into their target markets. Advertising to end beneficiaries such as blind people, deaf people, non-English-speaking ethnic minorities, homeless people or people with sexually transmitted diseases can be problematic. Often the advertising is aimed at intermediaries or is via unusual channels (such as tape-recorded newspapers, soup runs or newsletters to massage parlour owners); nevertheless, with these exceptions, advertising is similar to the commercial world.

Public relations

Public relations and associated publicity, however, is much more important in the charity services field. Charities seldom have the money for large advertising campaigns, so public relations is much more attractive. Also charities' services are far more likely to get editorial or news coverage than commercial products. Finally, charities have developed a professionalism in this area that probably outdoes their commercial counterparts. While it is infrequent, it is not unusual for charity services (such as overseas aid programmes, Braille services and services for homeless people just arrived in London) to feature on prime-time television news. The only equivalent coverage commercial organisations get is when problems beset them.

Personal selling

Personal selling, sometimes to beneficiary customers, or more likely to intermediary beneficiary customers, has become much more usual since contracts have become more common. Many voluntary organisation personnel feel uncomfortable about 'selling' their services but two reasons should encourage them, one altruistic and one self-interested. Statutory services purchasers have too little money to purchase all the required services. If the charity does not actively sell-in its services, too often no services will be purchased and the end beneficiary will be the loser, receiving no services. More self-interestedly, if the charity does not sell-in its service it will have less service income and the service unit will be that much less viable.

In the USA Evans and Schultz (1996) found four factors regarded as crucial by the purchasers letting contracts: reliability; effective communication; good follow-up; and help with specification construction.

Cowell (1984, pp. 176–7 and 1995) quotes seven guidelines for the personal selling of a service (based on George *et al.* 1983), which are still valid today. The guidelines were derived from empirical data that looked at the differences between selling goods and services. They provide an extremely useful checklist of the factors that are likely to be in the services purchaser's mind when they are considering whether to take up the service, adapting them for charity service:

1   Orchestrate the service purchase encounter. This needs to pay particular attention to the purchaser's needs and expectations; the service representative needs to put across technical expertise and represent the service.

2   Facilitate quality assessment. The representative needs to establish with the purchaser what the reasonable levels of expected performance might be, so that the purchaser can subsequently judge quality after the service has been used.

3   Make the service tangible. Here the representative 'educates' the purchaser about what they should be looking out for generally in the service field, comparing alternative services, but particularly emphasising the strengths and uniqueness of their own service.

4   Emphasise organisational image. Here the service representative needs first to assess the purchaser's understanding and appreciation of the charity in general and, while taking account of this, to present the positive realities of the charity and its general benefits.

5   Utilise references external to the organisation. Here the charity tries to encourage satisfied previous users to promote the service.

6   Recognise the importance of all public contact personnel in the service. Given that production/delivery of the service is simultaneous to its consumption, it is important to sensitise and train all personnel in their direct role in contact with customers; and it is also important to minimise the total number of people interacting with each customer.

7   Recognise the customer's involvement during the service design process to generate customer specifications, for example by asking

questions and showing examples. Unlike with a physical product, the customer can have an impact on the detail of the service provided, which will not only make for a better service, it will also increase customer commitment.

Where high fees are involved for a charity service (such schools, colleges, residential homes or employment rehabilitation centres) it can be particularly effective to encourage the end beneficiary (disabled person, frail person, homeless person) and/or the intermediary purchaser (local education authority adviser, government department official, housing benefits manager) to visit the physical location of the service, and so I would add an eighth guideline:

8   Where high-value/high-volume purchasers of service are involved, encourage the person to visit the service location.

Professional referral

Professional referral as a means of promotion is critically important to most charity services. Unlike the world of commercial services where brokers expect commission, statutory service professionals and charity professionals (even from 'competing' charities) regard it as an ethical requirement to refer clients on to the most appropriate service source. This includes charity services. This puts a premium on promotional work by charity services to such intermediary professionals as doctors, other health workers, social workers, educationists, police, embassy officials and newspaper critics. However, charity services managers, as opposed to the charity public relations officer (PRO), are often (but not always) reticent to push their services to these intermediary groups. It is almost felt to be improper or unprofessional. These attitudes need to be talked through against a background of low charity service penetration and the prospect of charity service closure as a consequence of falling numbers of beneficiaries.

Word of mouth

As with commercial services and products, beneficiary word-of-mouth recommendation is a very important method of charity service promotion. While this method cannot work among socially isolated individuals or permanently institutionalised groups, it is effective in many settings. Among relatively numerous beneficiary groups such as older people, hearing-impaired people and homeless people, peer group inter-action is very significant – more colloquially, the grapevine is very active.

Place – how the service is distributed

Issues such as where the service is located, its accessibility, how it is distributed to the beneficiaries and how widespread its coverage, are all crucial to effective charity service delivery. For example, as social policy has changed and residential provision in a whole range of service areas has given way to day provision, physical location has become paramount. Residential services in out-of-the-way places have closed in favour of day services in high population areas and near motorways and railway stations. Location within communities rather than out in the country is more attractive because of the element of normality. Most statutory contracts require services to include equal accessibility and equal opportunities, for example for wheelchair users, sensorily impaired people and people from minority ethnic communities. Unhelpful geographic location can be mitigated, for example, by providing transportation services to and from a client's local area.

The geographic distribution coverage of a service has a very real impact, but one which is often underestimated by charity service managers. Most services have a heavy geographic bias. National services based in London have disproportionate numbers of beneficiaries in the South East. National schools in Leeds have disproportionate numbers of students from the North. Even services in local communities can be geographically circumscribed either by the presence of community boundaries or main roads, or simply by walking distance.

Franchising

Distribution channels for charity services can throw up surprises. A combination of the Freepost facility available for blind people and the fact that the majority of blind people are older and housebound, means that the postal service, rather than the local library, is an ideal distribution channel for libraries for blind people. Turning to franchising as distribution, the voluntary sector has been effectively using this distribution method for at least 60 years. The majority of local charitable groups are independent even though they may be fully integrated into a network such as Age Concern, MIND or MENCAP. Services from these national charities are distributed via these independent local groups, which undertake to deliver services to a certain standard and are subject to (informal) inspection. Such effective cooperation between independent local groups and the national charitable body suggests that the commercial world, becoming increasingly interested in franchising and devolution, has quite a bit to learn from its charitable service counterpart.

Integrated services

If the voluntary sector has been leading (but, arguably, now behind) the commercial world on franchising, it also has some track record in the area of integrated distribution. This is where a charity provides several related services. Berry and Parasuraman (1991, pp. 137-41) argue that successful commercial service organisations run a range of services and, using positive customer experience of one service, cross-sell to another. Larger service-giving charities certainly do this, although sometimes unconsciously rather than by design. SCOPE will refer clients, say, from its social services on to the employment rehabilitation arm.

However, there is an important distinction between the commercial and charity experience. In the commercial instance, the more referrals made, the more financially advantageous it is for the company. For charities, the more cross-referral of clients from one service to others in the organisation, normally the greater the loss! Given the overall shortage of charitable donations to make up the shortfall, this is a significant inhibition to cross-referral, especially as fee income often comes tied to the first service and either cannot or is insufficient to be shared with the second charity service. To take account of this, charity service referrals can, on occasion, require reference back to the original (say) local authority referring professional, or contracting organisation, in order that fees can be agreed for the additional and separate service provision.

People in service delivery

This is the first of the three elements (people, physical evidence and promotion) that Booms and Bitner (1981, pp. 47-51) argue need to be added to the traditional marketing mix to make it relevant to services. Zeithaml, Bitner and Gremler (2006) expand on this.

Staff and volunteers

Recruitment, selection, training and support of staff and volunteers are crucial in delivering a quality charity service. While a charity manufacturer of goods also wants good staff, quality control should identify a poor product before it reaches the beneficiary. In services, especially charity services, where there is a high interaction between staff and customers, it is essential to get it right first time because a service is produced and consumed at the same moment and poor quality has an immediate impact. So commitment to quality and to beneficiaries is essential in charities.

The section on services in Chapter 4 defines what beneficiaries are looking for in judging quality, namely reliability, responsiveness, assurance, empathy and tangible evidence of effectiveness (Berry and Parasuraman 1991, pp. 15-21). This list makes it immediately apparent that the role of staff and volunteers in contact with beneficiaries is crucial. If they are not delivering all of these attributes, the service will not be excellent.

Because conventional quality control in a (charity) service only picks up problems after they have impacted on a beneficiary, effective quality control and a commitment to a marketing approach has to be embedded in the service personnel themselves. Expectations need to be set high because operational staff are the quality control.

If things do go wrong, speedy rectification is essential. Once again this comes back to operational service staff and their immediate managers who need to have sufficient delegated authority to put things right. If rectification is not speedy (such as changing the seat of someone who cannot see the stage, or changing a rehabilitee's learning group when she or he is unhappy), the whole customer service experience will be over (and ruined) before matters are put right.

Other customers

In a charity service, especially to beneficiaries, customer-to-customer interaction is a crucial element of the marketing mix and must be handled with care and sensitivity. There is something distasteful and unethical about 'managing beneficiary interaction', especially where beneficiaries are adults. But the adage that 'one person's freedom is another person's prison' applies. If the attitudes and behaviour of one or more beneficiaries upsets or, even worse, destroys the confidence of another, then the service experience and the service quality for the latter will be poor. The boundary between legitimate intervention with a beneficiary group and interference with a beneficiary's independence is a fine one. Successful charity services require staff who are well trained, professional and sensitive. Beneficiaries need processes of appeal, in some cases with the help of advocates, for those instances where they feel that staff or volunteer actions were unreasonable.

Putting the customer-to-customer interaction into a positive mode, there is no doubt that successful peer group interaction among beneficiaries adds to service quality. Careful segmentation of the beneficiary target market helps by bringing together people who are likely to have more similarities than differences. Sensitive service personnel, subscribing to the philosophy of the charity, can encourage a setting of personal development where beneficiary peer group support can improve the beneficial impacts enormously.

Physical evidence

Charity services are less tangible than physical goods. While the potential beneficiaries may not be paying for the service, or at least not paying the full cost, they may still have reservations about taking it up. They may take a lot of information about the offering on trust, but still not be reassured enough to sign up, simply because the service is in the future and is intangible. They may feel nervous about being trapped into a process they think they may not like or may not be convinced that the benefits will outweigh inconveniences.

Commercial services marketing has found that physical evidence experienced beforehand can encourage people to take up a service. In our field, some charities offer the opportunity to sample a service (especially where significant beneficiary commitment is involved, such as being residential, significant travel or long course commitment) prior to committing to it. For example, residential homes will encourage potential residents to stay for a week, schools will invite young people and parents to look around the building and meet staff, or rehabilitation staff will have open days attended by previous rehabilitees.

In these settings the physical environment of the service and its ambience are vital. Are facilities clean and tidy? Are they well equipped? Are they well furnished? There is some evidence from the commercial sector (Sewell and Brown 1990, p. 122) that staff confidence in their service, which they will ideally exude to potential beneficiaries, is enhanced by good physical settings.

Processes

There is an argument for saying that, in many charity services, such as schools, theatres, holiday schemes and group work, the process is everything. How well people are educated, entertained or empowered is crucial. Many of these activities are really part of the service product. The fundamental aspects of charity services' processes, such as how easy is it to find out about and apply for the service, really count. This is covered in greater detail in Chapter 4.

But particularly vital is customer involvement. There is the well-known dictum in education of the importance of being 'active in your own learning' to be successful. This is also true of charity services aimed at beneficiaries. Any service that metaphorically pours its service down the throats of clients or other beneficiaries is doomed. Constructing service processes that give beneficiaries the opportunity to influence service delivery will not only be more likely to enthuse them, but will also give higher quality interaction and benefit.

Philosophy

In charity services marketing this eighth 'P' is the beginning and the end of the mix. Chapter 4 looks at this in more detail. It is likely and logical that the starting point of philosophy will be the same for each service that a charity runs, to ensure a consistent and cumulative approach. The philosophy to be adopted will depend on the current era (compare Victorian charity values with today's), who runs the organisation (both volunteer and paid leaders), the extent to which beneficiaries are part of this leadership, the area of charity activity, and so on. But what is certain is that without an explicit philosophical position for the charity as a whole, and hence for each service, things will become muddled and contradictory. If independence of beneficiaries is explicit, even nursing homes for disabled 90-year-olds will create choices for residents. If empowerment is part of the philosophy, then carers in a school for multi-disabled young people will sit patiently while a pupil with cerebral palsy, severe learning difficulties and poor hand/eye coordination spends one hour feeding him or herself rather than being fed by a member of staff.

However, the complexities of achieving consistent translation of philosophy into practice are considerable. The British Parachute Association (BPA) is, rightly, totally committed to safety. Yet the association's journal has a quasi-independence (as is the case with many voluntary organisations), and includes the usual disclaimer 'the views expressed in Sport Parachutist ... are not necessarily those of the BPA'. Its December 1993/January 1994 issue printed a picture showing a skydiver in mid-air drinking from a can, with the headline 'Yorkshire Bitter can seriously improve your skydiving' and the caption 'Tandem master enjoys a swig' (Pentreath 1994, p. 9). A stark example of contradictory safety philosophies!

Charities such as Shelter, British Red Cross, Friends of the Earth, Save the Children, Birmingham Royal Ballet, Christian Aid, RNIB and Barnardo's have developed clear philosophies, which are transferred more or less explicitly into their services. This is essential to a charity's marketing approach if potential charity beneficiaries or their advocates are to be able to choose a service and have their expectations met.

Conclusion

Voluntary and community organisations are major players in the UK social and economic system (Kendall 2003). With the shift in the welfare state responsibility from provider to purchaser, the role of charity services is growing. Given charities' poor record of reaching only a small proportion of their potential beneficiaries, charity services need to adopt a marketing philosophy and practice with increasing rapidity if they are not to fail potential and actual beneficiaries.

The language of commercial services marketing is not attractive in the charity sector but many of the ideas and practices, suitably adapted, work much better than might at first be thought possible. However, certain important differences between charity and commercial services (such as permanent commitment to a particular customer group regardless of loss, the impossibility of hostile takeovers and the legal commitment to the objectives of their cause) require commercial marketing concepts and practices to be adapted. This need for adaptation provides particularly interesting challenges to marketers, whatever their background.

Key points

Positioning

- Distinguish between direct and indirect services and identify the relationship between them so that the service can be positioned effectively in the market.
- Understand your position in the market in relation to other players providing similar services.
- A programme of needs (marketing) research can be invaluable in terms of ensuring that service provision keeps up with demand and adapts as needs change.

Product

- Examine the quality, features, name, reputation and guarantees of the service being provided and monitor it regularly.
- Think from the service customer's point of view. Is the service reliable and responsive; does it have empathy?
- Avoid rushing into decisions to add to or close a product.

Price

- Service income has been squeezed by competitive unit-cost tendering imposed by central and local government.
- Charities need to be able to respond to this by understanding clearly the cost of their services and structuring their bids accordingly, for example discount/loss-leader schemes.
- If the perceived value of a service can be improved, it may be possible to alleviate the impact price to the customer.
- When pricing policies result in a charity losing beneficiary 'custom'

the moral, personal and practical implications are far more significant than in the commercial world.

Promotion

- While public relations and publicity are vitally important as a means of promotion, personal selling can be highly effective. Use Cowell's seven guidelines (see page 178), which focus on the potential purchaser's point of view.
- Professional referral is critically important, so effective promotional work to intermediary professionals such as doctors, social workers, newspaper critics and police is essential.

People

- Encourage staff and volunteers to 'get it right first time' and give them the authority to rectify the situation if it is not.
- By targeting sensitively, make sure that interaction and relationships between beneficiaries and between beneficiaries and staff is positive. Provide mechanisms for appeal.

Physical evidence

- Offer beneficiaries the opportunity to sample a service before taking it up.
- Make sure that the physical environment and ambience are appropriate.

Philosophy

- Ensure that the philosophy of the service is consistent with that of the charity.

8   Pressure group activity

As we saw in Chapter 4, product is a marketing term used to describe physical goods, services and ideas. Unlike commercial companies, voluntary organisations frequently market ideas either in their pressure group and campaigning work or through fundraising. In this chapter we look at pressure group activity and campaigning.

Background

In my experience charities go about their pressure group work very differently to commercial interests, and fairly differently to powerful interest groups such as doctors and lawyers. In essence this is because charities (and, for that matter, most voluntary organisations) are often not seen as sufficiently powerful or cohesive to be brought into the early stages of local or central government decision-making. It might surprise many people to learn that the broad voluntary sector comprises 9 per cent of gross domestic product (Kendall 2003); but voluntary sector interests span literally hundreds of disparate causes, compared with the interests of motor manu-facturers, which arguably span one or at most a few. Since 1997 successive administrations have involved the sector more, seeing it as having a more significant role in service delivery and civil renewal. But both sides' habits (government and charities) die hard, and few charities have gained the insider status traditionally held by business and professional groups such as the National Farmers Union and the Royal Colleges.

As charities are not automatically brought into the early stages of a democratic process, they tend to make greater and more frequent use of the media to try to inflate their perceived importance. By doing so they try to create a climate where decision-makers will judge it wise to do some 'cooption' work by, for example, agreeing to meet and discuss points of concern to defuse and dilute opposition and provide opportunities for cooperation, agreement and compromise.

So because of their lack of power and cohesion, charity pressure groups tend to be more public than their more powerful commercial counterparts.

Early changes

This widespread public face of charity pressure group activity is a fairly recent phenomenon, which began in the late 1960s and early 1970s, a period that involved a number of dramatic changes in the charity world. Charities were maturing as policy-proposing organisations that wanted to press their case. They were gaining new confidence in a putative pressure group role, even if the post-war consensus on the role of welfare state services had downgraded the charity service-giving role. But their access to, and influence on, government was very restricted (Field 1982) and did not compare with the power of the industrial lobbies (Miller 1991, p. 49). Increasingly charities realised, through research or direct experience, that welfare state services in their broadest guises were not reaching the ideals set for them, and felt powerless to intervene effectively. But the tinder-like atmosphere in which pressure groups operated was warming up. In particular, government was becoming more consultative (Miller 1991, p. 50).

Then came the launch of Shelter as a charity, which was the spark that lit the pressure group fire. While other voluntary organisations worked either quietly (the Child Poverty Action Group and the then National Council for Civil Liberties (now Liberty)) or noisily (the Campaign for Nuclear Disarmament) as pressure groups, Des Wilson and Shelter – launched via the television film 'Cathy Come Home' – rewrote the rules of charity pressure group activity. Just three years later David Hobman woke the sleeping giant of the National Old People's Welfare Council and turned it into Age Concern and, similarly, David Ennals transformed the National Association of Mental Health into MIND. In 1971 Sir Keith Joseph, then Secretary of State at the Department of Health and Social Security (DHSS), acknowledged charities' legitimate pressure group role by saying 'constructive criticism must always be welcome by the government. Strident or shrill criticism should not be necessary unless the government refuses to enter into a dialogue . . . I welcome guidance and constructive, widespread criticism' (Joseph 1971, p. 2).

Vigorous activity

And so the 1970s became a decade of vigorous pressure group activity, which was modified by the new climate of the 1980s. Narrow parliamentary majorities of the second half of the 1970s, which inflated the importance of backbench and charity influence, gave way to massive government majorities and so put the focus back on civil servants and ministers. The radical reappraisal in the 1980s of almost all areas of government policy gave significant opportunities for charity pressure groups to bring their influence to bear. However, radical policy reviews, combined with an overall requirement to cut public expenditure produced a heady cocktail which some charities were very nervous of drinking. There was at least one occasion when disability charities actually refused the offer of a ministerial meeting, so concerned were they that their views might fuel what was seen as certain regressive policy developments.

Policy reforms

After the 1992 election charity pressure groups were having to live even more dangerously. Both major parties were worried about the extent of public expenditure. Radical new policies that, in the 1980s were only on the drawing board, were being implemented, in particular community care, education reform, NHS reform, the remaining public utility privatisation and significant deregulation. These reforms were being implemented at a time of a massive increase in public expenditure deficit. This meant that charity pressure groups were largely defensive, trying to protect the gains of earlier years from cuts and reorganisations, and only seeking gains at the margin of change. As one cause or client group gained, another lost. However, the reduced government parliamentary majority made the charity groups much more powerful.

Labour government

The position on the resource front did not change for the first two years of the 1997 Labour government, and so gains to one group still nearly always resulted in losses to others. The increased emphasis on 'community' and stakeholders gave many charities, especially those in the social welfare field, a creative backcloth to policy development and proposal, but the more 'radical' the government managed to be, the more charity pressure groups had to ride a policy roller-coaster.

The large Labour parliamentary majorities swept away much of the power of backbenchers, so useful to pressure groups when majorities were slim. Ministers, their advisers and civil servants once again became the key focus of attention. This was aided by the marked growth in civil servants' willingness to interact with voluntary organisation personnel. This was so widespread that it must have had ministerial blessing. It was most noticeable in the Treasury, where civil servants and ministerial advisers initiated contacts, in marked contrast with previous decades, when the Treasury was very difficult to penetrate effectively. The reduced Labour parliamentary majority from the 2005 election gave charity pressure groups power they had not had since 1992.

New money

By the late 1990s and at the beginning of the 2000s the Labour government was injecting significant streams of new money, particularly in education, health and law and order – just the setting for vigorous pressure group activity and success. However, except in the field of education, local government did not fare so well and so activities such as social services provided fewer opportunities.

Accepted conditions

So, all the generally accepted conditions for successful pressure group activity suggested by Coxall (1985) remain.

For pressure groups there is the opportunity for:

- valuable advance information;
- influencing policies.

For government there is the opportunity for:

- getting advice and information;
- gaining acceptance, or even agreement for its proposals;
- quite often, gaining assistance with the administration of policies.

Campaigns: case examples

Campaign types

Adapting Ansoff's model (see Figure 4.11 in Chapter 4) gives four possible types of pressure group campaigns:

1 Defending established gains to existing groups.
2 Promoting existing gains to new groups.
3 Promoting new gains to existing groups.
4 Promoting new gains to new groups.

In times of recession and/or government determination to cut public expenditure, there will be heavy emphasis on type 1 campaigns. There is a high risk that successful type 2,3 or 4 campaigns will set off a process whereby other gains are eroded in order to provide substitutional budget. Therefore in times of recession and/or government expenditure cuts, these campaign types need to be undertaken cautiously, and are most likely to be used as further defensive outposts to type 1, or as a ground-breaking exercise to establish fertile soil to grow the campaigns effectively when a more favourable public expenditure climate returns.

In times of plenty, but with a cautious government, campaign type 2 is more likely to be successful. In times of plenty, but with adventurous government policy-making, types 3 and 4 are particularly attractive.

The typology laid out above, is just that – a typology. In other words, pressure group campaigns do not always fit neatly into one type, but most do. In the following examples, the free eye test campaign is type 1 (defensive), the arms control campaign is type 2, the disability income cost allowance campaign is type 3, and the campaign for lead-free petrol (CLEAR) is type 4. These examples give a first-hand feel as to how pressure group campaigns run in practice and they provide models to which I will refer in the following sections of this chapter. The first and third were campaigns in which I have been involved. This gives the advantage of intimate knowledge but the disadvantage of involvement, and thus I have tried to guard against subjectivity.

CASE EXAMPLE: LOSS OF FREE EYE TESTS

In the mid-1980s, the then Conservative government wanted to dilute what it saw as the opticians' excessive profits on spectacle provision. Its proposals included the abolition of the free eye test. This was a major concern for RNIB. Approximately 25 per cent of the eye test involves looking for signs of abnormality in the eye that would indicate disease, not infrequently blinding disease. It was RNIB's belief that if charges for eye tests were introduced, fewer people would have them. Several irreversible and potentially blinding eye diseases (such as glaucoma) have no painful symptoms, therefore the individual would be largely unaware of any deterioration before significant visual impairment had set in.

Allies

There were three main allies opposing the government proposals: the Association of Optical Practitioners (AOP) and the Federation of Dispensing Opticians (FODO) (both trade associations), and the British College of Optometrists (BCO) (the professional group). RNIB had an easy and relaxed relationship with BCO but was much more cautious with AOP and FODO, as they were essentially trade interests. BCO provided the neutral ground for the loose coordination of campaigning activities.

One powerful group that did not join in the coalition was the professional grouping of ophthalmologists, and in particular one of their influential leaders was actively oppositional. It is true that there are far too few ophthalmologists in this country and some felt that if opticians 'stopped trying to pretend they were ophthalmologists' by undertaking a certain amount of inspection for disease during the eye test, then their case for larger numbers would be better made. It is hardly an exaggeration to say that there had been a covert antagonism between these two professional groups for some years. Luckily there were some progressive ophthalmologists who were supportive.

Government proposals

The government put forward its legislative proposal which, it argued, would not reduce the numbers of people going for eye tests. First, it said that charges would not deter people – which seemed a strange claim coming from a government supportive of market forces, and

cont.

193

which gave the campaign ammunition for counter publicity. Second, the government said it would introduce exemptions, although initially it seemed that these were very narrowly cast.

Response

The coalition responded by arguing that fewer people would go for tests and that as a result eye disease would go unchecked. However, the difficulty was that the majority of the general public did not realise that the eye test checked for eye disease – they simply thought that it examined whether one was becoming long or short sighted. The campaign therefore carefully checked its facts with sympathetic ophthalmologists (as opposed to opticians or optometrists) and felt it would be absolutely correct to claim that fewer people going for eye tests would mean more people going blind. This provided much tougher news copy and RNIB appeared on radio and television to make these statements. The coalition then ran out of newsworthy material, but through academic contacts came across a research write-up of an experiment in a province of Canada which had introduced eye test charges. The numbers of people going for eye tests dropped dramatically. With this new research information the campaign regained the media offensive.

Tactics

Even though the government had a massive majority, the coalition worked hard on backbench MPs, arranging frequent meetings with key backbenchers, especially those involved with the committee stage of the bill. However, none of the government MPs voted against the bill at that stage. As the drama reached its climax, MPs of all parties were using RNIB briefs extensively and ministers were having to respond to allegations point by point. In the final vote, the new Secretary of State got the bill through by a majority of only eight. At one level this was a major achievement, considering the government's massive majority. However, you either win or lose in a pressure group campaign, and this was a loss.

Several years later a civil servant who was only indirectly involved told the campaign how close it had come to winning. He said that the civil servants had become pretty demoralised by the successful public

cont.

CASE EXAMPLE: LOSS OF FREE EYE TESTS continued

campaigning: 'you were always one step ahead of us'. This person went so far as to say that if the new Secretary of State had not arrived, the campaign would have won. Apparently he called all his civil service team in and made it clear to them that if he had initiated the bill, he would have kept eye tests free, but given that the government was now so far committed to this line of action he was damned if he was going to be beaten. Apparently this pugnacious leadership raised departmental morale, and the result is history. However, I am inclined to believe that, but for his arrival, another five members would have gone into the opposition lobby!

Relaunch

The campaign was relaunched in 1996/97, because the build-up to the 1997 election offered opportunities and it fitted in with a broader RNIB initiative to pursue one of its mission statements 'to prevent blindness'. The campaign idea product was refined to propose free eye tests for older people, among whom undetected eye diseases is most common. In March 1997 a Labour shadow health minister 'bought' this idea, 'paying' for it out of the £100 million planned efficiency savings. Unfortunately the shadow Treasury opposed and the proposal from the cancer charities for increased cancer screening won through and took its chance in the post-election resource bargaining. I make no comment on the relative merits of the service products of eye disease screening among older people versus cancer screening among the middle-aged. But perhaps the idea product aimed at the politicians, of offering the hope of more screening among the electorally more volatile middle-aged, was more attractive to politicians than screening for firmer-intentioned older voters.

However, this amended idea product was re-proposed to the newly elected government when RNIB met the new Secretary of State for Health in 1997. He showed renewed interest and asked RNIB to work with his civil servants. All the development work meant the coalition could present the arguments quickly and thoroughly. One might think that with the full backing of the Secretary of State the argument was won, but there were two major problems. First, civil servants were clearly worried that an increase in eye testing among older people would discover preventable blinding conditions (which indeed is the

cont.

CASE EXAMPLE: LOSS OF FREE EYE TESTS continued

purpose of screening!) but the prevention might require hospital treatment, which would further pressurise budgets and lengthen hospital waiting lists. Second, groups representing optometrists presented objections because they would receive too little money for doing the eye test. The Secretary of State had no sympathy with the latter problem and rejected the representations out of hand. RNIB never did discover how the other problem was solved, but the decision was made and everyone was delighted. The gain was, and is, a major contribution towards preventing blindness. It also re-established the principle of free eye tests for all, which was in danger of becoming extinct as a policy possibility after nearly ten years of abolition.

This case example shows how long a campaign may need to run in order to succeed and that a principled policy position (the idea product) can always be pulled down off the shelf, dusted down and re-presented!

CASE EXAMPLE: ARMS CONTROL

Another campaign that will certainly be a long haul is a joint one between Oxfam, Amnesty International and the International Action Network on Small Arms (IANSA), which aimed as a first step to achieve an international arms trade treaty (Le Goff 2004). Oxfam argued that the arms trade diverts resources that poor countries could otherwise use to promote development. In late 2003 the three organisations launched 'Control Arms' simultaneously in 70 countries through the organisations' regional offices. The immediate aim is an international treaty.

Tactics

According to research from the Small Arms Survey in Geneva, in just three years one million people die because of the arms trade. Control Arms was aiming to persuade one million people from all over the world to send in a photo or drawing of themselves to form a global visual petition. From the start the campaign made extensive use of the internet, thus providing a lot of regularly updated information. With an interactive site, many of the 'faces' appeared via the internet.

cont.

CASE EXAMPLE: ARMS CONTROL continued

In the UK the campaign kicked off with a mass graveyard created in Trafalgar Square with a slogan 'one person dies each minute from the arms trade' – in order to achieve significant media coverage. The campaign then published the report 'Lock, Stock and Barrel' that exposed loopholes in the British arms export guidelines which, it claimed, had allowed an eleven-fold increase in the export of weapons components since 1998, despite stricter controls on the export of fully assembled weapons. This forced the government to disclose more information on the kinds of components and where they were going.

Government support

The campaigners were surprised and delighted when the Foreign Secretary announced support for a treaty at the Labour Conference in 2004, saying 'I am pleased to tell this conference that we shall start work soon with international partners to build support for an international arms trade treaty.' Oxfam welcomed this by saying 'Straw's support brings tough international arms control much closer'.

Control Arms also involved a string of stars who would appeal to different target markets, including Emma Thompson, Michael Moore, Lilian Thuram, Bob Geldof, Daniel Bebe, Salif Diao, Joe Fiennes, Dido and Helen Mirren.

Pressure

To keep the pressure on the government and to get across newsworthy material the coalition brought out another report in 2005, 'Tracing Lethal Tools', which showed that it was easier to trace a missing suitcase around an international flight network than a pistol leaving a developed country for export. The report's release was timed to coincide with a UN marking and tracing conference and proposed a legally binding international tracing and marking system for small arms.

The clear, distinctive and memorable brand name 'Control Arms' was a good marketing move. Too many campaigns have no name, and representatives say 'we' when they are on the media, which means nothing to viewers or listeners. Using a clear brand name and message such as 'Control Arms wants an international arms treaty' doubled the message reinforcement. Analysis of other players showed that, counter intuitively, 2003/04 was a good time to launch. One might have thought that pressing for an arms control treaty at the time of the Iraq war was ill timed. But my guess is that the government and Straw expressed their support in part to mollify the sizeable number of people opposed to the war.

The use of a coalition was sensible for two reasons. First, each partner contributed different expertise and resources. Second, the coalition format distanced the Oxfam brand somewhat from the policy proposition to help retain the support of those who might have thought this was too political a stance for the charity. The involvement of a wide range of stars was also helpful in establishing associated legitimacy for the proposition, and the extensive use of the internet is helpful for any campaign, but especially an international one. Finally, the tactical timing of reports and other PR activity was excellent, forcing the authorities to have to explain what they intended to do to correct the 'nonsenses' and unacceptable behaviour that the reports revealed.

The third case example demonstrates an offensive pressure group campaign that primarily took place between 1984 and 1990 but, arguably, has lasted from 1970 to the present day. I shall keep this description to the six most germane years. It is an example of a type 3 campaign: new gains to existing groups.

Disabled people are among the poorest in our society. Some 70 per cent of them have to live on 75 per cent of the average wage or less. But not only are their incomes very low, they also have additional costs arising from their disability: for example, medical requirements to keep the house warmer than average; significant extra transportation costs and higher laundry bills through incontinence. There are well over 250 national and local organisations representing different groups of disabled people.

CASE EXAMPLE: DISABILITY INCOME AND COST ALLOWANCE

Coalition

Four groups are particularly concerned with disability benefits: the Royal Associaation of Disability and Rehabilitation (RADAR), the Disability Alliance, The Disability Income Group (DIG) and the British Council of Organisations of Disabled People (BCODP). Until the beginning of this campaign each group had been pressing independently and competitively for concessions for their particular group. It was easy for the government to be sympathetic to everyone but to 'divide and rule'.

The groups came together on the issue of financial benefits, prompted by the government's announcement of four major benefits reviews and a major survey into the income and circumstances of disabled people. This loose coordinating group rapidly evolved into a formal group – the Disability Benefits Consortium (DBC). The steering group comprised the original four groups as primary members and five of the major individual disability charities – RNIB, SCOPE, MENCAP, Age Concern and RNID. They argued, logically, that if they did not 'get our act together' the government would continue to divide and rule.

The aim of the coalition was to persuade the government to institute a comprehensive disability income and cost allowance based on a functional need rather than medical condition, which would be awarded on the basis of self-assessment by the disabled applicant. The coalition gave power and cohesion – just! Keeping together a coalition of organisations representing blind people, deaf people, physically disabled people, older people, deaf-blind people, people with learning difficulties, diabetes, cystic fibrosis, motor neurone disease and spinal injuries was extraordinarily difficult. Each organisation knew that there would not be enough new money to go around. Indeed, in the end there was less money.

Strengths and weaknesses

This coalition was strong in two ways. It was clear what it wanted in principle (the comprehensive disability income and cost allowance (CDI)) and it was able to expose the inadequacies of the existing disability benefits system. What it could not be strong on was detailed proposals for a new system with a realistic cost (as far as the government would see it). The CDI proposal was going to add between £4 billion and £5 billion to the then estimated £7 billion already being

cont.

**CASE EXAMPLE: DISABILITY INCOME AND COST ALLOWANCE
continued**

spent to help disabled people. In terms of need, that was a perfectly expenditure, it was unreasonable. Matters were also made worse because of demographic shifts. The majority of disabled people in this country are over retirement age, and the number of older pensioners was and still is rising rapidly. Therefore government expenditure on disability benefits had to rise rapidly in real terms just to leave an individual disabled person no worse off.

Tactics

The other very difficult aspect of pressure group work involving a disparate coalition is thinking tactics through clearly. The consortium managed to identify what it wanted to challenge, namely the arbitrary and inadequate means-tested special additions available to (mainly) disabled people under what was then called Supplementary Benefit. In essence, people on Supplementary Benefit who had additional requirements relating to matters such as hearing, nutrition and laundry were eligible for, and normally received, additional payments. The system was a complicated nightmare, had developed incrementally over the years, and was not well understood by disabled people.

Errors

With the benefit of hindsight, it turned out to be a tactical error to attack these additional payments. Referring to the typology outlined at the beginning of the chapter, the consortium was pressing for a new, better benefit reaching more people, and to support this it attacked the status quo. At a time of public expenditure shortage, this left the way open to the government to give the consortium a new benefit but offer much less money than was being sought, which is what happened. In crude terms, the government swept away the anachronistic system of special additions and replaced it with what it claimed was a simpler, more comprehensive system of additional premiums. The Disability Alliance, the DBC's analytical powerhouse, estimated that this made one million disabled people (out of six million) worse off. What was worse was that this new simplified system did not have the flexibility to give the relatively larger sums that very severely disabled people needed, and to an extent received, under the old Supplementary Benefit Additional Requirements system.

cont.

CASE EXAMPLE: DISABILITY INCOME AND COST ALLOWANCE
continued

Outcome

The massive outcry and organised protest, plus the substance of the argument, persuaded the government to act in two ways. First, the minister proposed what he called an 'Independent Living Fund', which had a very strange legal constitution but essentially had the flexibility to pay out relatively large sums to very severely disabled people. The second initiative that somewhat ameliorated the situation was the offer of a new benefit, the Disability Living Allowance (DLA). Its attractiveness to many groups was that it was to be awarded on the basis of self-assessment by the disabled person (for which the consortium was calling); it would go to groups of disabled people who had previously had relatively poor access to existing disability benefits (in particular, people with learning difficulties and people with visual impairments); and as a costs allowance it adopted the consortium's principle of being non-means-tested and non-taxable (it was money to repay disabled people for the extra costs they incurred because of their disability). The downside was that it was, and still is, only available to people of working age, and the majority of disabled people are over retirement age. The primary consolation was that, if the consortium and its constituent members had not been so active, analytical and vociferous, the results of the government's review might have been very much worse.

There are four other points to be drawn from this case example.

Manipulating information

The first is the extent to which any government will use information tactically in public argument with a pressure group. For example, in this case example and consistently since, the government has stressed the very large real expenditure increases on disability benefits over the years (which is true), but in such a way that encourages the general public to form the view that individual disabled people are getting a lot more money (which is untrue). The public will therefore implicitly ask why is there all this 'whingeing' by disabled people and their representative groups?

The primary reason for the large real increases in total government expenditure on disability benefits is the changing economic/demographic structure of our society, which results in increasing numbers of disabled people, because of growing numbers of older people, who are much more likely to be disabled. Individual disabled people in general are no better off.

I suppose it is inevitable that ministers focus on this overall growth and encourage the public perception that benefits for individual disabled people are improving when they are not. What is particularly disheartening is the way civil servants have been increasingly drawn into this duplicity since around 1980, and that this trend has increased since 1997. One example will have to suffice to justify what most long-term campaigners will tell you, namely that the game has got much rougher. In 1997/98 the government started its first concerted attack on incapacity benefits. During this particularly bloody battle, which culminated in more Labour MPs voting against the government than on any other issue in its first term, government informal briefings played a crucial part in winning hearts and minds. The most extreme example was a departmental press officer briefing at least four newspapers that, because of the benefits they received, disabled people were among the richest people in this country!

Timing

The second point to emphasise is that timing is crucial, especially related to economic cycles. The benefits review was undertaken not only at a time of public expenditure constraint, but also before the boom at the end of the 1980s. Government cuts were therefore inevitable and the only question was how big they would be. However, the subsequent review of disability benefits effectively took place in the middle of the boom and dropping public sector borrowing, and arguably this positive economic background might have persuaded the Treasury to put back into the system some of the money it had taken out during the broader benefits review decisions.

Research

Third, well-thought-out substantial research, especially when it is the government's own, does actually have an effect and leads to better decision-making. The major government disability research undertaken by the Office of National Statistics (ONS) was crucial to the consortium (and probably also to the DHSS) in being able to hold a fairly solid defensive line against a voracious Treasury. It was also very helpful in the design of the new benefits, even if they were not sufficiently well resourced.

Luck

The fourth point to emphasise is the importance of luck – good or bad. One important aspect of the campaign over the five years was the active involvement of individual disabled people in writing to and lobbying their MPs and joining in demonstrations. The largest demonstration early in the campaign involved disabled people linking arms across Westminster Bridge and a major rally in Trafalgar Square, which was very successful. It generated a great deal of media interest, especially from TV news crews. However, despite being filmed and recorded it was not aired on either national television or radio news and there was virtually no press coverage. Why? Because that was the day the Berlin Wall came down!

CASE EXAMPLE: CAMPAIGN FOR LEAD-FREE PETROL (CLEAR)

The final case example is an example of a type 4 campaign – new gains for new beneficiaries. There is no doubt in my mind that one of the key reasons for its success was that it was directed by Des Wilson, who is an outstanding exponent of applying a marketing approach to pressure group work.

The aim of this campaign was to get all lead taken out of petrol. The reason were two-fold – there was growing evidence that exposing young people to lead in petrol reduced their IQ levels, and leaded petrol was inexorably distributing three million tons of non-degradable lead across our land each year.

As well as having Des Wilson's skills and experience, CLEAR also had substantial funds for what turned out to be a fifteen-month campaign, which was nine months in the planning.

cont.

CASE EXAMPLE: CAMPAIGN FOR LEAD-FREE PETROL (CLEAR) continued

Tactics

Because the minister and his civil servants had recently made a decision to reduce lead by two-thirds on the recommendation of an expert working party, CLEAR decided that the internal corridors of power would be highly resistant to a change of tack to a complete ban. Rather, the tactic should be for a high-profile public campaign, to enlist mass support from the general public. One of the many advantages of this approach was that the campaigners could promote the straightforward case on their chosen ground – children's health and long-term environmental damage. They judged that they would be outmanoeuvred if they attempted to grapple with the technical complexities of achieving lead-free petrol and a debate over costs – it was enough to say that Japan and America were doing it.

Another advantage of keeping the campaign relatively simple was that it enabled it to build up quite a powerful coalition in favour of banning lead even before the campaign had been launched. The launch was, at first sight, conventional; an exclusive to a Sunday newspaper prior to the launch on the Monday. The main features were two studies, to give a news hook. The combination of careful planning, solid research and good prior media hustle meant that the newspapers, television and radio turned out. However, now come the professional and technical add-ons. On the same day, copies of a specially prepared handbook and a newspaper summarising the main points of the campaign were mailed to all MPs and other influential organisations. Des Wilson and two others then set off on a provincial tour, 'hitting' Coventry, Birmingham, Manchester, Liverpool, Leeds, Newcastle, Bristol, Southampton and Cardiff in a very short time. These cities were chosen because they had TV stations as well as local radio. Des called this technique 'barnstorming', after the American methods of political campaigning.

'Hitting' a city

Des Wilson described a typical 'hit' of a city. He and two colleagues would arrive in the designated city in the afternoon, give interviews to the local morning newspaper for the next day and the local evening newspaper for the following evening, then go in to the local radio station and record the news programme for 6 p.m. They then went

cont.

CASE EXAMPLE: CAMPAIGN FOR LEAD-FREE PETROL (CLEAR)
continued

across to the TV studios to do a recorded interview with one of the two local stations and one or two regional stations for an insert in the 6 p.m. news, and then went off to do a live interview on the other station. At 7 p.m. they met potential leaders of local groups, along with local personalities, ideally the MP and the leader of the council, and went into a public meeting which the advance guard would have organised and ensured was going to be full. A reception and possibly an appearance on a late evening radio chat show followed.

The next morning, there was another local radio appearance, followed by breakfast in a hotel with local leaders, perhaps a newspaper editor, leader of the council, and local church leader. They then went to the assembly of the most important local secondary school, followed by a special period with the sixth formers; followed by a late morning meeting of local women's organisations and, with a bit of luck, a chat with the local Rotary leaders. In the hands of a skilled operator like Wilson, this barnstorming gained enough critical news mass for the news story to achieve blanket coverage and to start regenerating news. It is the equivalent of 'burst' advertising, as opposed to a steady 'drip' of consecutive smaller stories and, as such, is much better at generating awareness.

Trump card

Towards the end of this tour Wilson played what he called his 'trump card', a confidential letter from the Chief Medical Officer at the Department of Health and Social Security confirming that, in his view, lead should be completely banned from petrol. It is possible to argue that getting hold of such a letter is a matter of luck, and indeed it is. However, it is also the case that leaks only tend to go to those whom the person doing the leaking thinks is going to (a) do something effective with the document and (b) protect the source. Nevertheless it *was* mainly luck. However, what makes Wilson a master tactician is the fact that he did not release the letter until well into the campaign – even though it was available from day one. He knew that the campaign could easily lose momentum after the first three or four weeks.

So what did he do with the letter? For reasons I do not fully understand, he no longer had a copy of the original letter. Therefore wide distribution

cont.

to newspapers and television might have created a challenge to its authenticity. So he chose to leak it to *The Times* and convinced the editor that the letter was genuine (which indeed it was). *The Times* printed the letter in full, attributing it to CLEAR and putting it on the front page. All these were conditions that Des Wilson laid out (and probably were only agreed to because it was one journalist speaking to another). Because it was front-page news in *The Times*, it was then picked up widely by radio and television, and within twenty-four hours the Leader of the Opposition was challenging the Prime Minister in the House on it.

Momentum

News momentum was building, but how could it be kept going? Wilson then produced a Coopers & Lybrand report on lead-free petrol which Godfrey Bradman, the main campaign funder, had commissioned back in 1981. Because it contained conclusions damaging to the government's position, once again it got good coverage; not least because it came from such a reputable city firm.

The campaign then felt confident enough to commission an opinion poll among the general public as to their views on the issue (remember that there had been major national publicity on three occasions over a five-week period as well as a great deal of local and regional coverage). If the results had been hopeless, they could have been ignored – but they were not. Seventy-seven per cent of the general public said that they wanted lead out of petrol even if the price went up by 'a few pence per gallon'. Once again this report provided significant coverage and, more importantly, the *Daily Telegraph* headed its story with the fact that the government was 'losing the argument'.

Des Wilson also pointed to the inept response of the oil and motor industries. Carefully crafted, polite letters to the oil companies and their trade association resulted in a brush-off. This gave the campaign another powerful weapon. It could claim that it had tried to engage in a dialogue with the oil companies but the companies had refused, which left the campaign with no option but to go public. It allowed Wilson and his colleagues to paint a picture of the oil cartel being uncooperative, secretive and only interested in its own commercial profits.

cont.

CASE EXAMPLE: CAMPAIGN FOR LEAD-FREE PETROL (CLEAR)
continued

Research

Later the campaign was helped by major research studies from the United States and Italy which, once again, gave more media coverage. In addition, Des Wilson later reported that the Associated Octel Company, manufacturers of leaded fuel additives, gave a considerable boost to the campaign by spending over £100,000 on major newspaper advertising under what he called the 'absurd heading' of 'the health and wealth of the nation'. He argued that this was totally counterproductive because it was unbelievable and in many detailed respects inaccurate, and gave the impression that the only way the oil interests could be heard was through buying space. This allowed him to build more newsworthi-ness in counter charges.

Meanwhile the campaign had commissioned two more surveys, which produced damaging results for the pro-lead lobby. The first survey found significantly high levels of lead in dust outside schools all over the country. This not only achieved national publicity, but it was also obviously covered very significantly in the local press. The second survey found that 40 per cent of the land in inner London and 20 per cent in outer London was unsuitable for growing vegetables because of lead. This study also got extensive coverage.

In fact, it was of great significance that the campaign involved increasing numbers of people from the scientific establishment to support the case. Des Wilson has argued that the government and the commercial lobby could arguably have fought off the pressure group campaign if it had not had this support. Similarly, the scientific establishment could have been squashed or at least ignored if it had not been reinforced by such an active public campaign. He argued that the coalition together was unbeatable.

Two additional points are worth mentioning. First, the Royal Commission on Environmental Pollution had decided to study the case and had concluded that the campaign claims were essentially correct. Second, the publicity was beginning to do so much damage to the government that Prime Minister Thatcher became involved. The government could do without claims that it was damaging children's health in the run-up to an election! On 18 April 1983 the Royal

Commission on Environmental Pollution published its report, calling for the elimination of lead from petrol. One hour later the Secretary of State announced in parliament that the government accepted the recommendation and would press for a Europe-wide ban! The previous day the News of the World had announced 'Premier Margaret Thatcher has decided to respond swiftly to the Royal Commission report'. I describe this because, while Wilson and his colleagues did not engineer this 'honourable' way out, it was very important in allowing a favourable final decision to be reached. Any pressure group campaigning will be more successful, more quickly, if the decision-makers who have to change their mind have an honourable and face-saving way of doing so – in this case accepting a recommendation from a Royal Commission.

Conclusion

These case examples give four very different illustrations of pressure group work. The following sections will examine how marketing can be applied to pressure group work and will use these and other cases as exemplars.

Other-player analysis and positioning

Other players

Competitor analysis and subsequent positioning is a critical success factor in pressure group work. Unlike charity provision of physical goods and services, the charity pressure group market is very busy and highly competitive. Charity pressure groups are competing with each other and the commercial and statutory sector interests for influence. Demand massively outstrips decision-makers' ability to supply. Every disadvantaged group quite rightly wants more and better resources and services. Every environmental charity has a distinctive priority of agenda points; if there are commonalities, they are still competing for the ear, the time and the money of decision-makers. Every arts organisation needs more money. Even if the interest of the more junior official (where the work is done) can be engaged, convincing the boss that time and effort should be committed to the issue is very difficult. A fair bit of pressure group work meets the ultimate bottleneck of the parliamentary legislative programme, where competition is at its most intense.

So a charity decision to press an issue needs much analysis of other players to identify interests that might be oppositional and powerful.

Many of the traditional texts on pressure groups seem to regard them as unified organisations – almost an irreducible unit of common agreement. This is far too simplistic. External observers tend to see unanimity, which is in fact a tactical pretence, covering over a variety of points of view. Take something as apparently narrow and simple as the campaign for financial allowance for blind people. In the early stages of this campaign the National Federation of the Blind regarded itself as the owner of the idea, and was not 100 per cent convinced that it wanted other organisations in the field of blindness to be active participants in the campaign, for fear they might hijack it. The National League of the Blind and Disabled backed the campaign in the early stages from the point of view of solidarity, but was not enthusiastic because it saw the leadership in another organisation of blind people. RNIB, in the very early stages, regarded the exercise as little to do with it, and disliked the methods used to promote the idea. So if those tensions can exist within an area that many people might regard as tightly bounded, with a proposition that is very precise, in a field in which one might imagine there are few differing voices – then just think what the situation must be like in pressure group activity in fields of greater economic and political significance!

Positioning

In fact it is hard to think of many situations in which a pressure group operates unaffected and unimpeded by other related actual or potential pressure groups. It is possible to imagine two related continua, which relate to each other vertically, and are consistent on the left-to-right plane (Table 8.1, overleaf).

For example, the eye test campaign started out as a coalition but over time became solo with positive acquiescence from the rest of the coalition. Control Arms is a coalition but over time Oxfam, because of its greater resources, took a leading active role. The Disability Benefits Consortium was a coalition. The CLEAR campaign was probably a solo one, with positive acquiescence from associated pressure groups. However, Des Wilson would probably argue that it was a coalition. In reality it may have shifted between these two positions at different

Table 8.1 Model of pressure group positioning options

Approach of leading pressure groups	Solo				Coalition	Partnership
	Opposition	Reluctant acquiescence	Neutrality	Positive acquiescence	Joint proposal	Partnership
Approach of related pressure groups	(active, competitive goals)	(relatively inactive, competitive goals)	(inactive but competitive goals)	(relatively inactive, cooperative goals)	(active cooperation on joint goals, relatively active pursuit of individual goals)	(active joint goals, inactive or nonexistent competitive goals)

stages, arguably starting as a coalition but shifting into solo with positive acquiescence as Wilson, and the resources he commanded, began to assume dominance. The free eye test campaign and the comprehensive disability income and cost allowance campaign are both coalitions with joint goals, but also with the individual organisations pursuing individual goals within the joint campaign.

In marketing terms, what does this model suggest with regard to positioning for successful pressure group work? It is possible for a pressure group to succeed in any position on the continuum, but clearly it would be much harder with associated groups only reluctantly acquiescing or openly opposing the individual pressure group's goals. So it is clearly important to try to avoid this situation either by modifying the pressure group goals to ensure that associated groups are at least neutral, or by building up better relationships with associated groups to explain how the individual campaign is not as competitive as it might appear at first sight.

Coalitions and partnerships

Superficially the right-hand end of the continuum would seem to be the most attractive for success. Both coalitions and partnerships give the advantage of considerably increased resources. For example, the Disability Benefits Consortium has the combined strength of 250 disability organisations, including all the major charity players, with considerable lobbying resources at their disposal. However, the downside is that the demands on the decision-makers tend to be much greater. For example, a satisfactory financial blindness allowance would cost the state less than £500 million, but a satisfactory benefit for all groups of disabled people as per the coalition would cost the state in excess of £7 billion. So if the magnitude of the demand increases with the size of the coalition, this goes a long way to cancelling out the impact of increased campaign resources. Another downside is that, although there are joint proposals, the individual organisations are still likely to be pursuing individual goals. This takes a lot of time to talk through and involves the coalition leaders in endless meetings. Coalitions will be successful more quickly and easily where the target 'only' needs to change its behaviour and the target is not required to provide significant sums.

Going solo

Probably the most successful pressure group campaigns are those that are essentially solo ones, with the positive acquiescence of associated groups, or at least their guaranteed neutrality. Such positioning allows the demand to be less costly to the decision-makers and well differentiated from other competing pressure group demands, it narrows down the number and range of decision-makers to target, and it simplifies the advocacy work and message.

Opposition

Analysis of the other players not only extends to allies who might become competitors, it very importantly also concentrates on the opposition. Here the CLEAR campaign spent much analytical time. The commercial lobby of motor manufacturers, petroleum companies and lead providers was obviously very strong in the areas of technical competence and behind-the-scenes lobbying. Therefore Wilson chose what he called the 'moral high ground' of health and long-term environmental gains: he took the argument out into the public arena, and in particular the editorial arena. In an analysis of strengths and weaknesses of the campaign and the opposition this tactic made a lot of sense. Commercial companies are very powerful in their behind-the-scenes lobbying and in their technical resources, but they are often very uncomfortable under public scrutiny. The CLEAR campaign, although it had technical resources, could not compete in this area, nor did it have access to the corridors of power. However, it had the highly effective public representational resource of Wilson himself, excellent contacts in the editorial media and a sufficiently well-argued proposition on the moral high ground.

Conclusion

In summary, other-player analysis and subsequent positioning are crucial to any effective pressure group work. This analysis needs to concentrate not only on the obvious opposition, but also on allies who might become competitors. The well-established SWOT analysis is ideal. The objective is to position the campaign in terms of its contents, alliances and methods in ways that will support the overall objectives but also concentrate on campaign strengths and opposition weaknesses. Pressure group work is an area where competition for attention and action is intense, and differentiation of the campaign is a necessary and often crucial requirement.

Targeting

It is surprising how often charities do not think carefully about the target groups for their pressure group work. Instead, good ideas tend to spring out of charity knowledge and practice and become inscribed in the organisation's formal policy positions; everyone feels a lot better when a new demand has been articulated, but nothing happens. Clearly it is not possible to promote every charity policy position, as it would be completely debilitating on resources to do so. However, even when a policy plank is selected for greater promotion, there is often little thought given to targets for the 'good idea'. Exhortations (such as 'GPs should do more of such and such', 'the Arts Council should spend more on such and such an area', 'overseas aid policies should be changed to do such and such' and 'pesticides in farming practices should be reduced') will only stand a chance of being effective if questions are asked along the following lines:

- Who are the beneficiaries?
- Who are the advocates of the beneficiaries?
- Who are the decision-makers?
- Who are the influencers of the decision-makers?

Beneficiaries

Philosophically, and on most occasions practically, this is the group to start with. This is the group for whom the pressure group exists. Its needs should be the primary (but not only) determinant of the pressure group proposal. However, it would be disingenuous to suggest that there is not an important interaction between all four target groups – beneficiaries, advocates, influencers and decision-makers. It is clearly no use spending significant resources on a campaign that will help beneficiaries but is unlikely to succeed among influencers and decision-makers in the long term, let alone the short term. Pressure group work should be judged on results, not on effort.

Pressure groups often spend too little time identifying the key target groups among beneficiaries. Even in those relatively few instances where all beneficiaries benefit from a pressure group proposal, it is important to work out which groups benefit in what way, because the application of the proposal is seldom uniform. Establishing the differential benefits is important for three reasons. First, those members of the beneficiary group who are likely to gain the most are more likely to be advocates (see the next section). For example in the eye test campaign, RNIB had relatively more to gain because a significant proportion of people with poor sight are in that position because of not having their eyes tested. So anything that might improve this situation will be a top priority.

Second, provided that the pressure group has a clear idea about the differential benefits of its proposal, it can make concessions to opinion-formers and decision-makers in ways that appear to be significant, but in reality result in little diminution of the benefit. For example, in the free eye test campaign, proportionally more eye disease is picked up in tests of the over-40s than the under-40s. If the government wishes to make concessions on its hard line 'charging for eye tests' position for political or economic reasons, then it is more important to continue to demand free eye tests for the over-40s than it is for the under-40s.

The third, and most important, reason for targeting and segmenting the beneficiary group in relation to any proposal, is to test it out. This can be done both through desk analysis and research. It is surprising how often pressure groups develop proposals for change on the basis of hunch or 'we know best'. A little desk analysis will show that a superficially strong demand will, in practice, only benefit relatively few beneficiaries. So the pressure group must ask very early on, 'Who will benefit from this proposal?' It must also have strong evidence that the beneficiary group will actually welcome the proposal, especially for major proposals. If you are not clear about your target beneficiary group, this most basic question cannot be answered! (See the section on market research later in this chapter.)

So segmenting and targeting your beneficiary group is important for deciding and backing up the campaign proposals, identifying advocacy groups, and identifying areas where concessions can be made in ways that will minimise impact on the campaign objective.

Advocates

Identifying and targeting individuals and groups who can be advocates for the proposition, but are somewhat distanced from the pressure group, is a key tool for success. For all sorts of reasons, charity pressure groups themselves can quickly be discounted. Even pressure groups such as Save the Children and Age Concern will meet the occasionally overt, and certainly covert, reaction from influencers and decision-makers on the lines of 'well, you would say that, wouldn't you'. Advocates somewhat distanced from the pressure group increase the credibility of the proposition enormously. For example, involving recent immigrants who have successfully settled in this country as advocates for a more sympathetic immigration policy can make the campaign much more credible. Involving sympathetic employers as advocates for employing disabled people can make influencers and decision-makers sit up and review the situation afresh in a way that yet another meeting with RADAR cannot. Influential independent scientists were crucial advocates for CLEAR.

Identifying advocacy groups that can support the proposition is not a well-developed art among charity pressure groups. When it happens the selection of individual advocates can too often be on the basis of the most important leader in this supportive group. It is important to identify advocates who are likely to be most credible to the influencer and/or decision-maker.

Decision-makers

The term 'decision-makers' is deliberately put in the plural; it is seldom that only one person makes a decision. There will be people above or below who have to sign up. Also, the real decision-maker is seldom the obvious person. The obvious decision-maker, such as the director of social services or the junior minister in charge is already visible. However, if the potential decision-maker is visible, it means that they are sufficiently well known to have a whole mass of responsibilities and rely primarily on recommendations from the bureaucracy. There has been an increasing trend for pressure groups to concentrate on local and central government political leaders as the objects of lobbying, which Miller (1991) argues is a mistake. Even when local or national government has a relatively small majority (and is therefore more open to influence at a political level), the majority of decisions are taken by the executive (civil servants, local authority officials, head officers of national associations).

But if the executive makes the decisions, at what level? Once again there is a tendency to assume that decisions are made at a much higher level than they really are. For example, the majority of work on a policy issue in the civil service will be undertaken at the level of what used to be called principal (now called 'number sevens'!), which is the fifth tier of the civil service hierarchy. Occasionally a higher-tier assistant secretary (number five) will be involved in shaping the policy and the decision on the basis of work done by the principal. However, these are the administrative civil servants, who have their equivalent in local government and other statutory organisations. The professional advisory arm, such as doctors, social workers, nuclear scientists, pesticide experts and construction engineers also plays a role. While the administrative part of the executive would claim, often rightly, that it makes the decisions, the professional advisers will be influential to a greater or lesser extent. A good rule of thumb is that the higher the status level of the profession or the greater the complexity of the subject, the greater the influence of the professional arm.

If all this seems very complicated, it is relatively easy to find out who the key decision-makers will be on any issue. The charity simply writes to the health authority's general manager, the director of social services or the only civil servant known in the relevant department. The reply will give all the information needed. It may be signed by an official; the next stage is simply to find out who is above and below them, and this will identify the decision-making unit – the target group. If it is signed by the minister, or the director of social services, there will normally be a reference on the letter with initials, or 'for further information ring extension ...' which, once again, gives information about the key decision-makers.

Influencers

The influencers also play a crucial role. They may even, on occasions, have the authority to overrule the decision-makers, although they will seldom do so. There are three stages when the influencers can have an important impact. In descending order of impact it will be at the start of the consideration, during the consideration and after the decision has effectively been made.

If a charity pressure group can raise an issue right at the start with a senior influencer such as a minister, director of education or chair of social services, in a friendly cooperative way, then this can spark an important catalytic effect. The senior influencer will then pass it on to the people who will work on the issue (such as a civil servant or local official) on the lines of 'Age Concern Eastbourne has raised with me the problem of the crossing outside Marks & Spencer being dangerously placed – could you see if there is something you can do?'.

Contact with influencers during the decision-making process has to be well judged, as it can make the executive decision-makers antagonistic because they will feel that the pressure group is looping over their heads to the top. However, it is not a pressure group's role to please executive decision-makers! If a pressure group senses a decision is going the wrong way, action obviously has to be taken. The contact with the influencers can either be friendly or adversarial. In the eye tests campaign, the civil servants were working to a brief to introduce charges – with that brief coming from the minister. Therefore the looping over to the minister was essential and adversarial. Because direct persuasion of the minister was not working, the pressure group work shifted into the public arena and 'advocates' were triggered to put pressure on the influencers, which in the eye test case were many and varied. They included the chair of the Conservative Backbench Health Committee, the Select Committee Conservative members of the committee stage of the bill, and influential government members in the Lords. While all this activity can in work terms seem impressive, the more activity there is and the more public it is, the more it is a signal that the pressure group is losing!

The least effective stage to approach influencers is just as, or just after, a negative decision has been made. This is normally the death throes of a campaign (although the CLEAR example above proves the opposite), when the positions of decision-makers and key influencers are highly entrenched.

It can be difficult to draw distinctions between decision-makers, influencers, advocates and beneficiaries. One can imagine a continuum, with decision-makers at the left-hand end, influencers next, then advocates and finally beneficiaries on the right (see Figure 8.1).

Decision-makers ⇄ Influencers ⇄ Advocates ⇄ Beneficiaries

Figure 8.1 Relationships of key target groups in pressure group activity

As one shifts along the continuum from right to left, some beneficiaries become advocates, some advocates shade into influencers and some influencers practically become decision-makers. A minister in a government department has the authority to make the decision, but does not often have the power (the detail of the argument). For this reason the minister is closer to the influencing rather than the decision-making side of the divide. However, if the decision is of great importance and/or politically sensitive, then the minister will shift over to join the civil servants at the decision-making end of the continuum. In exceptional circumstances, where the minister makes the decision against the advice of the civil servant, the civil servants may shift across into the influence part of the continuum.

Conclusion

Segmenting and targeting the market in charity pressure group work is often superficial or even non-existent, yet it is essential for success. It is important to segment and target not only among potential beneficiaries, but also among credible advocates. Also it is important to segment and target not only among decision-makers, but also among influencers. The relationship between these four groups is complicated but crucial. Not all beneficiaries benefit equally; some beneficiaries become advocates; some influencers can become advocates; some decision-makers can become advocates; and, depending on the stage of the campaign and its changing importance, people who were previously decision-makers may become influencers, and people who were previously influencers may become decision-makers! Nevertheless, this four-category model is vital for laying out the chess pieces of any charity pressure group work. Such analysis allows a proposal to be truly beneficial to the ultimate recipients, enables the pressure group to marshal and deploy its meagre resources more effectively, and will impress and ultimately influence decision-makers, who are generally dismissive of ill-thought-out, crude campaigning.

Market research

Market research is a key tool to effective pressure group success. It can help in four ways:

- as a testing mechanism among beneficiaries to ensure that the proposal really does meet their needs;
- (following from the previous point) as evidence to influencers and decision-makers of genuine and detailed needs of potential beneficiaries;
- as support to campaigns, in the form of opinion polls;
- as a method of analysing opinions and positions of key influencers and decision-makers.

The following paragraphs take these ideas in turn.

Testing mechanism

It is surprising and frightening how often charity pressure groups assume that their propositions are correct on the basis that 'they know best'. While it is understandable that charities believe that they know what is best for their beneficiaries from practical experience, it is still not good enough. A marketing approach requires that proposals are tested out among beneficiaries before they are launched. Elsewhere in this book the suggestion has been put that it is not enough that charity committees contain professional workers experienced in the field, and not even enough that a charity has representatives on its committees from the end beneficiary group. No one person can be representative of the full range of beneficiaries. Market research among actual and potential beneficiaries testing out alternatives can go a long way (but not all the way) to informing pressure group policy-makers.

Evidence

This market research can have a double impact, as use as evidence with both influencers and decision-makers. For example, the then Department of Social Security had long resisted arguments that blind people needed financial help with their mobility problems (which was available to physically disabled people). By bringing together the findings of the RNIB needs survey (Bruce *et al.* 1991) with government research among disabled people (Martin *et al.* 1989) it was shown that blind people were far less independently mobile than disabled people in general. This conclusion from market research transformed a proposal that had previously been regarded as a self-centred whinge into a hard, credible evidence based demand.

Opinion polls

Market research in the form of opinion polls can be a useful support, especially in media terms. Charity pressure groups have used to good effect opinion poll findings on the lines of 'over 75 per cent of the general public would be prepared to pay higher taxes in order to improve services for ...'. In the CLEAR campaign Des Wilson argued that opinion poll evidence of overwhelming public knowledge and support for the campaign increased the campaign's credibility with government negotiators. It is important not to over-emphasise the value of opinion polls, but they can be useful increments of influence.

Analysing views

Last, market research, usually qualitative, among influencers and decision-makers is crucial in assessing tactics. All too often pressure group leaders spend too much time writing and talking up their own case, and not enough time listening to influencers' and decision-makers' views. For pressure group representatives, to allow these two groups to express opposing arguments in their presence is almost regarded as a sign of weakness and to 'stare defeat in the face'. Far from it – listening to counter-arguments, in particular from decision-makers, assessing their individual validity and finding out how widespread that view is, is crucial in winning any pressure group initiative.

The proposal

This is the first 'P' – product – of the marketing mix. The bedrock of the pressure group idea product is the 'P' for philosophy. Just as in services, the various campaigns will become contradictory if the common philosophy of the organisation is not clearly integrated into the pressure group idea. In some instances the philosophy element of the mix can be very visible, as demonstrated in the British Mountaineering Council's campaign for the freedom to climb difficult and dangerous mountains (see Figure 8.2).

The only thing worse than falling off a rock face is not being allowed to.

North Wales Daily Post, 20th June 1990

The crags of Pen Trwyn in North Wales are home to some of the hardest rock climbs in the British Isles.

Attracting climbers from all over the world to a punishing test of strength and technique.

In summer 1990, the risk of falling rocks dislodged by climbers forced Aberconwy Borough Council to close the cliff.

Now Pen Trwyn truly was impossible to climb.

And so it would have remained if the BMC hadn't intervened.

Our Access and Technical Committees worked hard to find a solution which suited both climbers and the general public.

Using our Access and Conservation fund, we installed abseil stations on carefully selected routes on Pen Trwyn. Eliminating the danger of falling rocks at the end of a climb.

Thanks to the BMC, Pen Trwyn is once again open for business. And like many other threatened cliffs and rock faces, we believe it should remain easy to climb.

PROTECTING CLIMBERS AND THEIR MOUNTAIN ENVIRONMENT

Figure 8.2 Organisation philosophy is important, and policy, campaigning and practice need to follow it – advertisement and leaflet from the British Mountaineering Council (BMC/Cheetham Bell)

Details

The proposal (the product one is trying to put across), has to be constructed with as much care as any physical good or service. The earlier sections touched on the importance of having a high quality proposal which is well thought out, right down to the details. The detail may not initially be presented, but if the proposers are not aware of it, they cannot put the case in a way that will later stand up. What are the main features of the proposal? Where is the evidence that these are the most important ones for beneficiaries? What is the proposition called (is it clear, as in 'disability income' or 'Control Arms')? Is there a one- or two-sentence summary that makes it plain what is being sought and why? Keeping eye tests, and taking lead out of petrol are simple, memorable propositions.

Making all these decisions in developing the case, anticipating opposing arguments, is akin to new product development. It requires all the stages of developing ideas, screening them in relation to target decision-makers, proposal development, 'business' analysis (such as cost of implementation), testing out on people and preparing for launch. Des Wilson has talked of the phase of proposal development taking six months or so. This is ideal with a proactive proposal, but is impractical in defensive campaigns such as eye tests, where the pressure group is likely to have days or weeks rather than months in which to act. The Good Campaigns Guide has an excellent section on planning (Lamb 1997).

Price

One of the more sterile arguments is whether a marketing approach can be applied to charitable activities because the price is often absent or distorted or paid by someone other than the consumer. This is nowhere more so than in pressure group proposals. However, there most certainly is a price attached to any pressure group proposal, which a decision-maker has to pay. What is more, the decision-maker is often more aware of the price than the manufacturer (the pressure group). In Chapter 4 it is suggested that the idea products have impact prices. Whether the target groups of pressure group campaigns respond positively depends on their implicit and explicit assessment of the balance of costs and benefits. For example the price the government will have to pay if tough arms control is introduced in the UK will be significant – lost GDP, taxes and jobs. The political price of banning or allowing hunting has been interesting. Initially the government felt the price of not banning hunting was higher than banning. However, skilful direct action tactics by the countryside lobby put the price of banning hunting even higher.

Resource levels

Price is a useful analytical and practical mechanism in pressure group work in two senses. The first is literally how much resource (not always money) the decision-maker will have to apply if the pressure group proposal is implemented. Sometimes this is money in the form of tax concessions, increased financing of local government or increased or direct grant aid to the charity. However, often the resource is indirectly financial, through demands for higher quality and more extensive services to a particular group. In my experience the impact on the decision-maker of the actual price of the demand is underestimated and under-discussed by pressure groups. At one level this is justified, legitimately, on the lines of 'it's our job to present to you unfulfilled needs, not to make decisions about cost of implementation, including where you will get the money from'. However, adopting the moral high ground as Wilson did in the CLEAR campaign is dangerous. Decision-makers are no longer (if they ever were) impressed by arguments that other countries are doing it. If the officials in the executive do a calculation of the price of implementation that proves to be far higher than that put forward by the pressure group (if it is done at all), then the idea may be dismissed before the debate has even started. Or if the officials calculate a lower price than that implied by the pressure group's demand, and this is not made explicit until well into the campaign, the latter stages of negotiation will get very bumpy as the (unanticipated) differences emerge.

Even if the pressure group does not declare the true price of implementation in the opening stages of the initiative, it is important to discuss it with officials no later than what might be estimated as the middle stages of the campaign. This gives time for all parties to adjust their demands/likely concessions in an ordered way rather than face a last-minute scrabble with plenty of recriminations. In particular if the price of the demand is seen to be too high, it allows the pressure group, if it wishes, to re-phase and restructure its proposal in such a way as to set precedence for subsequent campaigns in its area. (It goes without saying that the officials will, unless converted, be very cautious about such restructuring!)

Personal cost

The second aspect of price, which is seldom thought through, is the price that decision-makers and, to a lesser extent, influencers will have to pay in personal terms. Both will be asking themselves how much aggravation they are going to get from other groups making demands if they are seen to support this particular one. This price therefore loops back to the construction of the proposal, preferably in such a way as to minimise the knock-on effects (unless this has been part of the agreement to gain, for example, positive acquiescence from other groups – see Figure 8.2, page 221). The other more personal price which decision-makers and influencers will be considering is their popularity and standing with other important people in their work setting – particularly with the treasury or finance department! Additional resources are hard to get at the best of times and will involve a great deal of debate, preparation of internal proposals and endless meetings. If additional resources are refused after the decision-maker has in effect internally signed up to the proposition, the financial boomerang may come right back and hit the official doing the origination. This boomerang is in the form of a request for budget substitution – which in less bureaucratic language means that they are asked to find the costs of this desirable new initiative from elsewhere within their own budget, by cutting something else out of their area of responsibility.

Conclusion

In summary, calculating the price of a request and openly discussing it, not too far into the pressure group initiative, is important. I asked a minister with whom we had been dealing for some six years on initiatives to which we knew he was committed what he felt were some of our less successful tactics. He described the situation in which we would troop in to him and make a proposal that his officials had advised him was a totally unrealistic price to pay in the medium term, let alone the short term. From his point of view we gave a really hard sell on behalf of the disadvantaged group we were representing and would leave, in his words, 'feeling good' and report back to our constituency to some degree of approbation. However, as far as he was concerned the whole meeting had been a complete waste of time, except that he had appeared 'reasonable' in listening to our demands! Even so, his view was a partial one, and one would hope that presentation of just, but expensive, demands would over time have some impact. However, if I am honest, on several occasions we had not thought the detail of the price through in the way we should have done.

Promotion

Promotion is something that charity pressure groups are particularly good at, but we do not always relate our public promotion to the required impact. Within the confines of pressure group action, the only purpose of promotional activities is to influence decision-makers and influencers.

Personal selling

While mass publicity is very much the first love and expertise of charity pressure groups, we do need to learn a thing or two from our highly effective commercial counterparts. Personal selling of the proposal by liked and/or respected personal intervention is likely to be far more effective than stand-up, and superficially victorious, battles with ministers on Radio Four's 'Today' programme. Des Wilson argues that contacts with people with the right skills or with the influence in the right places are crucial to any campaign. Charities have an enviable list of contacts and should put them to good use. Clear, well-written and, above all, honest briefings are required. (Charity goodwill and trust is a valuable resource, which cannot be squandered for short-term advantages.) If at all possible, charities should enlist contacts through direct and personal requests, making it clear what they want the person to do. At the very least, most sympathetic people will write a letter, especially if the charity drafts if for them. Much better, however, is yet further personal intervention with influencers. Third-party approaches to influencers can have a major impact. First, the third-party advocate is more likely to be respected by the potential influencer. Second, the influencer cannot help but think 'if ... is sufficiently concerned to take up their cause, this is beginning to become a significant issue'. Commercial pressure groups have the resources for slap-up lunches and dinners. Luckily charities seldom have to use this method and can get contacts direct via meetings.

Advertising and PR

If personal selling of the idea is the most effective method, advertising and public relations can also play an important part in a pressure group campaign that requires public support. Environmental pressure groups, particularly Greenpeace, have made very effective use of advertising campaigns. However, these are obviously expensive and charities rightly tend to favour editorial channels. The CLEAR and 'Control Arms' examples show how coverage can be generated. The story itself should normally be strong enough to command some news coverage in the early stages. The difficulty is in maintaining momentum. The trick is to find ways to turn what is a continuing message into a news story. This requires some form of news hook. Timely reports and research surveys give sympathetic editorial journalists the hook they need.

Both newspapers and television welcome graphic coverage in stills and footage. Once again successful charities can find visual events that are powerful and/or amusing enough to gain coverage. Dumping tons of non- recyclable drinks containers outside Schweppes headquarters; gravestones in Trafalgar Square; piles of bones representing slaughtered animals; disabled people linking arms across Westminster Bridge; banners hanging from scaffolding up the side of Big Ben; street theatre outside the Arts Council – all these and more can provide strong graphic images for the media and remain true and relevant to the pressure group campaign.

Channels of communication (place)

In classic commercial marketing this is place, the fourth 'P' of the marketing mix, and sometimes called distribution. In the activity of pressure group work, it is most easily encapsulated in the term 'channels of communication' and is perhaps the most crucial analytical tool in ensuring success. Having identified the target groups, the communications channel can be crucial in helping the message to be received positively rather than negatively. A vast array of channels is available. Personal communications (meetings and telephoning) always win over impersonal ones such as letters, radio and television.

Personal contact

Formal meetings with decision-makers and key influencers require not only a legitimate interest on behalf of the person or organisation making the approach, but also a very direct interest. However, contacts with more distant influencers such as government backbenchers when the majority is fairly small, can be more liberal in number and more informal. MPs and even members of the Lords are trapped in Parliament for quite lengthy periods and can be surprisingly ready to meet, providing it is in Parliament and at a time to suit them. Contact by advocates from their own constituency is a communications channel to be sought avidly. Building up constituency supporters of a particular pressure group proposal, especially in decision-makers' and influencers' constituencies, can be very effective. Charity pressure groups with service units in constituencies across the country are at a distinct advantage, as are those with local memberships. The Disability Benefits Consortium's campaign for a disability income was greatly helped by disabled people seeking meetings at MPs' surgeries and describing how lack of money made their lives even more challenging. Also, charities such as Barnardo's, Save the Children, MENCAP and RNIB are major employers in many constituencies across the country, and as such have almost a guarantee of access to local MPs.

Third parties

Finally, influencing through relevant third-party organisations such as the Association of Directors of Social Services, local arts associations and sports associations indicates, rightly, that the issue is not simply one being dreamt up and supported by national pressure groups.

Conclusion

The idea that the pressure group proposal is sacrosanct, with the validity of the idea shining through without need of a marketing approach, could not be further from the truth. A pressure group proposal is as much a product in the marketing sense as a physical good or service. If anything, it requires a greater degree of sophistication of market segmentation and targeting, competitor analysis, market research and positioning, as well as the remaining elements of the marketing mix of price, promotion and place. If these elements are attended to methodically and in advance of the launch, the chances of the pressure group proposal being accepted are enhanced considerably.

Key points

Positioning and other players

- Identify potential partners and, if necessary, modify your goals to ensure that associated groups are at least neutral and do not become competitors.
- Concentrate on campaign strengths and opposition weaknesses. Differentiation of the campaign is vital.

Segmenting and targeting

- To help set priorities, identify the beneficiaries, their advocates, decision-makers and influencers. How do they overlap and interrelate?

Market research

- To give credence to your campaign with influencers and decision-makers, support your proposals with evidence researched among your target beneficiaries. Use respectable independent research and opinion polls if they are available.
- Make tactical use of the most widespread opposing views, especially if they are shared by influencers and decision-makers.

Proposal

- Putting together the proposal is akin to new product development, and equal care should be taken. Find a simple one- or two-sentence summary which clearly and memorably describes what is being sought and why.

Price

- Discuss at an early stage how much resource, directly or indirectly, the decision-maker will have to apply if the proposal is implemented. This gives time for all parties to adjust their demands or likely concessions.
- Consider the impact price to the decision-makers of supporting this campaign.

Promotion

- Personal selling of the idea is the most effective means of promotion, but can be helpfully supported by advertising and public relations.

Channels of communication

- Use personal communications (meetings and telephoning) as well as letters, briefs, etc.
- Find advocates who can make contact with influencers such as MPs, especially through constituency networks.

9 Income and fundraising

The full income picture

Before concentrating on fundraising it is useful to look at the full income picture of charities. This is difficult for several reasons, including problems of agreed definitions, difficulty of gathering primary data, insufficient research, non-comparable data sets and the field's sheer size and complexity.

Having reviewed the various data sets (including NCVO's Almanac, CAF's Charity Trends, Charity Finance's Charity 100 Index, the Top 3000 Charities and Kendall and Knapp 1996) I would conclude that since 1990:

- sector income has grown and still is growing at a substantial pace in both actual and real terms;
- this growth has been fuelled by substantial growth in voluntary income as well as earned income, but the third stream, investment income, has performed poorly;
- the growth in public sector grants, fees and contracts has been slightly ahead of overall growth and their share of total income has grown from around just over one quarter to just over one third – a creeping state colonisation of our sector, which we need to watch but which does not yet pose a real threat to independence;
- despite substantial rises in the two main streams of earned income and voluntary income, sub-streams such as charity shops have shown more variation, and some organisations have skewed income profiles, with periods of faster and slower growth and, in some cases (because of being heavily dependent on business) actual decline;
- the smaller number of charities with annual incomes over £1 million dominate the financial income market, but the huge number of charities whose income is £1 million or under dominate

the direct service volunteer market. If one combines these two resource sources (money and volunteers), charities of £1 million and under have approaching the same impact resources as those over £1 million.

Sector definitions

It is not the purpose of this book to go into the variety of useful definitions of the sector and their impact on income size and sources (but see Kendall and Knapp 1996 in Appendix 1, Kendall 2003, and Hems and Passey 1996 in Appendix 2). However, in order to indicate what we are discussing it is necessary to mention some definition in outline. Kendall and Knapp, as part of the Johns Hopkins Comparative Non-profit Sector Project (see Appendix 1), refer to the broad voluntary sector (BVS) and the narrow voluntary sector (NVS). The BVS includes not only charities as we recognise them but also such non-profits as cultural and recreational organisations, schools, universities, hospital trusts, housing associations, trades unions and trade associations. The NVS is BVS minus recreation, education, unions and trade associations, but including housing associations and cultural organisations. See Appendix 1 for a detailed definition. Kendall (2003), on these definitions, estimates the overall economic indicators of the voluntary sector in 1995 (see Table 9.1).

Hems and Passey (1996), reporting the ONS data interpretation exercise, use the term 'general charities' to cover registered charities (with the Charity Commission) minus those that are effectively part of government (such as the British Council, Arts Council and grant maintained schools) and excluding exempt charities such as charitable housing associations, universities, schools and places of worship. 'General charities' as a pragmatic collection probably approximates with what most members of the National Council for Voluntary Organisations (NCVO) would think of as the charity sector, including all the 'household-name' national charities and local charities. See Appendix 2 for a detailed definition. General charities equate roughly with the NVS minus housing associations and cultural organisations. More precision has been devoted here to 'general charities' because much of the data in this chapter draws on the ONS survey of these charities reported and analysed in the 2004 NCVO Almanac (Wilding *et al.* 2004).

Table 9.1 Overall economic contribution of the UK voluntary sector in 1995

Economic indicator	BNS	NVS
Volunteer headcount ('000s)	16,311	7,852
Full-time equivalent (FTE) volunteers ('000s)	1,664	774
FTE paid employment ('000s)	1,473	503
Percentage of economy-wide paid employment	6.3	2.2
Total FTE paid and unpaid employment	3,137	1,277
Percentage of economy-wide employment including volunteering (all formal sectors)	12.3	5.0
Total expenditure (TE)	£47.1bn	£15.4bn
TE as percentage of gross domestic product (GDP)	6.6	2.2
TE including volunteers[a]	£67.6bn	£24.9bn
As percentage of volunteer-adjusted GDP[a, b]	9.2	3.4

Notes:
[a] Assuming volunteer hours can be valued using mean non-agricultural private sector wage.
[b] Denominator includes value of volunteering in all sectors (including private, public, third and informal).

Source: Kendall 2003, p. 22.

Income sources

Wilding *et al.* report total income for general charities in the UK in 2001/02 as £21 billion. One of the most descriptive tables of income from their report is shown in Table 9.2 (opposite). Approaching half (47 per cent) of the income of the total general charities sector is voluntary income, just over a third (38 per cent) is earned, a tenth comes from investment (10 per cent) and a twentieth from trading subsidiaries (5 per cent).

While the figures shown in Table 9.2 are only associational, not causal, it is interesting to note that charities with turnovers of more than £10 million are more likely to have several, more equal sources of income (35 per cent voluntary income (excluding legacies), 36 per cent earned income, 11 per cent legacies, 10 per cent investments and 8 per cent trading subscriptions), whereas those in lower income bands are much more likely to be heavily dependent on one source of income (£1–£10 million band organisations from earned income (42 per cent); under £1 million from donations (49 per cent).

Table 9.2 Total income by size of organisation, 2001/02 (%)

Income stream	Under 10k	£10k–£100k	£100k–£1m	£1m–£10m	Over £10m	All
Individuals' gifts & donations (gross)	23.2	15.6	11.1	12.1	15.5	13.6
Public sector grants	6.4	16.2	24.5	17.3	12.4	16.9
Lottery distributors' grants	4.4	3.2	5.3	2.7	0.8	2.6
Voluntary sector grants	7.4	8.2	6.1	5.3	4.1	5.3
Private sector gifts & donations	1.2	0.9	2.4	3.0	2.5	2.5
Voluntary income (ex legacies)	**42.6**	**44.1**	**49.4**	**40.4**	**35.3**	**40.9**
Legacies	**1.1**	**1.3**	**2.7**	**4.1**	**11.3**	**6.3**
Individuals' fees and payments	26.6	32.1	18.9	18.2	11.1	16.9
Public sector fees & contracts	0.8	4.9	12.2	19.6	22.8	17.7
Private sector fees & sponsorship	0.6	1.2	2.5	2.3	1.2	1.8
Voluntary sector fees & payments	2.0	2.1	1.7	1.5	0.8	1.3
Earned income (ex trading subs)	**30.0**	**40.1**	**35.3**	**41.6**	**35.9**	**37.7**
Rent from investment property/ land	2.6	1.9	1.5	1.6	1.2	1.5
Dividends from equities and securities	12.2	7.8	6.0	4.9	7.7	6.5
Interest on cash and bank deposits	11.4	4.7	2.4	1.7	1.1	2.0
Total investment income	**26.2**	**14.4**	**9.9**	**8.2**	**9.9**	**10.0**
Trading subs: gross income	**0.1**	**0.1**	**2.7**	**5.7**	**7.6**	**5.2**
Total incoming resources	**100**	**100**	**100**	**100**	**100**	**100**

Source: Wilding, Collins, Jochum and Wainwright, NCVO 2004, p. 86

Looking at the largest income sources for each charity band highlights some interesting differences:

- Annual income under £10,000 pa – individuals' fees and payments (27%)
- £10,000 – £100,000 – individuals' fees and payments (32%)
- £100,000 – £1 million – public sector grants (25%)
- £1 million – £10 million – public sector fees and contracts (20%)
- £10 million and over – public sector fees and contracts (23%)

In none of these sectors do 'individuals' gifts and donations' form the biggest income source, and in all but the smallest income group they are substantially behind these largest income sources.

A quite different picture emerges if one values the resource put in by volunteers, especially those providing direct service. The 2002 NCVO UK Voluntary Sector Almanac (Jas *et al.* 2002) gives revised estimates of the value of volunteers as £15 billion per annum, thus approaching the total financial income of £21 billion. However, this 'in-kind' income via volunteers, especially direct service volunteers who contribute directly to impact, contributes disproportionately more to the smallest charities, as is shown in Table 9.3. So the smaller charities are not as small in their impact as the spread of financial income would suggest. Indeed the table shows the total resources for general charities with an income of £1 million or less is approaching the contribution of those over £1 million; and for those under £100,000 is approaching one fifth of the total general charity contribution. This interpretation challenges the commonly held assumption that the largest charities attract an overwhelming majority of the resources.

Table 9.3 Income of general charities including costed direct service volunteer time (£ billion)

Turnover	Less than 100K	100k to £1m	£1m to £10m	£10m +	All
Financial income[i]	1.8	4.9	6.0	8.0	20.8
Costed direct volunteer time[ii]	3.2	3.4	0.8	0.7	9.1
Total	**5.0**	**8.3**	**6.8**	**8.7**	**29.9**

[i] Wilding *et al.* 2004. [ii] Jas *et al.* 2002

Trends

However, in terms of fundraised income, big is beautiful and the strong, well-known brands are long lasting. Charity Trends (Pharoah *et al.* 2004) reports on the ten largest fundraising charities, and only one (Comic Relief) is less than 40 years old. Also, Pharoah points out that half of these ten were in the original top ten in 1978 when the series started; and all of the original ten are still in the top twenty! Few company brands could match this longevity.

However, most of the figures in this chapter so far are a snapshot. How are the income sources of these general charities changing over time and are there any trends we should be picking up? Table 9.4 is illuminating.

Table 9.4 Comparison of the percentage changes in income source growth over two time periods

Types of transaction	Real % growth 1991–2001	Real % growth 1995–2001
Earned income	15%	18%
Voluntary income (excluding legacies)	31%	4%
Legacies	45%	17%
Total investments	55%	21%
Total income	32%	12%

Source: Bruce, using the CSO Survey of Charitable Organisations 90/91 and adjusting NCVO 96/97 Almanac figures for 94/95 into a 2001 RPI base and comparing on a like-for-like basis with figures in the NCVO 2002 Almanac.
The 2004 Almanac uses an updated methodology and its figures are not comparable.

Thirty-two per cent real growth over ten years and 12 per cent over six years are both substantial, but the latter shows a slowing of the total rate of growth. Within this overall picture voluntary income is still growing but at a much, much slower rate than in the first half of the 1990s. On the other hand, earned income, which was flat or declining in that early period is now rising by as much as 4 per cent per annum in real terms. Other figures in the NCVO Almanac, adjusted for inflation, show some interesting trends. While contracted out services by the state (thus bringing in fee income – 18 per cent of sector income) are a big part of the story, so is the purchase of service by individuals (17 per cent of sector income). Both these subsets of earned income are growing. Individually paid fees grew by 12 per cent in real terms over the six years but government fees grew by 22 per cent over the same period. Legacies have performed consistently well over the period, confounding those who said the increased cost of old age would leach out large sums – however we need more time to be confident. Investments performed well but these figures do not take account of the large stock market falls since 2001. All these figures are in real terms, that is, inflation adjusted.

Fundraising

There are many books on charity fundraising but Sargeant and Jay's excellent 'Fundraising Management' (2004) looks at the subject from a marketing viewpoint.

Sources

The lay person's view of charity fundraising fixes on activities such as rattling tins or chugging in the street; sponsored events such as marathons and walks; and the increasing amount of charity mail that drops through the letterbox. In fact, this overt activity produces a fraction of net charity fundraised income. Fundraising is much broader. Colloquially, even in many charities, fundraising is restricted to donations in their most straightforward sense of individuals, companies or trusts giving money. However, among professional fundraising charities it is synonymous with 'voluntary income' and covers all charity income (including gifts in kind) except fees, charges, sales of services and goods related to the charity's prime purpose; statutory income; and investment and rental income. Voluntary income or fundraised income therefore covers such activities as company donations, gifts in kind, sponsorship and secondment; charity and trust donations; and individual donations, sponsorship legacies, and charity goods. Arguably, and some charities do it this way, statutory grants and the 'gift' of voluntary work should also be included. The approach required for company sponsorships and donations has many similarities to that needed to achieve statutory grants. Again, recruiting volunteers has similarities with recruiting donors.

Statutory sector	*Commercial sector*
Grants	Donations
	Sponsorship
	Gifts in kind
	Secondment
Charity and trust donations	Donations
Donated profits of subsidiaries	Legacies
	Time and donations (e.g. sponsorship)
	Charity goods
	Voluntary service work
Voluntary sector	*Informal sector (individuals)*

Figure 9.1 Sources of giving

Figure 9.1 gives a graphical representation of the sources of giving (excluding fees and charges/sales, investment, rents and other income) and Table 9.2 (page 233) shows the spread of voluntary income sources. Individual donations and government grants (not linked to a contract) are the two largest sources, followed by trusts and legacies. Company donations and trading provide relatively little income. Looking at the position over time, all these sources are expanding and need investment if voluntary income is to be maximised.

The distribution of fundraised income laid out in Table 9.2 can be summarised as shown in Table 9.5, with the second column showing the percentage rise in real terms for the six years ending 2001, where known, using the same methodology as outlined above for Table 9.4.

Table 9.5 Distribution of fundraised income and percentage rise 1995–2001

Source	% of total income	Real rise 1995–2001
Individuals' gifts and donations	14	0
Public sector grants	17	3
Lottery distributor grants	3	
Voluntary sector grants (trusts etc)	5	6
Private sector (company) gifts and donations	3	18
Legacies	6	17
Private sector fees and sponsorship	2	43
Gross income from trading subsidiaries	5	44
Other income sources (e.g. fees, contracts and investments	45	
Total general charity income	**100**	**32**

Source: Column 1, NCVO Almanac 2004; Column 2, Bruce, adjusting NCVO 96/97 Almanac figures for 94/95 into a 2001 RPI base and comparing on a like for like basis with figures in the NCVO 2002 Almanac.

These figures are portentous. Perhaps most significant is the fact that gifts and donations only keep pace with inflation over the six years. Even more worrying is that Jas *et al.* (2002) reported that these sources declined in real terms by 3.1 per cent at the end of the period. This indicates the importance of the beneficial tax changes such as the Gift Aid extension in 2000, and there are some signs that the position has improved since 2001 (see Walker in Pharoah *et al.* 2004) Nevertheless the inability of our sector to increase individual giving at the same rate as other sources of income is one of its most important challenges. We need the money for services and we need it to match the growth in government money in order to ensure our continued independence.

The growth, albeit small, in public sector grants suggests that what many people feared – that grants would drop, with the missing money being funnelled into narrowly focused contracts resulting in reduced independence – has not happened. Voluntary sector grants and legacies are showing healthy growth, which is encouraging especially given the very low cost ratios involved in raising funds from these sources. However, the champions of the growth league are the companies, whose income growth, at long last puts them into contention as a significant income contributor to the sector (totalling 7 per cent). Trading has also shown similar healthy gains.

Individual giving

The above tables are derived from money received by general charities and analysed through their accounts. Table 9.6 ooks at how individuals say they give, as measured by an NOP public opinion poll commissioned by NCVO (reported in Hems and Passey 1995). The figures should be approached with care because they record what people *say* they did, which may or may not be what they *actually* did. The bracketed figures are for 1995 and the unbracketed figures are for seven years later in 2002, showing trends (Jas *et al.* 2002).

The second column shows the percentage of individuals who gave by the method detailed in the first column, so 21 per cent of people gave via street collections but, in total, these donations only made up 2.9 per cent of individual giving. As a general rule, the more personal the 'ask' the more likely people are to give (see high percentages in the second column). However, the average donation may be quite low. Planned giving is the ideal method from the charity's point of view for three reasons. First, it is easier to ensure that the charity receives tax back in addition to the value of the gift; second, the giving is normally regular and predictable; and third, the donor needs less servicing in terms of prompts and thus it is much more cost effective.

The table shows some significant trends. The percentage of people giving via street and door to door collections has declined considerably and the percentage of income these methods provide has halved. These

Table 9.6 Ways of giving

	% donors		% given	
Street collection	21	(28)	2.9	(7)
Door to door collection	16	(27)	3.5	(7)
Buying raffle/lottery tickets (excluding National Lottery)	14	(18)	5.2	(6)
Buying in a charity shop	12	(9)	7.4	(5)
Shop counter collection	10	(10)	1.5	(2.3)
Church collection	10	(12)	12	(12)
Sponsorship	8	(11)	12	(12)
Collection at work	6	(8)	4.2	(2.7)
Buying goods for a charity	5	(6)	3.1	(5)
Pub collection	4.9	(8)	1.7	(2)
Appeal letter	4.7	(3.5)	5.2	(5.2)
Buying in a jumble sale	3.5	(5.5)	1.7	(2.7)
Attending a charity event	3.4	(4.4)	8	(5.1)
Subscription/membership fee	2.7	(3.3)	3.7	(4.2)
Covenant	2.5	(3.2)	8.7	(10)
Buying through a charity catalogue	2.4	(2.7)	3.6	(3.6)
TV or radio appeal	2.0	(3.0)	1.9	(2.0)
Payroll deduction	1.9	(1.6)	1.6	(0.9)
Telephone appeal	1.0	(0.6)	1.1	(0.8)
Appeal advertisement	0.9	(0.7)	0.8	(1.3)
Affinity card	0.4	(0.3)	0.8	(0.1)
Stocks and shares	0.1	0.1		
Other	5.7	9.6		

Source: NCVO Almanacs 2002 (and 1995).

are fundraising methods in decline. Raffle tickets, church collections and sponsorship are holding their own. Buying in a charity shop, attending charity events and collecting at work are in the ascendancy, at least as far as percentage of total giving is concerned. The first two give some support to the idea that donors respond more to 'getting something back' from their donations. There are one or two more recent methods, such as affinity cards and telephone appeals, but even after some years of development they are not big volume contributors.

Expanding the donations market has been a concern for many years. The last decade has seen some interesting partnership initiatives to attempt achieve this. There have been several legacy consortia and the three-year Giving Campaign brought together the Treasury, Inland

Revenue and many charities to produce a number of useful achievements. These included the 'gift aid it' brand, the Giving Nation, and particular work among financial advisers to help raise richer people's individual percentage donations.

Fundraising methods

Fundraising methods are as various as the ingenuity of fundraisers and the volunteers who work with them. However, there are some widely understood broad categories of fundraising methods. The previous section indicated the importance of the different methods of individual giving in terms of their total contribution to charity voluntary income. In this section the main forms of giving from a wider variety of sources are listed in categories according to my estimate of the general cost-effectiveness of the method. The percentages are quoted to indicate the proportion of the gross income depleted by costs. In other words, a 20 per cent cost ratio means that every £1 of gross income raised costs 20 pence, so the net income is 80 pence. As a generalisation, charities accept higher cost ratios on giving methods that contribute larger volumes of income, often via many smaller donations.

Legacies

These are one of the largest homogeneous and most cost-effective income source for charities. Nearly one in ten legators leave a charitable bequest (Ford 1996). They provide 6–7 per cent of total charity income (or around 14 per cent of voluntary income) and this rises considerably in the largest charities. It is therefore surprising that legacies have been the Cinderella area of fundraising attention, except for a number of charities such as RNLI, Barnardo's, SCOPE, RNIB and the cancer charities. For these larger charities, sometimes achieving 40 per cent or more of their total income from legacies, the cost of an active promotional programme is 1 or 2 per cent. In 2005 *The International Journal of Non-profit and Voluntary Sector Marketing* published a special issue on legacies to charities, which contains a wealth of useful information (Pidgeon 2005).

However, legacy marketing would seem at best to be a rather forlorn long-term hope, and there is no certain, although plenty of anecdotal, evidence on why or how charities get them (with the exception perhaps of those charities, such as cancer charities, closely linked to the dying process). The charities with large legacy incomes must be doing something right! For example, RNIB has been writing twice a year to every legacy solicitor in the country for over fifty years, and almost 70 per cent of its voluntary income comes from this source.

Increasingly the larger legacy receivers, and some relatively new entrants such as SCOPE and the World Wildlife Fund (WWF) have been developing and implementing sophisticated legacy marketing plans. The hypothesis has been developed (but not yet proven) that loyal donors can be encouraged to make a final and substantial donation via a legacy. However, this hypothesis needs to be followed up with a great deal of care and sensitivity for the obvious reason that death is for most people quite a frightening prospect. A second hypothesis, supported by disability and disease charities, is that people who are beneficiaries or close to a charity's beneficiaries are more likely to leave a bequest, and evidence is coming through to support this.

Another approach taken by certain charities is distributing free leaflets describing how people can make wills in general, in the hope that this might encourage the will-maker to remember the charity promoting the leaflet. While this service started by spreading leaflets like confetti, the process has now moved into the realms of sophisticated direct marketing. This means that the cost per 1,000 of take-up of leaflets is measured, follow-up letters go to leaflet requesters and fairly sophisticated means are used to encourage people to pledge or declare to the charity that they have included the charity in their will. Charities can achieve a surprisingly quick return in the form of proved legacies in the bank. Several charities have achieved their first bequest in the bank in less than a year after recording legacy pledges. This is because the average time between making a last will and death is between two-and-a-half and four years.

Of the four marketing strategies (promotion to intermediaries such as solicitors, promotion to existing loyal donors, promotion to beneficiaries and promotion to people who want more information about will making) all seem to hold a good deal of promise. A good promotional programme for local or national charities with an appealing cause should be showing through within five years. One last statistic should give encouragement – whereas seven in ten people give to charity, only one in twenty leave any money to charity in their wills, so there is plenty of room for market expansion (Walker and Pharoah 2002). Certainly many charities think there are expansion possibilities. The Remember a Charity campaign is run by well over 100 charities with the support of the professional bodies of financial advisers along with law firms and banks. Its purpose is to encourage more people to leave money to charities via their wills. Dauncey (2005) describes the UK Legacy Campaign and its public influence.

Commentators have, for many years, been forecasting the demise of the charity legacy, primarily because of predictions that people living longer will use up their wealth paying rising care costs. There must be some truth in these arguments, but luckily there is so far relatively little evidence of these impacts showing through. Abdy and Farmelo (2005) has reviewed recent legacy trends.

Trust donations

Charitable trusts provide quick returns (six to twelve months) with low cost ratios of 10 per cent or less. Trusts and the Lottery provide around 8 per cent of total income; and smaller charities do particularly well by this method. However, the halcyon days (if they ever existed) of sending a standard request to all the large charitable trusts listed in a trusts directory are gone. An effective marketing approach requires the charity applicant to know the areas of interest of the trust and the typical levels of grant given; if at all possible to arrange a meeting, or at least a short telephone conversation with the trust administrator; and to produce an application personalised to the trust. Any prior contact with one of the trustees can often be a tremendous help.

Big gift fundraising

In its modern and sophisticated form, this is another highly cost-effective method, which should achieve a cost ratio of 20 per cent or less. In its most usual form it consists of recruiting an active leader of industry, a member of the aristocracy or acknowledged leader of the donating constituency, to chair an appeals committee of similar but lesser leaders.

More recently formal committees have been less attractive and the grouping activity has become more informal and segmented, but the principle remains the same. Each involved person helps the charity to make personal approaches to peers within their own area to seek donations. It is quite normal for a medium-sized national charity to raise £5 million by this method, and for a large charity to raise between £10 million and £20 million. Oxford University has raised £256 million this way!

The higher cost ratio is because of the extensive time involved in getting the campaign to the launch point. It will typically take two years of a full-time, fairly senior development director, plus the involvement of significant time from senior charity staff and trustees, to recruit sufficiently wealthy and prestigious donors.

While the sums may seem large, with a formal appeal committee the combination of two years' planning and around two years to achieve the donations and pledges means that the sum is essentially covering a five- to seven-year cycle, if one is to leave a fallow period before starting the process over again. It is also fair to point out that some of the valuable sources of income will be the trusts mentioned in the previous section.

This method is not without its problems. The appeal committee can become more interested in how the charity should be run than in fundraising; influential people can have a real block about asking others for money; the best people are over-asked and are not prepared to spend the time; and chairs/leaders are particularly difficult to recruit. So some charities have dropped the committee component and kick start the process by having staff leaders invite potential prospects to small prestigious or interesting gatherings. Initial take up may be low, but once one or two big gift potential donors have been drawn in, others will soon follow. The key is to give these people brilliant attention – the red carpet treatment – customer service at its most outstanding. This recruitment and support process can be closely linked to charity events such as exclusive dinner parties or receptions where 'asks' are made. The most important point to remember is to thank, thank and thank again! If someone has given a substantial sum, they deserve this and are hardly likely to repeat their donation if they do not feel sufficiently appreciated and involved.

Corporate giving

Companies and their associated trusts have gained in popularity as a source of charitable income over the last couple of decades, not least through the leadership of some of the major companies in encouraging a corporate philanthropy. In pure donations of money they (only) contribute just around 3 per cent per cent of charities' income and around a further 2 per cent via sponsorship. However, the figures in Table 9.5 (page 237) show that this source is growing fast.

Broadly speaking, there are four categories of corporate giving. *Donations*, which are very similar in form to those coming from charitable trusts (very few strings attached); *gifts in kind* in the form of goods, services or seconded personnel – once again with few strings attached; *company-specific sponsorship* activities, sometimes called cause-related marketing, where the company 'donates' money in a very public way, linked to its own business activity (such as 5 pence going to the RSPCA for every returned pet food label, or royalties to a charity for the use of its logo (such as WWF's panda on product labels) because of the anticipated benefit to the product). Cause-related marketing has grown quickly in the USA and is growing here, although Sargeant and Stephenson (1997) report low penetration among local businesses. Cause-related marketing is considered in more detail later, under 'Partnership marketing'. Finally, there is *company-specific staff schemes*, where the company sees morale and commitment advantages in involving their staff in charitable activities. Examples include BA staff redecorating a charity school, Asda store staff raising money for a charity over a year, or a general policy of encouraging staff to become involved in local charitable activity – this being seen as an investment in the goodwill of the local community (for example, Barclays will match, or even double match, a staff member's personal donation to a charity).

It will be immediately apparent that honing a proposal that takes account of the company's particular position and its corporate needs takes up more time (and therefore money) than reasonably straightforward approaches to trusts. This is why this form of fundraising can go as high as 20 or 30 per cent in cost ratio, not least because of the 'after-sales service' that has to be applied, especially in the last two categories. The company will expect significant publicity and public relations benefits to accrue which, once again, requires the charity to allocate time and funds.

Employee donations

There can be an argument for this activity being a subset of the previous section except that it is specifically employee rather than company directed. In its formal tax-advantageous form, the total contribution to charity income is small but the amount is growing significantly (Pharoah *et al.* 2004).

Some charities, such as Barnardo's, have had long-established programmes (50 years or more) of commercial company employees giving a deduction from their pay packet year after year to the charity. This form of giving (payroll giving) is encouraged fiscally through additional tax breaks. The cost ratio in the first year can be quite high, in the 40–80 per cent range, but if the donations are sustained, they become one of the most attractive long-term investments, reducing to below 10 per cent per year. However, experience of the longer-established charities in this field shows what the commercial business sector already knows – donors need to be nurtured over the years, otherwise they will be lost.

Special events

This is the glamorous end of charity fundraising: the film premières, charity balls, exclusive dinner parties, publicity-seeking awards. Well handled (and taking account of sponsorship), the cost ratio can be in the 20–50 per cent range, so they justify this current positioning in the list of fundraising methods. Local special events run entirely by volunteers can reduce this cost ratio. However, badly managed special events can, in truth, make losses even if the charity does not declare them as such.

Special events often use the same organisational methods as big gift campaigns; the difference is that special events are speculative business activities. Take one of the most straightforward ones, that of the film première. Its success depends on the film having generated the relevant early publicity; the ability to attract a prestigious Royal and the stars; the ability to sell the cinema seats at a considerable premium over normal seat prices; the ability to fill the seats with a majority of paying guests. In short, it is a nightmare. For example, trying to coordinate the diaries of royalty and the stars is difficult; quite a few stars are unreliable – you may not know until the last minute whether they will turn up – and it is very difficult to predict how popular a film première will be. And a film première is one of the easiest special events to organise!

However, special events are here to stay, not only because they can raise large sums, but also because many influential people in charities, especially leaders of big gift campaigns (see above), like them. If a charity's volunteer corporate leader, who is raising £10 million, particularly wants a special event it can be hard to resist!

Local fundraising

This is the least satisfactory heading because it can cover all of the above activities and many more (see Table 9.6, page 239). However, local fundraising tends to be organised separately and has significantly different cost ratios. Regional or national charities fundraising locally will typically have cost ratios of 40–70 per cent. These percentages are seldom declared, and would not easily be understood by the public. However, for a charity a '50 per cent profit' on expenditure invested is still very attractive and for many charities contributes large sums in terms of gross value – typically larger than any of the above methods, with the probable exception of legacies. Also it is widely believed that local fundraising leads to legacies as well as contributing to sustaining and increasing charity awareness – the lifeblood of the charity brand.

The stock-in-trade of local fundraising consists of collecting boxes, street and door-to-door collections and raffles, church collections, sponsored events such as swims or walks, social events, lotteries, shops and special events. All need a certain amount of paid staff involvement, but the trick is to maximise volunteer involvement to keep costs down. Virtually all large and medium-sized charities have some, or many, paid fundraisers promoting, supporting and even organising fundraising at the local level, with volunteers heavily involved. However, volunteer recruitment is becoming increasingly problematic, not because people are volunteering less, but because there is more competition among charities.

Charity shops (considered in more detail in Chapter 6) are often an essential component of local fundraising.

Direct marketing

Direct marketing, as its name implies, is where the charity tries to go straight to the potential donor through direct mail, press advertisements, radio and, increasingly, on television, telephone and the internet. There has in particular been an enormous expansion of direct mail activity, which every reader will have experienced. Direct response via press advertising probably reached its height in the 1970s and early 1980s and is used less now (at least for fundraising purposes). The cost ratios involved are some of the highest of any fundraising method, ranging between 60 and 130 per cent (a loss). Cynically one might say that the expansion of press advertising direct response in the 1970s and early 1980s and the associated direct mail explosion have in part been caused by aggressive promotion from the advertising agencies and direct mail agencies. However, that is not entirely fair, because it has been seen as reaching new fundraising markets with new products. For a minority of charities it represents their major source of income.

Direct marketing certainly has provided a major flux of marketing information and expertise into the charitable sector via the advertising agencies and direct mail agencies. To support this direct response work, an encouraging amount of market research has been undertaken among donor groups. Terms like 'market penetration', 'cost per thousand' and 'opportunities to see' have become familiar to charity staff previously oblivious to such useful techniques. Direct marketing has also been the bridgehead for introducing relationship marketing into charities (see Burnett 1996 and 2002, Sargeant 2004, Sargeant and Lee 2002, Sargeant and Jay 2004). However, it is important to recognise that there is a variety of strategies not-for-profits can use to relate to donors, which depend on charities' competencies and resources (Saxton 1996b).

Market analysis

There is tremendous pressure on charity fundraisers to perform. This is primarily because of the overwhelming requirement for resources to fund services to end beneficiaries. However, there are other more subtle pressures, which can be equally powerful. First, unlike so much of the rest of a charity's activities, fundraising is all about numbers. It has a measurable bottom line. It is almost possible to hear a sigh of relief from trustees and senior finance managers as the fundraising items come up on the committee agenda – at last here is something they can measure and be hard-nosed about. At the same time everyone becomes an instant expert when it comes to fundraising, even though this may be based on nothing more than personal views on receipt of charity direct mail letters or Christmas card designs!

This primary pressure (the desperate need for more funds) and the three secondary pressures of measurability, measurability in contrast with intangible charity services, and amateur 'expert' judgements, put enormous strains on fundraisers to perform well in a very short time. The successful fundraising charity has to resist pressures for instant success by giving fundraisers time to prove themselves and for financial investment to be given time to work, but must still be objective in the analysis of success and failure.

'Time to prove themselves' must include some careful analysis of the charity's current and potential fundraising markets, and the positioning of competitor charities. In this chapter we can, for the first time, use the term 'competitor charity' with an easy heart. There is no doubt that charities do, and by their very nature have to, compete vigorously for funds. (As an aside, this does not mean that charities do not cooperate over sharing fundraising experiences – commercial companies would be amazed and pleased at the constructive way that this happens in the charity sector through organisations such as the Institute of Fundraising.)

Methods of expansion

Once again we have the four-way marketing choice: existing donors with existing products, existing donors with new products, new donors with existing products, and new donors with new products. It is very important to be clear which of the four are being pursued in what combination and with what priority.

Existing donors

Unless there are strong contra-indications, priority should be accorded to the first choice – existing donors with existing fundraising products. In my experience voluntary sector managers, especially the more dynamic ones, have a tendency to be too dismissive of a charity's traditional experience and activity and over-confident about the new things they will introduce – this applies particularly to fundraisers, who as a breed are required to be optimists! As a generalisation, which is increasingly being supported and asserted in the commercial literature in relation to customers (Reichheld and Sasser 1990; Reichheld 1996; Berry and Parasuraman 1991; Zeithaml and Bitner 2003 and Zeithaml *et al.* 2006), it is more effective and profitable to encourage existing donors to give more and reduce the rate of attrition of donors than always to seek new ones. For example, a significant proportion of donors would give more if we asked for more, asked more frequently and thanked more sincerely. This process would be greatly facilitated if we were more effective at thinking about and valuing our donors (or even keeping track of them!). All too often the key volunteer leaders of big gift campaigns are 'under-thanked' and receive too little feedback about the impact of their efforts on the charity's work; this is similar with trust donors and corporate donors as well as individual donors.

Keeping track

Doing these things greatly enhances the chances of larger and more frequent subsequent donations. It may seem extraordinary that charities lose track of supporters, but we do. My guess is that two charities out of three would be unable to find the names, let alone the addresses, of supporters who attended a charity fundraising dinner as little as five years ago. Reichheld and Sasser's research (1990) shows that, depending upon the industry, profits can be improved by between 25 and 85 per cent through reducing customer loss by as little as 5 per cent. There is no comparable research for charity donors but I am sure it is the correct message for us. There is a very uneven equation between the high costs of recruiting a new (major) donor, be it an individual, a trust, a company or a legator, in comparison with the relatively small amount of gratitude, valuing and cost needed to keep the loyalty of an existing donor for longer (or for ever).

There is one last major reason for initially looking to the first of the four choices. This is that the fundraising products and the methods needed to deliver them are well known to the charity and, by using a marketing approach, they can be improved at little extra cost. In contrast, the time, effort and failure rate of moving to new fundraising products, methods and donors is high and should normally be a second choice.

Criteria for diversification

So far the arguments seem like a recipe for the status quo. What are the conditions for expansion into the other three choices? The most important criterion is under-utilisation of one of the more cost-effective fundraising methods with short lead times (including trusts and companies). Second, the charity may be over-dependent on one form of support (such as legacies or employee fundraising) and may judge that medium-term income stability requires diversification. Third, the fundraising market changes rapidly and methods that were very successful a few years ago are no longer so. The key judgement is to identify when a method is waning. Fourth, competitor charity activity can be influential, crowding the market. There was a period when Help the Aged was one of the few charities successfully raising money via sponsored events organised within schools; it only maintained that position by radically amending its product and method as competitor charities moved heavily into this market.

Donor behaviour

Commercial marketing literature seems to me to be at its least scientific in the area of consumer behaviour, reaching its low point with services rather than goods. The situation is even more problematic in the field of charity marketing, and donor behaviour in particular. For example, the probable difference between what one says one does, and what one actually does, must be vastly magnified in the field of donor behaviour. Halfpenny and Saxon-Harrold (1991, p. 6) list five factors that make it particularly difficult to collect reliable information about individual charitable giving:

1 Selecting a representative sample.
2 Different individual perceptions about what constitutes a charity.
3 Likely overstating of donation behaviour.
4 Difficulty in remembering what was given to whom.
5 The distorting effects of national/international disasters on donor behaviour.

The latter has particular impact. One just has to think back to the impact of the tsunami. Rados (1981) has argued that 'why did you' type questions are at best uninformative and at worst misleading, first because people do not really know why they give, and second because their reasons for giving are likely to be a complex interaction from any list of possible motives.

What the charity fundraising market needs are the long-established consumer buying behaviour reports found in commercial sectors, but it is difficult to see how these could be replicated in the fundraising field with its complex distribution channels.

We therefore have to fall back on opinion surveys and the experience of well-established fundraisers and academics writing in the field. It is both extraordinary and completely understandable that, with a product that is essentially an idea, we have no objective understanding as to why people buy (give to) the product. Several thoughtful lists of motives for giving have been hypothesised (including Lovelock and Weinberg 1984, p. 505 and Andreasen and Kotler 2003), but these are based primarily on experience of the North American donor market, which is different from the British one in many respects, not least because of North Americans' superior generosity towards charities and the different tax benefits of giving. Hibbert and Horne (1996) argue that 'the decision to give seems largely to be a response to a social learning and conditioning' and as a result situational stimuli are also very important in determining giving. Another useful British survey is a series of questions placed by the Institute of Philanthropy into the British Social Attitudes Survey (Institute of Philanthropy 2004). The Economic and Social Research Council is interested in donor motivation, and published a pamphlet on the subject in 2005 (ESRC 2005). Farsides (2005) and Hibbert (2005) both review the literature that discusses whether giving is driven by altruistic or egotistic motives. Farsides suggests that charities should treat donors with respect, offer them opportunities, not pressures, and genuinely care about their concerns. Hibbert looks at what justification non-donors offer and examines how neutralisation, as an explanation of deviant behaviour, might illuminate practice.

If we then overlay any list of likely motives with differing psychological, social and economic factors of the target market, one begins to despair of ever raising money at all! So how can we throw any light on this subject?

Market research

First, a charity fundraising marketer should not be put off from undertaking their own market research among the charity's existing donors. Quantitative research of this kind can be very illuminating in terms of age segmentation, sex and marital status – all attributes easily obtained from mailed questionnaires. Once this is achieved, qualitative market research, through depth interviews, and possibly group discussions, can begin to shed light on particular motivations of key donor groups towards your charity's cause. This approach has certainly helped many charities to identify those groups most likely to give to them, and the variety of reasons that lead them to do so goes a long way towards helping to frame the 'ask' (the proposition for which the charity is seeking funds and way help is asked for).

Finally, while it is probably a mistake to do so (having argued that lists of motives are almost certainly spurious), as a person with a foot in both the practitioner and academic camps I am going to give my list of motives or reasons for giving. It should be used with caution, as it is nothing more than a starting point for a particular charity's consideration. The reasons that bring a person to the point of donation will be complex and interactive rather than singular. Moreover, this list is for the UK situation.

- Being asked.
- A sense of compassion.
- Habit or tradition.
- My religion encourages it.
- As a means of recognition by peers/superiors.
- Knowing someone alive or dead who was in that situation.
- Being, or having been, in that situation myself.
- Because the charity recognises me and keeps me involved.
- To receive benefits accorded to donors and their immediate family.
- Embarrassment (too embarrassed to say no).
- To get rid of the asker.
- Life has treated me well, I have a responsibility to help others less well off.
- Community expectation (new science block for the school).
- Feel good, feel better as a person.

I finish with 'feel good', because if there was one over-arching reason for giving, I believe this is it. The task of the charity fundraiser is to establish what will make any individual or organisation 'feel better' afterwards.

The fundraising product

Fundraising products are essentially ideas. At first this seems strange because the money is required for very tangible activities – food for hungry people, education for disadvantaged groups, activity to stop whaling. But in the vast majority of cases the donor will be relatively distant from the physical goods or services created by their donation. I emphasise 'relatively' distant because there are some situations in which a donor can experience the object of their donation, such as contributing towards saving a picture for the nation and then viewing it. However, this personal experience is still relatively distant from the donation in both time and space. Normally the donor is 'purchasing' an idea they will never see put into practice, or if they do, they will normally have no rights or control over it. Transferred into the commercial scene, this scenario would be either unbelievable or fraudulent!

Nevertheless, fundraising idea product marketing has much to learn from service product marketing. Donating towards a fundraising idea has major similarities with purchasing a service, but also some differences. It is *similar* in that:

- the idea product is intangible;
- ownership is not generally transferred;
- the idea product cannot be resold;
- the idea cannot be easily demonstrated before donation;
- in most cases direct contact between the donor and the charity is necessary.

However, it is *different* to a service in that:

- the idea product can be stored (although it is questionable how meaningful this is);
- production and consumption do not really coincide;
- implementation of the idea is spatially and temporarily separate;
- the idea can be transported and even exported;
- the donor takes no part in the production.

(This is a comparison with the list of attributes of services given by Baker 1991, p. 554 and 2003.)

Constructing

Constructing a fundraising idea product is as simple or difficult as answering all the basic interrogatives. In other words, what is the proposition? Who is it going to benefit? How will it work, and what will the outcome be? However, selecting the proposition from the wide range of activities that the charity is undertaking must be in relation to whom the fundraising idea product is being aimed at. In other words, the benefits of the idea product have to be selected and promoted according to the old marketing mnemonic of AIDA – attention, interest, desire, action.

In essence the fundraiser takes the beneficiary service product and:

- reshapes it into an idea product;
- selects for featuring those beneficiary benefits most likely to appeal to the donor;
- makes the idea product as tangible as possible (Bruce 1994).

Reshaping

How does the fundraiser reshape the product? – by examining the benefits it provides to the beneficiary and selecting those most likely to appeal to the donor. For example, a visiting service to older people may have several effects, including maintaining independence and relieving loneliness. The fundraiser will be more effective as well as legitimate by choosing the attribute most attractive to the donor. What is illegitimate is to choose to feature an attribute which is not part of the beneficiary offering simply because it will appeal to the donor. Some fundraisers in the disability and overseas aid fields have done just that, for example through inviting pity and showing pathetic images to donors when the benefits for beneficiaries are those of empowerment, not dependency .

Tangibility

Virtually all fundraising experience suggests that the more specific the proposal can be, both in its description and outcomes, the better. An idea product of 'helping people overseas' is not nearly as attractive to the donor as '£15 will buy two hoes, two spades, a scythe and 25kg of seeds to enable a family to plant and tend their land, providing them with enough food to be self-sufficient' (Oxfam leaflet).

But however specific and concrete the idea, it is still essentially intangible and the charity fundraiser has to employ the techniques used by goods and services marketers to address this problem. They need to give evidence of tangibility both when asking for money and subsequently, by way of reassurance. Tangibility can be indicated through simple devices such as personalising individuals who are typical of the group of beneficiaries; providing photographs of the work in action; gaining testimonials from people who have been helped, through films and videos of the work; and even producing samples of the work. Examples include an overseas aid charity including a small packet of hydration salts in their direct mail letter, a blind charity enclosing a sample of Braille, or Oxfam encouraging the general public attending exhibitions to operate an appropriate technology water pump.

After-sales service

However, the 'after-sales service', as a service marketer would call it, is extremely important. If someone has purchased something as fragile as an idea, they will need subsequent reassurance to establish and maintain trust, which is perhaps the most vital aspect of the relationship between a charity and its donors. Wherever possible (and it is not always so), the fundraising marketer will give donors progress reports with either explicit or implicit opportunities to achieve continuing financial support. This formula, which is a product attribute, is applicable to every method of fundraising apart from receipt of a legacy!

Service component

Because idea products alone are so intangible, fundraisers have introduced service components such as fundraising dinners, sponsored walks and film premières into their fundraising. There has to be an idea product at the core of any of these events, but the presenting product is effectively a service that encourages the exchange between the donor and the charity. Introducing the strong service component makes life very complicated for the charity marketer as described above in the section on different fundraising methods and in the case example of the fundraising dinner in Chapter 1. In the service component, the three extra 'Ps' of service marketing – people, physical evidence and processes – come into play. For example, the attitude and behaviour of charity staff in personal contact with donors become crucial to successful outcomes; similarly the effect of other participant donors is crucial. If 10 per cent of the participants of a sponsored walk are what might colloquially be called 'lager louts', what does that tell loyal family supporters about the charity? Will they continue to be loyal?

Physical goods

The most concrete form of fundraising products are physical goods, as described in Chapter 6. They are items that the purchaser donor would almost certainly have bought anyway (such as Christmas cards or goods from a charity's catalogue), but they choose to buy them from the charity at similar prices, but with the added value of the charity branding.

Simultaneous multiple products

Any marketer who has not by now gained a graphic picture of the complexity of managing charity work, as attested to by Drucker (1990, p. 83), is likely to do so under this section! For example, it is not unusual for charity fundraisers to be marketing a fundraising idea, a fundraising service and fundraising physical goods at the same time. An obvious example is the fundraising dinner. Here the core fundraising *idea* to, say, equip a new classroom, has to be established with a clear target sum, and the idea has to be effectively communicated to supporters before, during and after the dinner. However, the *service* of the dinner itself has to be marketed (which aristocrats, dignitaries or stars are going to be there and what opportunities will there be to meet them?). Who will be your peers at the dinner and are they the kind of people you wish to meet? Can the answer to the latter question be indicated by the prestigious venue, the price and the menu? Will there be entertainment, and if so, do you declare who will be providing this in advance even though it may put some people off?

On the evening itself, how do you staff it with sufficient charity representatives to provide back-up, but not so many as to make the diners feel that there are charity freeloaders? Given that many tables will be booked by one person on behalf of about a dozen other people, how do you get their names and addresses for follow-up work without appearing unduly nosy? These are just some of the service marketing challenges that have to be met and designed beforehand.

There will also be the obvious *physical goods* aspect of the service, such as the quality of the food, and there will almost certainly be a raffle of donated items which is often the most profitable element of the event. This requires auction prizes that will appeal to those people attending, who in turn have to have enough money to purchase them, and should be advised in advance about what items are likely to be auctioned, but advised in such a way as not to scare them off!

And somehow in the middle of all this convivial and quite frequently inebriate enjoyment, the idea product of the equipment for the classroom has to be made as tangible as possible because memories lapse and people are not there simply to have a good time – they came with the purpose of raising money for your core idea product.

Price

Some of the previous examples will begin to indicate the complexity of pricing decisions in the marketing mix when it comes to charity fundraising offerings.

Levels

Something as simple as a price level poses difficulties. The fundraising idea can be defined in such a way as to get different price levels, and these are in part determined by the likely acceptability to potential donors. For example, Help the Aged's appeal for overseas, '£12 to make a blind person see', seems an incredible bargain. Is it actually too cheap to be believable? If it is, then the text of the appeal needs to explain why it is such a good bargain. Also, such a low price might depress the total income level achieved for the idea. Therefore the charity has to consider upping the price by including the legitimate extra overhead costs, or by encouraging people to help restore the sight of ten or even one hundred people.

Efficient fundraisers will develop a portfolio of fundraising products covering different aspects of the charity's work and different price levels from, say, £5 for a small item of physical goods for a charity beneficiary, right the way up to £1 million to build a new wing to a school.

Terms

Payment terms are complex even for charity fundraisers familiar with the field. These include a one-off payment, regular cash payments, standing orders, covenants, Gift Aid, special charity cheque accounts, payroll deductions, credit cards, sponsorship units, legacies and share gifts. Some of these methods allow the charity to reclaim tax that the donor has already paid (albeit only at the standard rate). As a general rule a charity will wish the donor to enter into a method of planned, continuous giving that will maximise a tax addition to a charity and lock the donor in over time. However, deciding how to achieve this without scaring the donor off can be a complicated and sensitive process.

Promotion

Promotion, which consists of advertising, publicity and public relations, is the very stuff of charity marketing. However, publicity and public relations are considerably more difficult to achieve in the area of fundraising than in the area of service giving. Television, radio and the press are far more hard-nosed about editorial coverage of fundraising activity than they are about service-giving work. Perhaps the pleasant exception to this is the local press. Press, radio and/or TV support of fundraising activity is very much an art rather than a science and, in comparison with commercial products, suffers a chronic lack of under-funding. In part this is because the money simply is not there, and in part it is because the detailed causal link between the advertising of fundraising activity and the final take has not been established. Ali (2001) writes persuasively on this area.

Personal selling

Personal selling receives a very high profile in charity fundraising. Although it only comes from estimates of experienced fundraisers, I am inclined to believe the assertion that personal approaches to donors are five times more effective than telephone approaches, which in turn are several times more effective than written approaches – effective being described in terms of the number of donations achieved and their total value. But what are the attributes of these 'personal sellers'? Bayley (1988, pp. 14–16) describes the key attributes as:

- proven leadership;
- involvement;
- commitment (to the charity, or at least to charity in general);
- community recognition (here community can be one of interest as well as geographic).

Incentives

When we move into the field of sales promotion (or, as charity managers would call it, 'recognition and rewards'), once again the commercial world of money-off initiatives and on-pack competitions seems relatively simple. Major donors, loyal donors and outstanding volunteers are all offered access to a range of incentives. These can be categorised in three main ways:

- status;
- access;
- process.

Status incentives are very varied, but they all provide the donor or volunteer with enhanced status, certainly in the individual's mind and usually more widely among their peers. For example, powerful volunteer fundraising leaders may be made vice-presidents of the charity – prestigious offices only offered to relatively few people. Such offices are sinecures, they do not allow the rewarded person significant involvement in decision-making, at least outside their own area of experience and expertise. Another form of status recognition is naming something, such as a classroom, lifeboat or residential block, in honour of a major donor. Some charities create member grades depending on the length of donor service. Most charities invite major donors to receptions to hear about the charity's work. Some have a donor book where major donor names are recorded and some still list major donors in their annual reports, including people who have left a legacy.

Access incentives operate at the higher levels of donor (or volunteer) contribution level. For traditional, historical reasons charities have ready access to at least the aristocracy, and quite often to royalty. While members of royalty do not always wish to be associated with direct fundraising, they are very happy to meet major supporters at discreetly and decorously arranged receptions. While I would not pretend that access opportunities are a sufficient incentive to secure extraordinary donor effort, they are certainly recognised informally as rewards that can provide peer group recognition on a fairly significant scale. At a 'lower' level, other access opportunities can be provided, such as meeting the charity directors, chief executive, chair or committee chair. For the really interested and committed donor these meetings can be equally if not more satisfying because they learn more about the work and the impact of their donations. Big gift campaigns also provide access incentives in that, for example, business leaders know that they will meet business leaders from other sectors, and 'junior' business leaders will meet 'senior' ones.

Process incentives bears some relationship to status recognition in that it often involves appointing people to committees, but the appointments are working ones rather than sinecures, and generally have lower conventional status. However, they do provide opportunities for committed donors and volunteers to become more heavily involved in the work of the charity, such as certain forms of fundraising or publicity on the basis of their knowledge and expertise. Other forms of process recognition include inviting loyal donors to service establishments or offices and meeting the workers involved in direct service delivery, but on a regular basis.

All these incentives contribute to a relationship marketing approach. Charities are particularly well placed to be able to achieve such relationships, although they are often singularly oblivious and indifferent to these needs of their volunteers and donors. Many donors welcome the opportunity to become more involved in the charity, giving them personal development and the charity more effective advocates. Burnett (1992 and 2002) develops comprehensive arguments on 'relationship fundraising'.

Place/distribution

When selling ideas, their distribution or delivery becomes a much more dominant direct responsibility of the fundraising marketer than their commercial FMCG counterpart. The 'medium is the method' of direct marketing fundraising. Similarly, the voluntary fundraising committees, special events, fundraising, retail shops, postal appeals, jumble sales and collecting boxes are all a part of the method of distribution of fundraising – getting the fundraising idea product out to the potential donor. *Location* of both the fundraising idea product and the potential donor can be crucial. Most charities have strong and weak geographic areas of support, which will have been determined over the years, through, for example, the presence of a stronger service delivery capacity, the strength of the fundraising network in that area or the traditional strength of the fundraising leadership.

Accessibility of donating opportunities is crucial, as are *distribution* channels. In this respect charities connected with faith networks achieve a massive competitive advantage because of their good geographic coverage. National charities spend a great deal of time and effort in extending and strengthening the distribution of their fundraising arms across the United Kingdom.

Conclusion

Fundraising has been the bridgehead through which marketing has increasingly established itself in the charity world. This has been achieved because commercial marketing is relatively easily and effectively translated into fundraising, and because fundraising and public relations have traditionally involved advertising agencies, which have exported marketing concepts and practices.

However, charity fundraisers have adopted these marketing principles and practices in sophisticated ways, often unique to the charity world. This is particularly true of price and promotion in the marketing mix, along with product as an idea.

In contrast with this sophisticated understanding and application of marketing techniques in the product mix, the understanding of donor behaviour in any scientific, objective fashion is in its very early stages. Arguably fundraisers are selling donors nothing but ideas for quite high prices and with virtually no understanding of donor behaviour! It works because donors trust charities to translate their donations into necessary and cost-effective action. Consequently donor trust of charity objectives and activities is one of the most precious and powerful attributes the individual charity, and the sector as a whole, possesses. Anything that substantially dents that trust will spell disaster.

Key points

Each of the main fundraising methods – legacies, trust donations, big gift campaigns, corporate giving (donations, gifts in kind, sponsorship, company-specific staff schemes, payroll deduction), special events, local fundraising and direct marketing – requires a particular marketing approach.

Choosing the method

- Allow fundraisers sufficient time for proper market and competitor analysis.
- Give priority to expanding existing donors and existing fundraising products where these are successful.
- Diversify if existing methods are weak for some reason, for example under-utilisation of methods with short lead times, over-dependence on one form of support, market changes, increased competition.
- Remember that donor behaviour is complex, but quantitative research supported by careful qualitative research can be helpful.

The product

- Constructing the fundraising product and promoting it is similar to a service. What is the proposition? Whom is it for? How will it work? What will the outcome be? Be as specific as possible.
- For the marketer, it is important to note that the fundraising product can operate at a number of levels simultaneously – primarily an idea, but also a service and occasionally a physical good.

Price

- Develop a portfolio of fundraising products at different price levels to attract as wide a group of donors as possible.
- Make payment terms as straightforward as possible to avoid alienating potential donors.

Promotion

- Personal selling is probably the most effective means of promoting the product.
- Reward major and loyal donors or outstanding volunteers with incentives providing status or recognition, access and process.

Place

- Location/distribution of the product is crucial, as is ease of giving.

10 Identity and positioning

Charity identity (increasingly being referred to as the charity brand) and charity positioning are inextricably linked. The charity identity has to reflect its role faithfully, and the role depends heavily on the positioning of the charity in the public's mind in relation to local and national statutory services, commercial organisations and, particularly, other charities. This chapter is the nearest that this book comes to strategic marketing planning, which in the business world has (with some justification) taken over the area known as strategic planning in the charity and statutory organisation worlds. In North America this colonisation has also occurred in the not-for-profit area. However, in the United Kingdom strategic planning in charities is well established and, provided that it assumes a marketing/customer orientated approach, seems to me to serve satisfactorily.

Trust and confidence

Before looking at individual charities it is useful to look at the image or identity of the whole charity sector, as viewed by the public and beneficiaries. The Deakin Commission on the future of the voluntary sector (NCVO 1996) emphasised the importance of public confidence in charities. There is conflicting evidence for this. The fact that around 70 per cent of the public donate to charity and donate billions of pounds each year suggests a very high degree of trust and confidence. However, there has over the years been a decline in trust of many institutions. This does not seem to have hit voluntary organisations so hard (Euro-barometer in Wilding *et al.* 2004) but it is an area where we must be vigilant, as trust is the source of our sector's legitimacy (Henley Centre 1996, Bruce 1998 and Wilding *et al.* 2004).

More worrying was research by Fenton as early as 1995, which reported a survey of 1,000 members of the public in which donors (95 per cent of the sample) were asked about their trust in charities:

- 56 per cent did not believe that donations reached the people they were intended for;
- 52 per cent believed there was corruption in charities, with people pocketing funds;
- 49 per cent believed that too many charities had plush offices, shops, etc.;
- 34 per cent believed too many charities did similar things;
- 17 per cent believed charities were run by disorganised amateurs.

Fortunately there is some evidence that young people are not nearly so negative (Lynn and Davis Smith 1991; Gaskin *et al.* 1996).

Despite the encouraging views of young people, one has to ask why the population of donors is so critical. Could it be unfair media portrayal, so often blamed by groups (such as politicians) who feel they are underrated? Deacon *et al.* (1994) give us no hope here. Having surveyed charity media coverage closely over six months, they concluded that 'there was a remarkable absence of reflective or negative commentary about voluntary activity in news coverage...'. So if journalists should choose to attack charities in the same way that they have attacked many other institutions, we could be in for a rough ride. Indeed charities I meet believe this increased criticism is beginning to happen.

This prompts the question: does it really matter? It could be argued that trust is important for any organisation with customers. But for charities it is much more important. As we have seen in pressure group/ advocacy work and in fundraising, the products are essentially ideas that have to be taken on trust. If donors do not trust a charity, or charities in general, then the donations are at risk. If voters, politicians and civil servants do not trust charities, will they embrace our campaigning ideas? Will new beneficiary customers come forward in large numbers?

So it is incumbent on charities, if they are to have a sympathetic audience, to put and keep their houses in order. Each charity that exhibits low standards is likely to fuel customer mistrust. Thus the way in which we develop (consciously or unconsciously) our individual charity identities or brands is important not only to the particular charity, but to the whole sector.

Charity identity (brand)

The charity identity is the very personality of the organisation as perceived by the target markets. I use it as an alternative to the term 'brand', used in commercial marketing, where individual lines of physical goods have brands and brand names (for example Persil). Generally speaking, as far as services go, the brand is associated with the company (for example Virgin) (for a discussion of commercial brands see de Chernatony 2003 or Aaker 2002). I prefer to use the term 'charity identity' because of the commercial overtones of the term 'brand', which are unattractive to the charity world. From now on I use these terms inter-changeably. Sometimes the term corporate identity is used.

It is useful in understanding the importance and value of a charity identity or brand to look at the commercial world, where brand equity is the financial value of a brand and is based on factors such as the extent of brand loyalty, name awareness, perceived quality, the strength of brand associations, other assets such as patents and trademarks, and communication and distribution channel relationships. You can see the financial value of brands when, in company takeovers, the purchaser appears to pay well over the odds for another company just because it has highly valued brands. For example, Nestlé paid far more than the strict value of Rowntree assets in order to purchase the Rowntree name and its individual brands. While it may not appear on the balance sheet, a strong, well-supported brand can be said to be a company's most enduring asset.

The charity brand and brand image (the charity identity) is just as, if not more, valuable and has to be carefully nurtured to gain maximum success.

Constituent parts

If the charity identity is the very personality of the organisation, what are its constituent parts? The most obvious constituent is the charity name, but other valuable elements include the logo or representative symbol, well-established slogans, publicly sited buildings, especially shops, signs, vehicles, publications, staff (their presentation, attitudes and behaviour), supporters and beneficiaries. Indeed the whole representation of the charity to its target markets constructs the identity. The *physical representation* of the charity to the general public and potential beneficiaries (via name, logo and so on) can be firmly controlled by the charity. But because services are so dominant in the charity field, the *direct experiences* of the large numbers of supporters and beneficiaries are crucial in establishing the charity identity.

Why is charity identity so important?

If we learn from the commercial world of brands, it is because well known identity/brand *simplifies choice* for potential customers (in our case mainly beneficiaries and supporters). It guarantees *quality* and it allows *self-expression* (McNeal and Zeren 1981, p. 35). As a guarantee of quality it is important to all charity customers but especially for targeted decision-makers (Parminter 1997). More fundamentally, it allows customers to distinguish between charities in general and between charities operating within specific fields (say, children). Charity brands have rightly received increasing attention over the last ten years (see Hankinson G. 2004; Hankinson P. 2000; Bruce 1994 and 1998; Pidgeon 1996) because of the value and values locked up in them.

It is more difficult for smaller charities to create strong identities because they have fewer resources and often an unsupportive organisational culture towards marketing. Nevertheless it is vital, and Dixon (1997) describes how Crisis, a medium-sized UK charity for single homeless people, has achieved this using a marketing approach. Small local charities can boost the strength of their local identity by joining an appropriate national umbrella network, such as Age Concern or MIND.

Charity customers face a bewildering choice with 180,000 or so registered charities, plus all the other not-for-profit organisations such as hospitals. A strong charity brand will be chosen more often by customers, not only within the market sub-sector such as overseas aid or disability, but also across the whole not-for-profit market. A strong charity identity will also give customers reassurance about the quality and effectiveness of the work undertaken, a tag to help customers instantly recall their favourable perceptions. A strong charity identity will also attract certain kinds of customer. Greenpeace supporters are likely to be very different from Age Concern supporters, who in turn are very different from Royal Opera House supporters.

If that is why a strong brand is useful to customers, why is a strong charity identity so important to us? First, a strong brand gives us a high *awareness*, which is obviously a necessary, but not sufficient, requirement for a large donor base and a large beneficiary take-up rate. Perhaps more importantly a strong charity brand gives us *customer loyalty*. Customer loyalty is crucial because it is estimated to be up to ten times more costly to recruit a new customer than it is to keep an existing one. And this is at the heart of the benefit of a strong charity identity, namely that the marketing spend is much more cost effective when a charity has a strong identity with its concomitant large customer base.

A final reason for our need for a strong charity identity is that it allows what the commercial marketers call brand extension – launching new products under the brand name. In essence this allows the charity with a strong identity to extend its work into a different but related area on the back of its good reputation. The extension could be into a new geographic area or into a new work function. For example, following the remarkable success of Band Aid, through Live Aid, a number of events and organisations were launched with the word 'aid' in the title. Commercial marketers would argue, and I think they are right, that WaterAid's launch and present success will have been helped by the acquired communication strength of the word 'aid' and the generally good reputation of other events and activities under the 'aid' headline.

Customer positioning

It is also important to be clear that charity identity or brand image is not what *we* think it is or want it to be, but rather how it is actually perceived by existing and potential customers (customer positioning). Of course, we must have aspirations for our charity identity, but they must be realistic and they must develop out of the reality of our current *perceived* charity identity, otherwise the claim will be incredible to customers. As charity positioning is the target market's perception of the charity it is clear that any attempts to reposition have to be researched after re-launch to check whether and how they have been received. I never cease to be amazed by the number of re-launches that are claimed to be a success by the charity without any supporting evidence from customers.

In concise form, then, I would define a charity identity or brand as 'the interaction of the target market's values with the received knowledge and experience of the charity'.

Individual values

Individual values are crucial. If a potential supporter does not believe that there is a role for charities and that such provision should be supplied by the state, then their reception of the messages coming from a charity will be considerably different from someone generally supportive of charitable endeavours. The distinction between knowledge and experience is also important. The charity can do much to control the information going out to target markets and, all things being equal, potential customers will take the information at face value. However, once a potential customer (either beneficiary or supporter) has turned into an actual one, they will judge the charity identity to a greater extent on the basis of their experience, rather than on the more straightforward charity messages transmitted via advertising, publicity and public relations.

Target markets

For analytical, planning and service delivery reasons, it is important to distinguish between various target markets. Chapter 3 lays out a typology of customers, consisting of beneficiaries, supporters, stakeholders and regulators. That is not to say that there will never be any overlap between two or more of these groups which, for example, in mutual aid organisations beneficiaries are supporters and vice versa. However, for the majority of charities, in most situations, these groups are distinct.

A further important distinction is between *potential* and *actual* customers. As was described in the previous section, because charities are service dominated, actual direct experience of the charity has a powerful and distinct impact on how it is regarded.

As in the commercial world, charities spend a great deal of time, money and effort in addressing potential supporters, and often do much less with their existing supporters. Not only can this be expensive (see Chapter 9), it can also undermine charity identity.

On the other hand, charities are sometimes less assiduous in promoting to their potential beneficiaries. This is for a variety of reasons, not least the frequent difficulty of securing effective channels through which to reach them. However, an underlying inhibitor is that, in general, the more beneficiaries a charity recruits, the more money it 'loses' (the more it has to achieve through other forms of income generation). There is therefore not the same incentive for charities to reach out to potential beneficiaries as there is for commercial companies to reach more consumers.

These conclusions are particularly important in relation to charity identity, because lost or undervalued supporters obviously do a great deal to undermine a positive charity image; and loss of opportunity among potential beneficiaries similarly reduces the charity's ability to promote its identity.

Why is charity identity development so difficult?

Commercial managers and academics have been open enough to acknowledge that in certain respects charity management, and charity marketing in particular, is very difficult because of our multiple customer groups (Drucker 1990, p. 83). Charity identity development, or what in commerce would be called brand development, is perhaps the most difficult area. Why? Because in the charity brand one has to have a consistently presented identity acceptable to all four customer groups – beneficiaries, supporters, stakeholders and regulators. If one 'says' different things to different customer groups this will become obvious and the charity will put in jeopardy that most valuable charity asset – trust.

Priorities

Why should we be tempted to say different things to different groups? The answers are not pleasant and represent a part of charity history we should like to forget. In this analysis I dwell only on beneficiaries and individual donor supporters. Beneficiaries often have no choice but to accept the charity offerings, but donors may go to any number of competitor charities and have their needs met. So for certain periods of their history some charities have sacrificed their overriding commitment to beneficiary needs and given priority to donor desires, which can sometimes undermine beneficiary needs. Examples of this were the emaciated children on the direct response adverts of overseas aid charities that left no dignity to the beneficiaries, or the disability charities that used pathetic images of beneficiaries to gain more donor support.

So in developing their identities, charities have to accept that they (a) cannot maximise their brand strength with all customer groups and (b), in my view, have to give priority to beneficiary needs and desires even though this could weaken the appeal to the supporter group. While this may seem morally obvious and legally required (by charity law) it is not infrequently challenged by fundraisers. The most subtle challenge is to argue that supporter needs are 'equal' to those of beneficiaries. In my experience this results in messages which undermine beneficiaries.

Professionalism

It is reassuring that Tapp (1996), in an admittedly small survey, found that 'much of their [charities] day-to-day management is, however, concerned with such issues as maintaining a consistent style and tone of voice, and careful reviews of policies and actions to ensure they reflect their personality'. However, Pidgeon (1996) is not so sanguine about charities' ability to be professional in their approach to identity/brand development. He concludes from his considerable experience in charity direct marketing that, unlike his agency's commercial clients, charity clients were often almost unable to brief him in depth on 'the brand, the brand values and the position the brand holds in the market place'.

Both sets of evidence are reconcilable because, in my experience, charities have got better at ensuring 'consistent style and tone of voice' but seldom get to grips with (often unspoken) core values, what we stand for and what other relevant players stand for. These aspects need to be articulated, written down and formally agreed.

What constitutes the charity identity?

In discussing identity it is useful to distinguish between the presented identity (through one-way messages from charity to potential customer), perceived identity and experienced identity (where the customer and charity interact, normally in a support service setting or a beneficiary service setting).

Presented identity

Presented identity is the sum of the messages we send out to actual and potential customers: our purposes, values, activities and effectiveness.

ιe consistent presentation of the name and logo. Pidgeon
s that, while commercial organisations view their brands
comp.~   ively and consistently, charities view their identities
narrowly, simply as the graphic representation of their names and logos,
normally consistently displayed. In my experience Pidgeon's view is
correct.

Name

Of the attributes presented to customers, the name is clearly the most
powerful element of the identity mix. The value to charity identity of
names such as Save the Children, Help the Aged and Guide Dogs for the
Blind is massive.

Berry and Parasuraman (1991) propose four criteria for assessing the
power of a brand name, which would seem equally relevant to a charity
name:

1 Distinctiveness – the name immediately distinguishes the firm from
   competitors.
2 Relevance – the name conveys the nature or benefit.
3 Memorability – the name can be understood, used and easily
   recalled.
4 Flexibility – the name accommodates organisations' inevitable
   strategy changes.

The most dramatically successful names in the charity world fulfil all
these criteria. Guide Dogs for the Blind fulfils the first three but is left
with very little flexibility to do anything else but provide guide dogs for
blind people. The British Red Cross fulfils all the criteria except for
relevance. It is very distinctive, memorable and flexible but the majority
of people simply do not know what the Red Cross does in this country.
What was the World Wildlife Fund (WWF) and is now the Worldwide
Fund for Nature has had continuing challenges associated with its name.
It has always been distinctive but not very memorable, and on occasions
insufficiently flexible. It has solved the problem by using the initials
WWF wherever possible, which works particularly well given its
international remit.

However, it is important to point out that names can be very
successful even when they do not fulfil every criterion. Greenpeace must
be one of the most successful names and is certainly distinctive,
memorable and flexible – but it does not convey, at least immediately,

what the organisation does. However, the dramatic exploits of the organisation have more than overcome that problem.

Berry and Parasuraman also argue that where a name has significant weaknesses as well as strengths, a decision to change it should still not be taken lightly. This is certainly the case with established charities that have a tremendous stock of awareness and goodwill built into their brand names, deriving in the main from decades, sometimes hundreds of years, of investment. In commercial marketing this is called brand equity and is sometimes valued on the balance sheet.

Logo

Also powerful in identity is the charity logo. WWF's panda, the Red Cross logo and so on are very powerful elements of the identity mix. In the case of WWF, the panda logo is probably better known than the name of the organisation and as such is extremely valuable – indeed so valuable that it is 'sold' on to commercial companies in joint promotional activity. Commercial exploitation of charity names and logos is a contentious area, with passionate advocates on both sides. Some argue that the proper commercial exploitation of names and logos is not only valuable in income terms, but is also useful in spreading the message. Others argue that the purity of a charity identity is absolutely crucial in encouraging and maintaining supporters' and beneficiaries' trust, and that commercial exploitation degrades the identity. As in most cases, the true position is probably somewhere in the middle – commercial exploitation is beneficial providing that the criteria for acceptable use are strictly laid down and, even more importantly, strictly monitored. The Vegetarian Society has from time to time suffered because its 'licensing' of vegetarian products has not been sufficiently strictly monitored.

Publicity and PR

However, the rigorous and regular presentation of the name, logo and associated slogans is not enough to establish the strength of many charity identities. The content of publicity and public relations initiatives is crucial. For example, powerful TV images of Oxfam workers giving practical help in disastrous situations of food shortage in a developing country, television reportage of feeding centres run by Crisis at Christmas, and the continuing powerful images surrounding Shelter, nearly forty years since the TV film 'Cathy Come Home', all contribute significantly to charity identity.

However, you need to keep an eye on *all* your communications channels, not simply advertising, publicity and public relations. It is extraordinary how charities use opportunities for branding poorly or lose them completely. For example, until 1986, RNIB had 60,000 talking book tape recording machines in people's homes – unbranded. Before you smile too broadly, make sure you check the appearance of your invoices and publications, find out what how your organisation's switchboard sounds like to strangers, and so on.

The *physical expression* of the name and logo through signs, publications, advertisements, physical products, etc., often establishes the difference between the ordinary charity and the professional marketing one. Great discipline is required to have a common physical representation, especially in charities where individualism and dynamism are often a hallmark!

Perceived identity

Even if a person has little contact with a charity, the perceived identity can be different from the presented one. Individuals have many preconceived ideas about charities in general ('I don't think they should exist'); groups of charities ('We concern ourselves too much with animals and not enough with children'); and individual charities ('My mother collected for Barnardo's and I have always had a soft spot for them'). So charities have to devote considerable energy to finding out what their target groups think about them and must create their communications with this information in mind.

Experienced identity

Service marketers place much emphasis on the belief that in service companies the customers' experiences are as, if not more important than the presented messages in establishing a brand perception and organisation identity. They argue that an excellent branding strategy can make a strong service stronger, but it cannot rescue a weak one. If that is true of commercial services, it has to be true of charities and hence should go some way to reassuring cynics who regard promotion of charity identity as superficial misrepresentation.

Charities such as WWF, SCOPE and the RSPB have literally millions of supporters. If mass membership charities treat their members with disdain by bombarding them with unwanted letters, triplicate or even quadruplicate mailings, addressing them as Mr when they are Ms, politely reprimanding them because they have not yet donated when they have, then no amount of presented advertising and publicity is going to convince any of these supporters that their charity identity is anything other than poor. The charities quoted above go to great lengths to care for their supporters, which can turn them into a massive force of advocates in the population at large.

One cannot underestimate the positive advocacy powers of committed supporters in charities. Hinton (1993, p. 22) described the motivating effect of supporter conferences in Save the Children and gave impressive anecdotal evidence of supporter commitment these conferences and other volunteer support schemes encourage.

While the positive impact on charity identity of committed supporters and the negative effect of disaffected ones is great, the same applies to the expressed views of particularly pleased or disaffected beneficiaries. The positive advocacy impact of newly blind older people enjoying reading novels that they felt they never could read again (via talking books) produces the most amazing amount of gratitude and positive commitment. Equally, however, a letter from an RNIB customer who had inadvertently been charged twice for a technical aid that broke within the warranty period and had to be replaced, has to be read to be believed!

Direct experiences and subsequent word-of-mouth recommendation from beneficiaries and supporters are crucial in establishing charity identity.

Research

Marketing research and analysis are crucial in establishing, amending or repositioning a charity identity and position in the market. While it is possible to subdivide further, the views and commitment of four main groups of people need to be gained, namely beneficiaries, supporters, stakeholders (especially staff) and regulators.

Beneficiaries

Research among beneficiaries has been mentioned many times in this book. As far as the charity identity and position is concerned, it is vital to understand how actual and potential beneficiaries regard the charity, and particularly to obtain such basic information as what percentage has heard of it! Staff and trustees tend to imagine that the charity is very well known, particularly among beneficiaries. Market research often brings home uncomfortable truths. Research among beneficiaries is far less prevalent than one might imagine or hope. It is difficult to imagine how a charity can develop its identity and positioning, let alone provide core services, if it is unaware of the detailed needs of the actual and potential beneficiary groups. Penetration estimates, usage patterns and opinions among beneficiaries are fundamental inputs to charity identity and positioning, as well as service development.

Supporters

Research among existing and potential supporters is more widespread. Once again this is probably because of advertising agencies' influence and involvement in the fundraising market and the subsequent recruitment of marketing professionals into charity fundraising. Virtually all the large charities undertake attitude research among their actual and potential supporters. This reveals strengths and weaknesses of the charity identity. On age profile, most charities have an older age skew among supporters, while a few (such as Oxfam) will have relatively more support among younger and middle-aged people. Some charities score particularly high in terms of honesty, efficiency and cost effectiveness. Others (such as Greenpeace and Shelter) have stronger identity areas in the field of innovation and pioneering work. Whatever the results, research among supporters will tell the charity how it is regarded, how well it is getting its messages across and the extent to which it can or ought to shift supporter understanding of its identity.

Surveys

Most of the larger, more marketing-orientated charities commission regular quantitative awareness and attitudinal surveys among the general public. Typically these surveys are undertaken by one of the large commercial survey companies, involve a sample of around 1–2,000 people and occur once or twice a year. Another method is bench-marking, where a group of charities jointly commissions larger and more frequent surveys. The surveys cover prompted and unprompted awareness. The latter is sought by a question along the lines of 'Please tell me the names of ten charities that come to mind', the purpose being to identify the charities that are most prominent in the mind of the general public. Although all research will have inherent weaknesses, these regular awareness surveys provide a valuable tracking capability, for example, asking identical questions among comparable samples at six-monthly intervals enables significant rises and falls of awareness (perhaps related to promotional activity) to be identified.

Unprompted awareness

An example of unprompted awareness measurement is that undertaken by Omnimas among more than 1,200 people, which asks 'Can you tell me the names of all charities or other fundraising organisations you have ever heard of?' No names are read out to the respondents, but when they appear to 'dry up' the interviewer prompts with the question 'Any others?' three times. The results are then analysed and reported in total, and broken down by sex, age, social class and ITV regions. The national total results in mid-2004 are shown in Table 10.1.

Big promotional campaigns, especially advertising, can uplift awareness figures significantly. While Oxfam has consistently been the UK's best known charity, it is now being beaten by Cancer Research UK, after its creation through the merger of the Cancer Research Campaign (CRC) and the Imperial Cancer Research Fund (ICRF).

Prompted awareness

Prompted awareness, as the term implies, is where a list of charity names is read out and people are asked if they have heard of them. This form of measurement achieves much higher scores, for example Oxfam's and Cancer Research UK's awareness level rises to around 90 per cent.

Opinions differ on the usefulness of such general awareness tracking studies. My view is that unprompted awareness figures are a useful measurement of rising and declining popularity over time, and are especially useful when broken down into geographic areas, age, sex and socio-economic status. While one cannot guarantee that a spontaneous

Table 10.1

	%
Cancer Research UK	39
Oxfam	28
NSPCC	22
RSPCA	22
British Heart Foundation	13
Barnardo's	12
Red Cross	12
Macmillan Cancer Relief	11
Save the Children	9
Marie Curie	8
RNLI	8
Age Concern	7
RNIB	7
Help the Aged	6
Salvation Army	6
SCOPE/Spastics Society	4
PDSA	4
MENCAP	3
Guide Dogs for the Blind	3
Christian Aid	3
WWF	2
RSPB	2
Shelter	1
MS Society	1
MIND	1
Action for Blind People	1
Action Aid	<1
RNID	<1
Samaritans	<1
St John Ambulance	<1

mention reflects a positive attitude towards the individual charity, given people's generally warm view towards charities this seems to me to be fairly likely. Making that assumption, charity unprompted awareness levels, over time, provide a useful relative measure of a charity's popularity. However, as with so many such measures, they give few clues as to *why* a charity's popularity is growing or declining; but they do prompt the charity marketer as to whether there is a general charity identity problem, and the extent of it.

Stakeholders

Charities are, rightly, increasing the amount of research they undertake among stakeholders. As the name implies, these are the people who have a particular stake in the effective running of the organisation (other than the broader groups of beneficiaries and supporters). Stakeholders consist particularly of staff and committee and council members, but also include the leaders of key external groups or organisations that work closely with the charity – for example, government ministers and civil servants, local authority representatives and major funders. It is particularly important to note that a welcome trend among charities is to include representative beneficiaries or, even better, formal representatives of beneficiaries onto the charity councils and committees. This tendency sets charities apart from the vast majority of commercial organisations and provides a unique marketing opportunity. While the beneficiary representatives cannot be truly representative of every person the charity is helping, they do provide quite a different kind of insight and input into trustee planning and evaluation of charity services. In terms of the commercial marketing rhetoric of 'involving customers' and the growing interest in relationship marketing, the commercial marketing sector has much to learn from these progressive charities.

Research among stakeholders commissioned from independent outside agencies, and undertaken with guarantees of confidentiality, can be of inestimable value in understanding how the charity is really regarded. For example, government ministers and civil servants will often, in public give (superficial) accolades to an individual charity. However, in the privacy of their own offices, being interviewed with guarantees of anonymity, they may give quite a different story! It is important that these views, if they are widely held among stakeholders, are fed through to the charity.

Stakeholder research will also get under the surface of known differences between distinct groups of stakeholders. For example, disability charities founded by parents of disabled children (such as MENCAP and SCOPE) have real and understandable differences of opinion between parental representatives, the generation of disabled adults in committee leadership positions (who were originally their children) and stakeholders who believe that the remit of the organisation should be broadened outside the specific client group. Stakeholder research can begin to identify the extent of the opinion differences and likely areas of common ground, in ways that are less easy to achieve in formal committee situations.

Staff are also stakeholders and, given the dominance of services in charities, staff views, attitudes and behaviour contribute significantly to charity identity and positioning. If senior charity managers do not understand the true views of staff (at all levels) about the charity's operation and, in particular, the projected identity and positioning, then, all too quickly, staff will be asked to project messages that they do not believe in.

Other-player analysis

Commercial marketers would call this competitor analysis, but in most situations such a term is inappropriate in the charity setting. I would define it as follows: 'The term "other player" signifies any organisation whose activities in supplying other similar products (goods, services or ideas) might have a significant impact on the charity's own activities'. Thus other players consist of other charities, commercial organisations, statutory organisations and, in some situations, what the Wolfenden Committee (Wolfenden 1977, pp. 22–7) calls the informal sector of family, friends and neighbours.

Macro environmental analysis

Before getting into detailed other-player analysis, especially if the review is a fundamental one, it is important to undertake a broader environmental analysis of trends that may impact on the charity. These are generally identified as either *social*, *political* and *technical* or *economic*, *legal* and *environmental* impacts. Social changes would include such things as changing age structures (the ageing population); political changes (broadly defined) include such things as changing government policy to encompass greater purchasing of welfare state services from commercial organisations and charities, or new policies such as care in the community. Technical changes might be the impact of more sophisticated, user-friendly and cheaper computers: for example, allowing disabled people to become more independent of personal helpers, or the impact of more sophisticated recording techniques on orchestral recordings, making them sound very different from live concerts. Changes in the economic environment might include the impact of a recession or a boom on the charity – moving into a recession may impact on charity income in some areas (individual giving), may be delayed in other areas (company donations that come out of previous years' profits), or may be relatively unaffected in other areas (legacies).

Other charities

For the relatively few charities that undertake other-player analysis, other charities tend to be the main focus of attention, in terms of service giving, fundraising and pressure group work. As far as service giving to beneficiaries is concerned the particular charity sub-sector (such as charities concerned with ageing, the dramatic arts, overseas aid or the environment) tend to be the most important for consideration.

When it comes to fundraising, the net will inevitably be cast wider. Significant charity other players can be identified in a number of ways. For example, people leaving bequests tend to name several charities and the charities legacy department will be able to say who these are. Research among donors can provide similar evidence. Another way is to look at areas of a charity's fundraising strengths and identify any other rising star charities in this area. For example, if an individual charity has a great dependency on legacies, which are the other major bequest-receiving charities and which have grown the fastest? Is it possible to identify why? Are they in your charity sub-sector?

Commercial organisations

At first sight, analysis of commercial organisations might seem irrelevant. However, this is far from the case, especially in the field of physical product and service product offerings. Most charities have implicit or explicit policies of cross-subsidy between various physical and service products offered. Some actually make profits for the charity, although these are best handled through a related charitable company. Commercial entrepreneurs are quick to spot market opportunities, creaming off profitable potential areas of charity activity and leaving the charity (perhaps correctly?) with the products that require heavy subsidy. For example the changes in social security payments for residential care for older people in the late 1970s and early 1980s provided commercial companies with significant profit opportunities in running care homes. The commercial sector of this market expanded dramatically, while the charity residential homes sector remained sluggish. In the fields of technical aids for disabled people, certain government funding schemes have provided major market opportunities that have been taken up by commercial companies rather than charities, especially in the high technology field. During the late 1990s/2000s this trend reversed and many commercial providers, especially smaller ones, exited. This is not to argue that such commercial provision is wrong – far from it, because the charity sector alone is unlikely to be able to fulfil market need. It is unprofessional, however, when the charity is blissfully unaware of the marketing opportunity and the commercial organisation expands or declines until it is a fait accompli.

Statutory organisations

While lack of analysis of commercial other players can result in missed opportunities, lack of analysis of statutory organisation other players can be disastrous. Most charities are providing service products (and occasionally physical products) contiguously and in interaction with statutory providers and/or funders. With a few exceptions (including the Royal National Lifeboat Institution), the charity provider is smaller and has to act in a complementary fashion to the statutory provider. For charities in the social welfare field, the reorganisation of social services departments in the early 1970s into generic providing arms (rather than specialist ones for older people, children and mental welfare) caught many charities on the hop.

The transfer in 1990 of many Department of Employment programmes from national responsibility to the responsibility of local training and employment councils (TECs) had major impacts for NACRO (the National Association for the Care and Resettlement of Offenders). It resulted in NACRO reducing its centres from 70 to 41 and its places for unemployed people from 13,000 to 6,000, and making 600 staff redundant. The changing quantity of arts funding and the changing balance between national and regional distribution has had a major impact on many arts organisations.

The dramatic shifts in health and social services away from virtually sole provider into a situation where the statutory authority is a commissioning agent asking other organisations to tender competitively for services caught many charities relatively unaware. Many social welfare charities had spent thirty years learning to embrace a new dogma that encouraged them to pioneer new services and pass them on to the state. They had to relearn rapidly, and decide whether to compete with other charities and commercial organisations to win contracts, sometimes for the very services they had passed on to the state in the 1950s, 1960s and early 1970s. For example, local voluntary societies for the blind passed over their assessment and rehabilitation services to local government in the 1960s. Suddenly some social services departments were asking them to put in bids to take them back. NCH Action for Children anticipated the contracting trend early, responded positively and as a result has grown faster than most other children's charities. In the early period the Children's Society decided on the opposite course of action Anticipating, interpreting and acting on these trends in a way that fits your charity's philosophy is a crucial contribution of other-player analysis.

Positioning the charity

The preceding chapters have looked at positioning of individual products, whether physical goods, services or ideas. However, we are looking here at the positioning of the organisation as a whole, and the reinforcement and development of the identity of the whole charity. To a great extent the overall identity and position is the sum of the decisions on the different individual charity products. There therefore has to be overall guidance and decision-making in relation to individual activities. Also, there are separate and 'whole organisation' decisions to make on charity identity, such as in the selection or retention of the charity's name, logo and unique contributions.

Porter (1980) argues that commercial organisations should position themselves in one of three ways: through strong differentiation from competitors, through cost leadership (not necessarily the cheapest price but the price that sets the standard in the market) or through focus. Andreasen and Kotler (2003) argue that organisations should strive for any one of four long-term market positions: market leader, market challenger, market follower or market nicher. Chew (2003) critiques these propositions while maintaining their overall importance.

Differentiation

There is no doubt in my mind that if a charity can achieve it, the route of differentiation and distinctiveness is the one to take, providing that the cause is acceptable or potentially acceptable. For example, in the overseas aid field, the combination of name, reputation and activity are inherently stronger for Save the Children and Help the Aged than they are for Action Aid. In the UK volunteering market, the two major charities have sought differentiation. Both Community Service Volunteers and Volunteering England exist to promote volunteering. Community Service Volunteers does it through the direct placement of people into volunteering situations, and using the experience gained to promote volunteering policy. Volunteering England was set up to provide an information, research and development resource on volunteering in general, and chose to be distinctive by deliberately not involving itself directly in volunteer recruitment and placement. This, it argued, ensured that its advice would not be skewed by involvement with a particular volunteer programme. In other words, Community Service Volunteers and Volunteering England are differentiated from each other in a relatively narrow field.

Positioning of the largest charities providing a multiplicity of services at first looks straightforward. Across the whole charity sector, Barnardo's, RNIB and SCOPE are distinctly differentiated by the nature of their client groups. Market positioning around a beneficiary group may be good differentiation and attractive to supporters. However, the vagaries of social policy changes mentioned above can cause problems. For example, statutory services have increasingly preferred to work with generic groups of clients, for example disabled people rather than people with cerebral palsy. They would prefer to do business with generic charities rather than organisations dealing with what they see as narrow interest groups. Single-interest groups' response to this situation is to argue that such a positioning is important, because other people do not view the world from the position of the single interest.

However, trying to get across the very wide range of services these charities provide for one beneficiary group and thus differentiate themselves from smaller charities operating in their sub-sector is very difficult. Emphasis on any one particular service, such as residential centres, talking books or employment rehabilitation, might differentiate the organisation, but it works against the charity by making it appear specialist and may restrict its room for social policy manoeuvre. For example, children's homes are no longer part of Barnardo's repertoire, and SCOPE no longer provides employment rehabilitation. For these large charities the only tactic open to them is that of market leader.

Niche marketing

For some charities, niche marketing is attractive, for example the Macmillan Cancer Relief's Macmillan Nurses against the giant Cancer Research UK, or Crisis at Christmas in relation to Shelter.

So the world of charity identity and positioning is nothing if not complicated! Steady evolution, if not on occasions revolution, of a charity's identity and position is required. It was only a matter of time before organisations with names and identities such as the Royal Home and Hospital for Incurables, the National Old People's Welfare Council and the Spastics Society had to update their identity and position.

Relaunch or repositioning

The charity world has been alive with launches, relaunches and repositionings, probably for as long as charities have existed. But the last forty years have seen a particularly large amount of activity. Among the trends that have encouraged this have been the growing size and scope of statutory services (up to the 1980s) and their fundamental reorientation in the 1980s and 1990s; the accommodation of charities to these changes, initially by handing over services to the state; their, partly consequentially, increased role as critics of statutory services on behalf of disadvantaged groups (the rise of overt pressure group activity); the increasing adoption of commercial techniques, especially in fundraising activities; the impact of a new breed of charity leaders who, partly personally, changed the whole dynamic of charity activities (such as Jackson Cole of Help the Aged, Des Wilson of Shelter, David Hobman of Age Concern, David Ennals and Tony Smythe of MIND); the increasing adoption of more professional management practice, initially in the 1970s from the statutory services, and in the 1980s and 1990s from commercial organisations; and the rapid rise in the number of charities.

To give comprehensive and detailed examples from these exciting years would make a book in itself. What follows are a few short examples, which indicate some of the aspects of a relaunch. However, these should not be taken to indicate that charity identity development, or brand development is common. Indeed Tapp (1996) argues that such development work is scarce.

CASE EXAMPLE: LAUNCH OF SHELTER – THE NATIONAL CAMPAIGN FOR THE HOMELESS

The launch of Shelter in 1968, tied to the publicity rocket of the TV drama documentary 'Cathy Come Home', is already a legend. Des Wilson, as director, brought all the marketing and public relations skills that good journalists have, plus his public presentational skills. Reference is made to this launch earlier in the book (see page 189). It essentially pioneered the way for charities to become overt pressure groups and campaigning bodies while retaining charitable status.

CASE EXAMPLE: NATIONAL OLD PEOPLE'S WELFARE COUNCIL RELAUNCH AS AGE CONCERN ENGLAND

The National Old People's Welfare Council (NOPWC) was set up in the mid-1940s as a coordinating body of local old people's welfare committees – all under the arm of what has since become NCVO. In 1970 the NOPWC became independent of NCVO and appointed its first director, David Hobman. I joined at the same time, as Appeals and Public Relations Officer.

When a charity has such an indistinct, old-fashioned and unmemorable name as the National Old People's Welfare Council, there are no prizes for changing it! Nevertheless it felt quite difficult and brave at the time, with an organisation that was rather encrusted with tradition. However, the process of name selection was unusual. NOPWC got eight advertising agencies to bid for the charity account of a princely £1,000 per annum, with part of the pitch requirements being the proposal of up to ten new names for the charity. These eighty names were reduced to one, exclusively by market research, with the executive committee of

cont.

CASE EXAMPLE: NATIONAL OLD PEOPLE'S WELFARE COUNCIL RELAUNCH AS AGE CONCERN ENGLAND continued

trustees accepting the one recommendation – Age Concern. Then came the job of persuading the 200-plus local independent Old People's Welfare Committees to adopt the name, which required a big selling job. Within a year one-third had done so; within five years, 90 per cent had changed. These local adoptions were crucial in the overall success.

However, it is important to point out that this name change coincided with other major repositioning activity, including the organisation becoming much more proactive in its development of national coordination work, becoming much more active as a pressure group and rejuvenating the network of local Old People's Welfare Committees.

As a result of this repositioning and relaunch the charity has moved from being small and completely unknown to becoming one of the largest and best known in the country. It is worth noting that it took three years (until 1974) for the new name even to register on unprompted awareness scales; and, despite the fact that Age Concern has around 1,000 local groups, it took twenty-five years to equal the awareness rating of its competitor Help the Aged.

The first conclusion from this example is that relaunching a charity with a new name is a long-term undertaking. (The Royal Society for Mentally Handicapped Children, relaunched as MENCAP, is another example.) The second conclusion from the Age Concern relaunch is that, with the benefit of hindsight, it was perhaps wrong to rely entirely on the market research conducted to reduce the options down to the final one. It was probably not coincidence that the name most preferred by the research sample, Age Concern, sounds quite similar to Help the Aged, which was already a well-known and established charity at that time. However, because the two names are relatively similar, this makes market differentiation for both charities difficult.

CASE EXAMPLE: RNIB REPOSITIONING

RNIB repositioned and relaunched in the mid-1980s and repositioned in the early 2000s. In 2001 the charity transformed itself from being an organisation 'for' blind people into a membership organisation 'of ' blind people. The constitution was changed to require that a majority of trustees (all elected) be blind or partially sighted and come from a membership of blind and partially sighted people. The decision was driven by philosophical and social policy considerations, such as blind people should be in charge of their own affairs; RNIB's legitimacy as a campaigner and pressure group would be enhanced; and that its legitimacy as a representative service provider would also be enhanced.

This increased legitimisation was important, not only in the UK but also in Brussels and Strasbourg in negotiating with the EU. Being the first major service disability charity to require legally that a majority of its trustees be disabled it also made it distinct from other disability service charities as well as service delivery charities within the visual impairment field.

CASE EXAMPLE: ROYAL COMMONWEALTH SOCIETY FOR THE BLIND'S RELAUNCH AS SIGHT SAVERS

An example of a relaunch which almost 'just happened' was the adoption by the Royal Commonwealth Society for the Blind (RCSB) of the cover name Sight Savers. RCSB had successfully achieved a Blue Peter children's TV appeal for its work. This programme is one of the most influential on a charity's fundraising, image and awareness strength among young people. However, the programme makers were worried that it would be difficult to get the charity's rather ponderous title across to the young audience, who were to be enthused to raise millions of pounds. They came up with the name of Sight Savers, which the charity has subsequently adopted as its public cover name. This is perhaps an example of what one might call serendipity marketing!

CASE EXAMPLE: BARNARDO'S

Barnardo's had a similar image problem to RNIB. Market research had showed that the image of the then Dr Barnardo's was still too Victorian. But with an unprompted awareness level of 20 per cent, Barnardo's would have been foolish to seek modern anonymity as a replacement to Victorian fame! The brilliant marketing solution it came up with was to drop the 'Dr', thus losing an element of its name that over-contributed to the formality of the image and referred people automatically back to the Victorian founder. It also developed a new logo, using all the market research activity described above.

Barnardo's discovered that its identity among the general public had not shifted as much as it would have wished and in 2000 it launched a further integrated advertising and PR push, which gained the Chartered Institute of Marketing's Campaign of the year award. Barnardo's relaunch still seems to me to be one of the most thoughtful examples of a major national charity relaunch/repositioning that we have seen for a while.

Conclusion

Charity positioning and charity identity (brand) are fundamental considerations in a marketing approach. With around 12,000 new charities being registered each year and resources scarce, competition for attention from all customer target markets is intense. Consequently launches and relaunches are frequent, but only exceptionally reach the public eye. Such relaunches require a fundamental marketing approach, rather than action on the whim of the advertising agency, chief executive or chair. The charity identity ideally has to be memorable, distinctive, descriptive and flexible, but above all it has to reflect a reality rather than an advertising agency's dream. Relaunches have to reflect real advances in the charity's work if they are to be fundamentally sound.

Above all there are no quick fixes. Charities do not have, and in any event should not spend, the millions of pounds that a commercial company would devote to a relaunch of one of its major brands. Charity identities are built up slowly, methodically and painstakingly over decades. Managers with a marketing view will be more than conscious of the heritage of their charity. Changes are likely to be incremental rather than revolutionary. They will certainly need to take account of the changing social, political, technological, environmental, legal and economic environment in which we work. They will also have to take account of supporters' needs and wishes. But if charity is to mean anything, and if marketing is to mean anything in the charity world, it will be the needs and wishes of the end beneficiaries that will drive us forward.

Key points

Identity

- The physical representation of the charity (logo, name, the 'brand') should be firmly controlled.
- The charity name should be:
  - distinctive;
  - relevant;
  - memorable;
  - flexible;

  but do not risk sacrificing existing goodwill and awareness by changing what might seem to be a weak name without proper consideration.
- Be aware of the commercial value of the logo, but control its use carefully.
- Take particular care over the physical expression of the name and logo – in advertisements, publications and signs.
- The message given to and perceived by supporters and beneficiaries is crucial in establishing identity. Make sure they have positive direct experiences.
- Research among beneficiaries, supporters, stakeholders and staff is crucial in establishing, amending or repositioning identity and market positioning.

Positioning

- If possible, build market position by distinctiveness and strong differentiation.

PART III

Key Marketing Approaches for Charities

11 Relationship marketing

What is relationship marketing?

Since the first edition of this book, relationship marketing has grown in both stature and importance. It is no coincidence that this covers the same period as the major growth in services marketing, where the customer and provider interact more intimately and over a longer period than in goods marketing. Nor is it a coincidence that relationship marketing has developed out of business-to-business marketing, with its fewer, more personalised customer-supplier relationships. What has slowed its acceptance is mass consumer goods marketing, where it is difficult to conceive of an individual customer relationship, simply because of the large numbers of customers involved. However, even that difficulty has receded because of sophisticated software programs that can identify individual customer needs and preferences. Supermarket store card systems know more about our shopping habits than we do! Closer to home, donor customer relationship management systems know enough about donor histories to strengthen our donor relations.

Marketing with attitude

In essence, relationship marketing is marketing with attitude! The attitude is not to concentrate on one-off transactions but to keep in mind a series of transactions, in other words build up loyalty that arises out of a continuing relationship between producer and consumer. Relationship marketing is thinking longer term about each individual customer – for example, not concentrating as hard as we used to on acquiring new customers but instead concentrating our mindset on keeping customers once acquired. We have all had experience of financial services organisations that woo us with highly competitive borrowing or savings rates. Once we have signed up, they then ignore us while offering even better rates to new customers from which we are excluded or only hear of by chance. This single transaction marketing can work when customers have inertia. But as customers get more adept at swapping around, single transaction marketing becomes expensive and less profitable than keeping existing customers satisfied and therefore loyal.

As with any new development, initially relationship marketing was threatening to the established marketing order. On the other hand, relationship marketers often had a zeal that led them overstate their case. Now that we are well into the new millennium the importance of developing, maintaining and sometimes ending customer relations is part of the marketing woodwork. This led O'Malley and Tynan (2003, p. 38) to assert 'to do relationship marketing well is simply to do traditional marketing better'.

A more formal and comprehensive definition is offered by Groonroos (1997, p. 407), one of the fathers of relationship marketing, who says:

> 'Marketing is the process of identifying and establishing, maintaining, enhancing and, when necessary, terminating relationships with customers and other stakeholders, at a profit, so that the objectives of all parties involved are met, where this is done by mutual giving and fulfilment of promises.'

Tools

But to do this we need to use the full range of marketing tools. For example, I remember when I left Unilever to join the National Old People's Welfare Council as head of fundraising and PR, to help David Hobman relaunch it as Age Concern. Initially my only staff member was an older volunteer who looked after the 200 or so donors. She knew a lot about many of them and when she wrote sending the annual report and asking for money she would personalise all the letters in response to news she had received in previous correspondence. Most people had been giving for years, a repeat donation record a relationship marketer would applaud, and certainly some indication of the strong relationship between the donors and her and the charity. However, they gave very small sums and because of their quasi friendship she was loath to ask for more than they had given in the previous year.

The next year we applied the marketing mix, offering a choice of specific fundraising products, making them as tangible as possible, and used a price range to give the donors options as to what they would like to give (in other words adding in a traditional *transactional* marketing overlay). The average donation soared and we lost very few donors. Unfortunately the volunteer retired a few years later and we ceased to be so personalised in our communications. We lost donors because the *relationships* had weakened – a tiny but real example showing the importance of integrating transactional and relationship marketing.

Profitability

Before continuing it is important to address those few words in Groonroos' definition – 'at a profit'. In a commercial setting this is an important caveat, but in the non-profit world it seems wrong. We can simply substitute the words 'while fulfilling the objectives of the organisation', as in the definition 'marketing is meeting customers' needs within the objectives of the organisation'.

Readers interested in the origins and relationships of traditional and relationship marketing and how they have converged, should read O'Malley and Tynan's (2003) excellent article in *The Marketing Book*.

Establishing relationships

All the elements of the charity marketing mix are important in a relationship marketing way of operating, but three are pre-eminent – product, segmentation leading to targeting, and people.

Product

How product is developed and constructed to meet needs – its features, benefits and guarantees – is clearly vital to establish and maintain a good producer-customer relationship. This applies to goods but is especially critical for charity services and to ideas in the form of pressure group work, campaigns and fundraising. If an idea product – whether a campaign or a fundraising one – is shown to be wrong or flawed, it is likely that the customer (government, public, donor) will not trust the charity on its next approach.

Segmentation

Segmentation leading to targeting is critical if the 'right' group is to be chosen as customers. If the choice is 'wrong' – say the group cannot be reached effectively, or its needs do not match the product benefits as well another target group's –it is predictable that many producer-customer relationships will not even begin, let alone be maintained.

People

In the case of services and idea products, people, in the form of *staff/ volunteers* and *other customers*, are very important. As has been covered earlier, staff or volunteers who are under-trained or do not have or understand delivery standards will not give customers a quality product. In these situations, unless customers are desperate and have no alternative, they are unlikely to come back. As charity beneficiary customers can be desperate and have no alternatives, we need to be careful not to assume that a continuing relationship is confirmation that all is well.

As far as other customers are concerned, if one visible group does not get on with another and the service delivery is such that they consume together, then the product offering will be undermined, and the likelihood of repeat purchase (the relationship) will be damaged. (For example, inviting culture vultures and IT girls to the same fundraising reception, or a hotel serving blind people booking in a group wanting to enjoy a rock weekend at the same time as a group competing in a chess tournament.)

Strengthening relationships

Product, segmentation and people are crucial elements to get right to establish a positive and continuing relationship. There are other things we can do to strengthen relationships.

Marketing research

Marketing research, including market research, is perhaps the most important way of strengthening relationships. Market research asks existing and potential customers what they think about the offering and how they are treated, and marketing research puts the customer view into a wider context, such as actual take-up behaviour with the charity and take-up patterns with other providers. Such research keeps a close eye on the customer, their needs and wishes and checks how well customers perceive the charity's offerings are meeting those needs and wishes. It helps the charity to understand how it can improve relationships from a customer viewpoint.

Spotting problems

Marketing research is fundamental to maintaining and improving relationships but it is future orientated. How do we do something *now* when an individual is dissatisfied? And, first, how do we know that there is a problem? With services we stand a greater chance if service delivery staff are trained to recognise tell tale signs of dissatisfaction – a stony faced customer, the slight hesitation from the customer in responding to a deliverer's question asking if everything is alright. But to feed back dissatisfaction, customers need to know the level of service they can expect, and so deliverers need to emphasise this as well as the acceptability of a customer raising problems.

Encouraging complaints

I have not come across research in our sector on whether complaining helps strengthen relationships, but this is the view in the commercial world. For example when Colin Marshall was trying to encourage BA to be more customer orientated, BA discovered that half the dissatisfied customers who had *not* complained changed to another provider. However, of those who did air their problems, only 13 per cent defected. BA concluded that encouraging complaints was good for business, and that the superficial peace for staff of customers suffering in silence was not good business.

These lessons would seem to be appropriate to charity fundraising in general and charity direct marketing in particular – areas of our work with short relationships, high levels of allegiance switching, and large numbers of competitors. If the commercial arguments apply to fund-raising, then the moral arguments come to the fore with services to beneficiaries – it is immoral to believe our beneficiary customers have problems we do not know about in individual cases, and could probably rectify if we did. We have to encourage them to tell us *and* be geared up to solve the problem.

Service recovery

Zeithaml and Bitner (2003) outline a virtuous circle: 'fail safe' the service (get it right the first time); encourage complaints; act quickly to rectify problems; treat customers fairly; learn from recovery experiences; learn from lost customers; and feed all this back into the fail safe stage – improve the service overall.

This list seems to me 100 per cent applicable to fundraising, where we are often insufficiently attentive to our customers – especially in direct mail where we talk about 'only fifty people complained'. We tolerate barely adequate reply services from fulfilment houses that know next to nothing about our work, and the majority of charities do not respond to a donor's request for fewer mailings.

We also need to adopt such approaches with beneficiary customers, but the knock-on effects have to be weighed up. In the commercial world (and the charity fundraising world) spending extra money to keep customers loyal in order to benefit from their lifetime value makes sense. But in the charity world keeping beneficiary customers loyal usually increases financial 'losses' through increased subsidy. Some charities might even privately reckon on the advantages of service failure in keeping in check what otherwise might be an uncontrollable or unserviceable flood of beneficiary customers. Many of us remember when having to wait one or two hours in the GP's surgery was quite a dampener on going to the doctor. Now appointment waiting times are much shorter.

But there are 'ways and ways' of keeping supply and demand under control when we have too little resource. The best technical way is through narrowing the target group, not delivering unacceptable standards of core service. Returning to the GP example. The NHS did not encourage GPs to provide a poor medical service as a method of dampening demand. Instead they reduced demand by forcing people to wait a long time, thus discouraging them from going to the doctor. While perseverance may be a poor way to segment and target, it is better than encouraging a poor core service. So a housing advice centre might only take walk-in clients two days a week, or make it clear it will only provide walk-in advice for people in imminent danger of being made homeless or from a certain catchment area. Within these constraints they should do everything they can – everything in the Zeithaml and Bitner list – to improve their service within the objectives of the organisation.

Customer appreciation and recognition

These two different but related areas are among the most valuable tools voluntary and community organisations have for building strong customer relationships, provided they are applied genuinely and sincerely. Appreciation and recognition can and should be applied to all four customer groups – beneficiaries, supporters, stakeholders and regulators.

Appreciation

We all know from personal experience that being appreciated by others is a powerful motivator. At its most straightforward it means being thanked fulsomely and genuinely. It is important to be specific ('thank you for raising so much money and special thanks for those long hours you spent with your collecting tin on windy street corners') and timely (leaving thanks or appreciation too long takes the gloss off it and can make it look like an afterthought).

Recognition

Appreciation can be all the more powerful as it turns into recognition, which can be applied to all customer groups. Because *beneficiaries* receiving services have to be active in the consumption process, they become part of the production process and the success. For example, a rehabilitation service for substance misusers cannot be successful unless participants cooperate and contribute; and so for each small step forward the participant can be appropriately recognised and congratulated. This recognition can stretch from the informal interchange between staff and rehabilitee all the way through to public recognition in a group setting. It helps to cement the customer relationship and strengthen the likelihood of a successful outcome.

Similarly *supporters* and *stakeholders* in all their guises, including donors, volunteer service workers and staff, are far more likely to remain loyal and do more if they are appreciated and recognised. Formal recognition through awards is becoming increasingly common but there are many ways of giving recognition, from senior charity representatives' personal thanks through to nominations for formal honours. Individual bonus payments are becoming more common, although they can have unintended consequences, such as demotivating others, who may feel they contributed to the bonus receiver's success.

Spreading bonuses widely is unaffordable but spreading thanks and appreciation widely, but appropriately, is not. It might at first sight seem improper to appreciate *regulators,* for example the Charity Commission, but they undertake many useful capacity building activities for their sector, which can be acknowledged.

If there is one common complaint I have heard regularly over the years, from all branches of charity customers, it is that of feeling underappreciated. Charities that thank and appreciate will succeed better by benefiting from increased motivation and enthusiasm.

Relationship strategies

Berry and Parasuraman (1991) have proposed different levels of relationship marketing, which Zeithaml and Bitner (2003) and Zeithaml *et al.* (2006) have elaborated upon. Level 1 concentrates on *financial bonds*; level 2 *social bonds*; level 3 *customisation bonds*; and level 4 *structural bonds*. Many charity relationship strategies will have initiatives that span the first three and sometimes even level 4.

One example is Age Concern England's insurance products for older people. It gives its key intermediary customers (local Age Concern groups) a percentage of the value of each policy they sell (level 1, financial bond); has dedicated staff who liaise and have regular meetings with groups of local Age Concerns (level 2, social); produces special packages tailored to the size and composition of the local group (level 3, customisation); and gives local groups representation as of right on the national Age Concern board (level 4, structural).

These relationship strengthening devices do not stop stresses and strains showing between local and national levels. But they make it virtually impossible for any local group to walk away from the national organisation (even though local Age Concerns are independent charities) and has made it impossible for Help the Aged to tempt any local Age Concerns into its network even if it had tried.

Financial bonds

Most individual and organisational membership schemes use financial bonds in the form of fees, unless there is concern that charging a fee may deter some people from joining, and so would mean the organisation would not be truly representative. As this is the 'price' of the marketing mix, all the previous caveats apply (such as not thinking through the impact on recruitment and differential membership fees or the impact of the hidden price). Arts charities show their sophistication in this area through their pyramid pricing structures, which buy varying levels of service and involvement – £10 per year to be on the mailing list, £30 for preferential booking and £100 for preferential booking and invitations to first nights.

Social bonding

Social bonding opportunities are often not maximised in the charity world because of concern about an organisation appearing wasteful or improperly applying funds for receptions or other events not totally tied to the organisation's raison d'être. But the beneficial outcomes of lifting morale and encouraging people's loyalty to the cause through a modest spend on social gatherings usually far outweighs the financial cost.

An example might be membership of a loose knit pressure group/campaigning alliance where it is difficult to keep members focused and even loyal to campaign goals. Rumours often spread that a constituent organisational member is about to be picked off by the government through the promise of a preferential 'deal', which ramps up mistrust among other members who then consider breaking ranks. In my experience, in alliances where members have 'played' as well as worked together, the increased social bonding increases trust levels, which helps prevent splintering. A quick telephone call to key leaders, giving brief assurances that no side deal is being done is taken on trust, because members know each other well enough to make a judgement.

Customisation

Customisation is a strong suit of arts charities and in the informal memberships of major donor circles of some of the more successful fundraising charities. This involves knowing the individual members' interests and preferences and shaping your product (service or idea) accordingly. This can range from telling library members who you know like detective thrillers when the latest version is available in Braille, through to being aware that a major donor is a director of Arsenal and, after discussing how the team is doing, asking if they could get a ball signed by the players for subsequent auctioning. Customisation is as much about thinking your way into your customers' interests and enthusiasm as it is to do with spending large sums.

Structural bonds

Structural bonds appear to be on the increase, particularly by giving members various forms of voting rights. The argument goes that this not only enhances the legitimacy of the charity but also binds the member into the charity more. At RNIB I was a passionate advocate of a broad based membership of blind and partially sighted people with voting rights. This was for several reasons, including the RNIB philosophy of empowerment, the increased legitimacy/clout a large membership brings to the pressure group table of the EU and any British government and, very importantly, because a voting membership provides a structural link between the individual blind person and the charity. But, as the term implies, structural links have a permanency and must be well designed not to lead to unintended consequences such as entryism (for example, at the RSPCA, where pro hunt lobbyists attempted to join up and influence the charity's policy using members' voting rights).

Membership

More and more charities are using membership schemes – a powerful example of relationship marketing – which can be used to cement and develop relationships with all groups of customers. The four-level model referred to in the previous section is useful, because it provides a framework that ensures the charity has maximised all its possibilities for relationship building within a membership scheme. It is not unusual for one or more categories to be missing, but through simple omission rather than by design. Arts charities have led the way on membership schemes, with environmental non-profits hard on their heels. Social welfare charities have also been waking up to the benefits of membership schemes in the last few years.

Conclusion

Relationship marketing is fundamentally important to voluntary and community organisations because of their huge reliance on trust and goodwill from their customers, whether beneficiaries, supporters, stakeholders or regulators. However, it is not an alternative to traditional transactional marketing with all its tools. It is an attitude, or way of thinking, which puts individual transactions into a serial framework. Thus it uses all the traditional tools of traditional transaction marketing, but needs additional tools such as the four-level model described and applied above. Adopted in this way, relationship marketing is vital to understand and apply if charities are to meet the needs of their customers successfully.

12 Partnership marketing

A partnership marketing approach is becoming important for charities. I define partnership marketing as 'the marketing of a product or offering jointly with another organisation or grouping which can be constituted from the voluntary, statutory, commercial or informal sectors'. Alternative terms for partnership are alliance, collaboration, cooperation, joint venture or networks, with each term having advantages and disadvantages and being more or less applicable in different situations. When the partnership is between charities and companies it is often called cause related marketing or CRM (not to be confused with customer relationship management – also CRM!).

Partnership marketing in practice

It can be hard to imagine a marketing partnership with the informal sector of family friends and neighbours. A simple example might be Groundwork collaborating with a group of neighbouring households around a park that is being upgraded. While the two groups may never use the term marketing, they are jointly agreeing how the park is currently being used (marketing research) and how it might be used after considering different options for upgrades (new product development). Partnership marketing is easier to grasp when it is between a charity or charities and another organisation(s) in the voluntary or statutory sector (such as a local RNID organisation for deaf people running a series of mobile clinics in local Age Concern groups, or a citizens advice bureau and local authority jointly running advice centres across a borough).

Mindset

Partnership marketing, like relationship marketing, is more a different mindset than it is a different branch of marketing. The traditional and previously dominant paradigm of transactional marketing of physical goods has given way to a much broader concept and application of marketing tools to customers, via goods, services and ideas, with single or joint deliverers. In the case of partnership marketing the changed mindset is that organisations and groups that previously nearly always thought of themselves as competitors or at least separate, can achieve their customer oriented goals more effectively through partnership or collaboration. A well-known example from the commercial world is British Airways' collaboration with previously competitor airlines across the world, now called 'partner airlines').

Partnerships and alliances

While it may not have been called partnership marketing, the practice has been around in our sector for hundreds of years, for example churches collaborating with the state to deliver social welfare services. What is less clear is whether these partnerships are currently static, growing or declining. If the commercial world is any reflection (and we do learn from, and follow, many commercial developments where they are reactions to wider societal and global changes), partnerships involving the sector will grow rapidly in both size and number. For example Accenture Consulting reported 26 per cent of the revenues of the Fortune Top 500 Companies came from alliances, up from 11 per cent five years earlier, and that many executives believed the rising trend would continue (Piercey 2003).

Anecdotal evidence would suggest that alliances are not (yet?) growing at this pace in our sector, but a number of drivers are encouraging more alliances and partnerships.

- Many of our customers, especially beneficiary ones, have multiple needs that charities often cannot meet on their own (for example homeless alcoholics).
- A significant number of our intermediary customers are not prepared to deal with many individual charities concentrating on single causes; they want instead a holistic approach by a holistic deliverer (government can get exasperated by a string of children's charities or cancer charities making separate representations about similar issues).
- Donors often ask for more cooperation between charities (for

example trusts including evidence of cooperation in their grant-making criteria)

- Statutory commissioners often believe they will get a more effective outcome if charity providers would cooperate more.

However, all of us who have tried to encourage such partnerships and alliances know how difficult and time consuming they are to establish and maintain. How can a marketing approach help?

A marketing approach

Marketing can help charity partnerships or alliances in two ways. First, they can help to ensure the alliance produces offerings that keep a dominant focus on its intermediary and end customers. Alliances often have so many interests to square that they end up producing offerings that satisfy the constituent members but not the partnership's customers. By using the charity marketing framework of the marketing mix supported by marketing research, positioning and segmentation leading to targeting, and understanding take-up behaviour, the charity member(s) can keep the work focused on end customer needs and wishes.

Second, a relationship marketing approach can help manage the interactions between, and commitment from, the alliance members to ensure it stays healthy and viable. The four levels of bond strengthening mentioned in the last chapter (financial, social, customisation and structural) are particularly useful tools.

Case examples

This chapter now goes on to explore some practical examples, to show how these two marketing approaches can contribute in practice if used by a critical mass of the partnership. Examples cover the four types of partnership – charity plus charity, charity plus statutory body, charity plus commercial company and charity plus informal sector grouping.

Charity plus charity

The Disability Discrimination Act 1995 (DDA), implemented progressively between 1996 and 2004, established new requirements on providers of goods, service and facilities to ensure that their offerings are accessible to disabled people and employers do not discriminate against disabled workers and applicants. The passing of the Act was itself a fascinating pressure group marketing saga, with both the government and charities paying unexpected prices in the marketing mix, including the embarrassment of the resignation of one government minister! However, this study picks up the story at the crucial point where the Act was passed and the focus had to shift towards implementation – a stage that many previous charity pressure group alliances ignored, assuming that winning new legislation was the end of a campaign, when in fact it is only the beginning.

Much worthy legislation withers on the statute book. The DDA was particularly vulnerable because it only requires providers of goods, services and facilities to make 'reasonable adjustments' to make their offerings accessible. While the guidance gives examples of what such 'reasonable adjustments' might mean, these examples are not comprehensive. In practice the definition depends on custom and practice, precedent and the courts. It was therefore vital that the implementation got off to a flying start.

CASE EXAMPLE: DISABILITY CHARITIES CONSORTIUM

A number of disability charities (including MENCAP, Scope and Leonard Cheshire) were properly enthusiastic about the opportunities the DDA provided, and several had plans to offer advisory services to commercial and public organisations on how to comply with the new law. In this way every piece of advice implemented would not only mean more access in that individual case, but would also add to the body of evidence of what is 'reasonable'. However, informal market research among public and commercial organisations indicated that they were confused by the variety of needs of disabled people: the requirements of blind people are different than for partially sighted, which are different from deaf people, which are different from people with learning disabilities, which are different from people with mental health problems. This research also discovered that the providers did not relish the thought of RNID turning up one week, MIND the next, MENCAP the next, RNIB the week after and so on.

cont.

CASE EXAMPLE: DISABILITY CHARITIES CONSORTIUM continued

Partnership

As a consequence the Disability Charities Consortium (DCC) was set up, a partnership called comprising RNIB, RNID, MENCAP, SCOPE, Leonard Cheshire, MIND and RADAR. Its purpose was to deliver pan-disability advice to employers and providers that brought together the various sets of expertise for different disability groups at one service point.

The DCC brought the marketing information together well (research, segmentation, other-player analysis and positioning). The marketing mix proved more challenging. The new product development was problematic because each charity's advice services had different prices, processes, physical evidence and levels of people skills. Philosophy was one of the few non-problematic areas because all the charities had an empowerment approach, which regarded the disabled person as the central focus.

Luckily the DCC was forced to make decisions on the marketing mix by the arrival of a tender specification to provide a national advice line (Disability Access Rights and Advice Service – DARAS). The DCC won this contract, which gave the consortium the confidence and enthusiasm to feel it could solve the challenge of an agreed product range for other opportunity areas. Customer research among advice line users was positive. So, broadly speaking, the first contribution of marketing to partnership working was successful, namely its conventional use in helping to design and deliver customer focused offerings.

Relationship marketing

However, its second contribution, in the form of relationship marketing, did not work well enough. The financial bonds were in place, in that all six DCC members contributed according to their means. There were social bonds because the charities' representatives had been working together on the bill for three or more years and so relationships were settled (strengthened during the campaign stage in pubs near parliament!). However, insufficient customisation of the offerings, linked to changed representation, led to the downfall of the initiative, but not the consortium.

The group members were all chief executives. A new chief executive

cont.

CASE EXAMPLE: DISABILITY CHARITIES CONSORTIUM continued

at RNID led to a crucial change in policy for the charity. Rather than accept a generic product (advice on all forms of disability) he took the view that deaf people's interests were best served by an impairment specific approach, even if that risked annoying companies and public bodies. The contribution of the charities that made up DCC had been customised to the extent that contribution levels and reward levels had been differentiated. But it was impossible to have a constituent charity with a rival product. One solution would have been expulsion, with a continuation of the joint generic product. However, the DCC had developed other valuable roles, particularly around lobbying, which depended on all six charities staying round the table. Also, both RADAR and RNIB had wanted to develop their own generic products and the demise of the six charity generic offering allowed them to do so.

New product

This initiative was a new product (Ansoff), in a new market, being developed by a new configuration of producers – it doesn't get much harder! The example contrasts with the often almost sickeningly successful case studies in so many management books. It emphasises the contribution of relationship marketing to partnership working between charities. It did not succeed but at the end of the day it is not marketing that makes judgements, but people representing the best interests of their organisation and customers. Marketing cannot guarantee, only contribute to, bringing these into harmony.

Charity plus statutory body

The Pension Service is the arm of government responsible for delivering a wide range of financial benefits to older people. Many are means tested. Research shows that many eligible people do not claim, for a variety of reasons, including not knowing about what is available and having insufficient advice. Also, some older people whose memories go back to the 1920s and 1930s were and are cautious about engaging with government officials and government offices over means tested benefits because of perceived stigma.

CASE EXAMPLE: THE PENSION SERVICE AND CITIZENS ADVICE, AGE CONCERN AND RNIB

Pension Credit

The launch of a new benefit for pensioners – Pension Credit – was a key initiative for the government in its attempt to tackle pensioner poverty. In order to boost take up, innovation was required. The Pensions Service approached a number of charities to see if they could help reach a wider audience and offer complementary support to help prevent potential applicants from feeling discomforted at approaching government officials for means tested awards.

Citizens Advice, Age Concern and RNIB agreed to cooperate and signed national partnership agreements with the Pension Service. Initially the charities' contribution was to give the Pensions Service staff space in their service centres to run surgeries, with the charities having briefed their beneficiary customers on the benefits of attending. That has now expanded into secondments from the Pension Service, and charities providing direct services. This includes data collection from older applicants and even certain levels of authorisation of benefits via these 'alternative offices', as they are known. The charities are reimbursed for their service contributions and their role is laid out in Pension Service leaflets, which go to over six million pensioner households.

Benefits – charities

The benefits for the charities include expanding their service delivery to beneficiary customers without having to use fundraised income; being able to integrate their other service offerings into the encounters; gaining new quantitative and qualitative evidence of older people's circumstances which, with privacy protection, can be used in their pressure group and lobbying roles; and increased awareness of the charities and their work through the Pensions Service's promotion activities.

Benefits – Pension Service

The benefits to the Pension Service include reaching people it might otherwise not have been able to reach; raising the proportion of eligible people claiming (which is one of its performance targets); expanding its service without employing more people directly – another

cont.

> **CASE EXAMPLE: THE PENSION SERVICE AND CITIZENS ADVICE, AGE CONCERN AND RNIB continued**
>
> government target; involving the third sector – another government policy; and using its resources cost effectively, for example not having to rent more premises in local neighbourhoods while still being able to deliver deeper into local communities.
>
> **Benefits – older people**
> The benefits to older people include more poorer people claiming their entitlement and so having more money; less anguish for those claiming who still associate means testing with humiliation (because of a third party, the charity, explaining the 'rights' base of the claim); and easier claiming because the service is often being delivered at a location where the claimant is going to be anyway.
>
> **Doubts**
> This 'win – win – win' approach may seem eminently sensible and obvious now, but it was not for the leading charities at the time. It took a lot of talking through and assessing the proposals before they were reassured on a number of fronts. First, that the prime loyalty to their end customer (older people) would best be served by this subcontracting rather than an expansion of staffing of the Pension Service; second that the arrangement would not damage their impartiality and ability to lobby; and finally, that cooperating actively to deliver means tested benefits was acceptable when the charities, in principle, favoured universal provision.

Conclusion
This case of partnership marketing shows the use of the full service marketing mix, in particular the creative way of overcoming the hidden price of perceived stigma, and the alignment of philosophy; and it shows the importance of the relationship marketing approach, in particular the financial, structural and customisation bonds (as each of the three charities delivered in slightly different ways).

Charity plus commercial company (cause related marketing)

Cause related marketing (CRM) is the best known form of charity partnership marketing, in part because of the dynamic promotion of the concept and practice in the UK by the CRM unit of Business in the Community (BITC) but also because the charity's partners, companies, have recognised the huge benefits for business.

The BITC website includes many examples of successful CRM, most involving children's and cancer charities, causes which dominate the area of CRM. However I have chosen an environmental cause because it shows that less 'popular' causes can gain effective partnerships if the right affinity is present; also this is a holistic example – it raises money and awareness for each partner but also benefits schools and local authorities.

CASE EXAMPLE: YELL

Recycling

'Yell – the yellow woods challenge' is a partnership between the Woodlands Trust and Yellow Pages. The aims are to encourage recycling, encourage children in particular to recognise and understand the importance of woodland conservation and recycling, and to raise money for the Woodlands Trust and its work to protect woodlands.

The partnership encourages schoolchildren to collect old Yellow Pages directories for recycling, with all participant schools receiving free, curriculum linked, environmental education packs. Schools compete for cash prizes of up to £2,000 for the number of directories collected per pupil. For every pound of prize money awarded to a school, Yell gives the Woodland Trust a pound. The scheme works closely with local government recycling officers to encourage their involvement and produces a 'teacher's toolkit'. The company has invested over £500,000, with £86,000 going to the Trust and the same to schools, with more investment planned.

All round benefits

The benefits to Yell are an environmental profile, a lot of free editorial publicity, especially in local papers, and positive relations with local authorities. For the Woodlands Trust the publicity is extensive, the public education of the schoolchildren linked to the Trust is very

cont.

> **CASE EXAMPLE: YELL continued**
>
> valuable, the funds are welcome, as is the increased profile with local authorities. The local authorities benefit from the publicity on recycling and have an extra 600 tons of recycled material added to their achievement. The schools and the children benefit from the educational opportunities as well as the cash injections from the prizes.

Another example of CRM is a campaign from Shelter and Coke. In late 2004 Shelter launched a campaign with Diet Coke to raise awareness of housing issues amongst young women and raise money to support Shelter's services.

The partnership included an on-pack CRM promotion, a celebrity film festival party and an eBay auction, all to tie in with the launch of Diet Coke's Mini-Break 250cl cans.

> **CASE EXAMPLE: SHELTER AND COKE**
>
> **New product**
>
> In April 2004, Diet Coke launched a new 'Mini Break' handbag-sized can, positioned as the perfect size for people 'on the go' and as a lunchtime drink. It was keen to market these cans to young women, and chose Shelter as a charity with relevance and resonance amongst its target group, and one that would fit with its young brand image. Shelter was also particularly keen to reach this target group. Young women have significant sympathy and support for their work, but they are a group with a poor perception of their own risk of housing problems.
>
> Young women face many housing problems. Whether leaving home for the first time, finding a safe and affordable flat or room to rent, buying their first home, or even escaping violence – the challenges and dangers they face are massive. Shelter was keen to find new ways to reach this group – to promote the availability of its services to young women, but to do so through a fun and attractive partnership.
>
> **Celebrity designs**
>
> Diet Coke approached celebrities Denise Van Outen, Sadie Frost, Alesha Dixon from Mis-teeq, and Atomic Kitten star Jenny Frost to create designs, based around their idea of 'sanctuary'.
>
> *cont.*

CASE EXAMPLE: SHELTER AND COKE continued

These designs appeared on four limited edition Mini Break cans sold in all Boots stores from 1 November 2004. One million cans were produced. Shelter received 10p for each can sold, plus an agreed bounty payment.

Each celebrity focused on their idea of home and friends as their own 'sanctuaries', and these themes were used in exclusive interviews and media activity to promote both Shelter and the Mini Break.

Designer Pauric Sweeney then turned the designs into exclusive handbags, which were auctioned on eBay in December 2004 to raise further funds and awareness of Shelter.

The cans and promotion were extremely successful and sales and fundraising targets were exceeded before Christmas 2004.

Media coverage

Vogue held an exclusive reader offer in partnership with Top Shop and Diet Coke. Readers were invited to a fundraising fashion night of 'Christmas Fashion' in aid of Shelter.

Further national and regional media coverage included pieces in the *Mail on Sunday, You, Hello!, OK!, Now*, the *Daily Star, Entertainment Today, Cosmopolitan* and *Glamour* magazine. Trade press coverage was achieved in many marketing and charity publications, including *Marketing Week* and *Fundraising News*. Fundraising and communications activity continued into 2005.

While CRM looks to benefit everyone, the approach is not without its risks and problems. Sometimes there are obvious reasons for a company wanting the halo effect of association with a good cause – such as it has a bad reputation. Also, the activities the company wants to support and promote may not be the charity's highest priority and, in the extreme, can lead to mission drift. Charities can also sell themselves too cheap. The Yell scheme cannot be a knockout winner for the Woodland Trust because the costs of administering the scheme must eat heavily into the money given.

However, the public seems to welcome CRM (the vast majority of consumers have participated in a purchase backed by CRM and most approve (BITC 2004)). It would also appear to work for the company, as about half of consumers in BITC's report said that, because of a CRM offer they had either switched brands, increased usage or tried or enquired about new products; with a similar proportion saying that the charitable association made them feel better about the company or product.

Guidelines

In order to mitigate risk and maximise success BITC has developed CRM guidelines, which focus on key principles of integrity, transparency, sincerity, mutual respect, partnership and mutual benefit; and six key elements of successful CRM: planning and preparation, negotiating the partnership – in particular aligning objectives – the formal agreement, managing the programme well, communicating the programme well, and monitoring and evaluating the programme. In particular BITC talks about the ABC of CRM namely Affinity, Benefits and Communication. *Affinity* means there should a good fit between the cause and the product. In the Yell case it is easy for the customers to see the affinity between protecting trees and recycled paper made from trees so that fewer trees have to be cut down. *Benefits* means making sure the benefit to the charity and company is clear and balanced. *Communication* means making the benefits clear, compelling, sincere and honest.

Charity and the informal sector

Most charities are working at the local level, with individuals and small groups. This presents an opportunity for a partnership marketing approach that is primarily about adding more tools to help what has traditionally been called community work or community development.

CASE EXAMPLE: GROUNDWORK UK

Groundwork UK is one of the many national charities working locally. Groundwork West London has a contract with Hammersmith and Fulham to work in local communities, including the Field Road Housing Estate, which has very limited green space and play areas.

cont.

CASE EXAMPLE: GROUNDWORK UK continued

The old Margravine Gardens play area and the estate was no longer suitable as a play area but was used as such because access to more suitable spaces involved crossing busy roads. Through consultation with local residents and imaginative involvement of children in drama workshops the project built up a picture of how the gardens could become a safe, different, creative and exciting place to play.

The project went back to the residents, local parents in the nursery and groups of young people to check that the resulting plans had interpreted what people were saying, and to get an informal agreement or sign off. To make sure the informal agreement was broadly based, the project also put on a special event in the gardens where the proposals were on show.

The partnership between Groundwork and the local residents and children has had a successful outcome, with more people playing more safely and more creatively. The marketing framework helped that outcome through joint design of the offering (the play area) and its features as well as other elements of the marketing mix such as agreement on the philosophy behind the offering and consideration of other elements of the framework such as understanding the target groups for the area (such as the importance of including children with special needs).

Conclusions

What conclusions can we draw from these case examples? In particular what do they tell us about when we should enter or create partnerships or alliances? And what do they tell us about which are the critical parts of the marketing framework?

First, partnerships need to be explored when, having explored all the obvious internal solutions, we are still having trouble increasing any or all of:

- the quality of our offering;
- the volume of our delivery;
- the penetration of our offering.

Resources

A partnership essentially brings extra resources to our operating activities and our ability to serve our customers. These resources come in many forms such as money, expertise, plant, distribution channels and recruitment. But as we have seen, partnerships are complicated and risky and we should normally only turn to them when efforts on an internal solution have failed to deliver the results we want and/or the extra resource benefits are established.

Choosing partners

Choosing the right partner(s) is problematic but, fundamentally, partners should only be chosen if they can help materially in one or more of the three areas above. Additional selection criteria include affinity, benefits, trust, commitment, reputation and shared goals.

Making it work

To make the partnership work to the best advantage of our beneficiary customers and their intermediaries we need to apply the full marketing framework of segmentation, targeting, marketing research, other-player analysis, positioning and the marketing mix. Within the mix, product composition and quality, philosophy, distribution and promotion are likely to need particularly close attention.

Six elements

For the process of establishing and maintaining the partnership or alliance BITC's six key elements are helpful – planning and preparation, negotiating the partnership, the formal agreement, managing the programme, communicating the programme, and monitoring and evaluating it.

13 Marketing: the way forward

Charities face a dilemma. The need for them is acute – arguably greater than any time over the last fifty years. But coincidentally their role has become much more complicated, even muddled, and probably will not become clear for another five or ten years.

Our niche markets of pioneering and pressure group activity remain. However, the statutory authorities, far from wanting to take on new, proven services, are busy contracting out traditional mainstream provision; not simply to charities but also to quasi-governmental organisations such as hospital trusts and opted-out schools, and to commercial companies. Often this contracting-out is under competitive tender. Charities are unsure when and where to compete, or even whether and from what perspective to engage in this rapidly evolving mixed economy of welfare. In short, charities are being buffeted by much larger political and economic forces. Traditional strategic positions and traditional operational techniques are not guiding us through this storm.

I hope that this book has shown how marketing as a philosophy, as well as a strategic and operational tool, can help and provide us with a means of steering successfully through these rough seas of change and, more fundamentally, help to keep our course true to our reason for existing.

Dominant ethos

While financial and production disciplines are as important as they have ever been; on their own, or even in combination, they are not enough. Commercial organisations, let alone charities, are not successful in anything but the short term when they are finance or production led. The increasingly dominant ethos in the commercial world is to be marketing led.

The applicability to the charity sector of the marketing ethos, of starting with the needs and wants of the customer, is strikingly obvious. Indeed critics might say that this is what we have always done. I think that position is arguable, but would need to write another book of a more historical nature! What is important is that charities, like marketing, have at their heart the needs of beneficiary customers, whether they are called clients, students, patients, users, audience or patrons; and so we have a philosophical fit between marketing and charities.

A changing world

Marketing is also well suited to cope with the increasingly competitive and rapidly changing world of the mixed economy of welfare, since marketing was developed as a means of coping with an increasingly competitive commercial and production environment around the middle of the last century. It defines its product offerings of goods, services and ideas not only in terms of the customer, but also in relation to other providers. So it is particularly good at helping in situations where the boundaries between services and sectors are changing – a challenge now crucial to charities.

Such a philosophy is also well suited to the growth of consumerism in the charity world. It is an approach that concentrates on customer needs and uses techniques such as marketing research. It sits well with a model that sees customers as having rights, and with a reality of rising charity customer expectations.

For charity workers still worried about its origins, it is important to emphasise that marketing as a practice is value-neutral. It can be used for good or ill – to promote smoking or to discourage it. As a philosophy it is not value-neutral. It is bad marketing to promote harmful products that clearly do not meet the needs of customers.

Tools

Last, it is important to emphasise that marketing is not some wonder ingredient – nor is it just icing on the cake. It is a holistic operational approach that enables charities to adapt their goods, services and ideas in ways that fundamentally take account of the needs of their end customers, but which also take account of what other providers are doing. As the previous chapters have shown, its key analytical tools are as follows:

- marketing research;
- customer segmentation;
- positioning of offerings (in relation to other providers);
- other-player analysis.

Crucial to the success of the offering are the eight 'Ps' of the charity marketing mix:

- philosophy;
- product;
- price;
- promotion;
- place;
- people;
- physical evidence;
- process.

All these transactional tools need to be placed in the framework of a continuing relationship with customers which, on occasion, will be developed in partnership with other organisations.

Conclusion

Using a marketing philosophy and marketing techniques in charities will not in itself redefine the boundaries between the various sectors of the evolving mixed economy, nor will it, in itself, redefine the role of charity. What it will do is help individual charities to operate successfully during and after this period of turbulence in a way that will be true to the people and causes to which they are committed. In short, marketing in charities is a powerful philosophical and practical force for positive development and progress.

Appendix 1

Johns Hopkins' structural operational definition of the broad voluntary sector (Kendall and Knapp 1996, pp. 18–19)

'Organisations appearing to meet all of the following criteria were regarded as voluntary bodies for the purposes of cross-national comparison.

Formal. Only structural entities with constitutions or formal sets of rules, perhaps (but not necessarily) registered with a public authority or voluntary intermediary body, were included. This ruled out the large set of informal household and neighbourhood support activities, which are particularly important in the community development and social welfare fields.

Independent of government and self-governing. Groups were required to be constitutionally or institutionally independent of government, and self-governing – that is, with their own internal decision-making structures, and not directly controlled by a private (for-profit) entity or by the state. This criterion does *not* exclude from the sector constitutionally independent organisations heavily dependent on the private market or the government for their resources.

Not-profit-distributing and primarily non-business. Organisations were ruled out if they were empowered to distribute net earnings to controlling persons (even if on solidaristic principles) or had a commercial orientation which made them indistinguishable from for-profit firms. Cooperatives, financial and other mutuals (including building societies, most friendly societies and motoring organisations) were among the exclusions.

Voluntary. A meaningful degree of voluntarism in terms of money or time through philanthropy or voluntary citizen involvement was required to qualify an agency as belonging to the sector.

Two further criteria were adopted for the purposes of statistical mapping only. *Party political* organisations were excluded. And *sacramental activities*, taken to include places of worship and the central infrastructure and support bodies of the churches, were omitted – although they are recognised in the classification scheme.'

Appendix 2

Office of National Statistics' definition of general charities within the UK voluntary sector (Hems and Passey 1996, p. 10)

'General charities are defined in national accounting terms "non-profit-making bodies serving persons" (NPMBs). The four key criteria are:

1. *Independent governance*
General charities are separate from government and business. This criterion excludes the following types of organisation:
- Those bodies allocated in national accounts terms to general government, such as:
    - registered charities which are also non-departmental public bodies or quasi non-governmental organisations including the British Council and the British Museum;
    - educational establishments, including universities and voluntary aided schools, which are recognised as exempt or excepted charities and are predominantly funded by government;
    - financial institutions which are allocated to the corporate sector in national accounts, eg Charities Official Investment Fund (COIF).

2. *Non-profit distributing*
General charities do not distribute profits to shareholders. This criterion excludes cooperatives.

3. *Objects have a wider public benefit*
General charities provide a wider public benefit that goes beyond any membership. This criterion excludes:
- mutual types of non-profit organisation which are solely for the benefit of their members, such as:
    - friendly societies and building societies (which may also be seen as financial institutions);
    - housing associations;
    - sports and social clubs;
    - independent schools;
    - trade unions.

4. Non-sacramental religious bodies/places of worship
This criterion excludes organisations which are predominantly sacramental religious bodies or places of worship from a general charities definition.

The definition of general charities within the UK voluntary sector therefore includes:

- the household-name, national charities, such as Shelter, Save the Children Fund, Action Aid, Royal National Institute for the Deaf, Royal National Institute for the Blind;
- local charities.'

References

Aaker, D.A. (2002) *Building Strong Brands*, Simon and Schuster: London

Abdy, M. and Barclay, J. (2001) 'Marketing Collaboration in the Voluntary Sector', *International Journal of Non-profit and Voluntary Sector Marketing*, 6(3), 215–230

Abdy, M. and Farmelo, C. (2005) 'The 2004 Legacy Market Audit: Recent Trends in Legacies', *International Journal of Non-profit and Voluntary Sector Marketing*, 10(1)

Ali, M. (2001) *The New DIY Guide to Marketing*, ICSA: London

American Marketing Association (1985) *Marketing News*, 1 March

Andreasen, A.R. and Kotler, P. (2003) *Strategic Marketing for Non-profit Organizations*, international edition, Pearson Education International: New Jersey

Ansoff, H.I. (1965) *Corporate Strategy*, McGraw-Hill: Toronto

Arbuthnot, S. and Horne, S. (1997) 'The Marketing Activities of UK Charities', *Journal of Non-profit and Public Sector Marketing*, 5(1), 63–79

Baker, M.J. (1987) *The Marketing Book*, Heinemann: London

Baker, M.J. (1991) *The Marketing Book*, 4th edn, Macmillan: Basingstoke

Baker, M.J. (ed.) (2003) *The Marketing Book*, 5th edn, Butterworth Heinemann: Oxford

Balabanis, G., Stables R.E. and Phillips H.C. (1997) 'Market Orientation in the Top 200 British Charity Organisations and its Impact on their Performance', *European Journal of Marketing,* 31(8), 583–603

Barclays/NGO Finance '100 Charity Index', *NGO Finance Magazine*, 76, Plaza Publications: London

Bayley, T.D. (1988) *The Fundraiser's Guide to Successful Campaigns*, McGraw-Hill: New York

Bennett, R. (2003) 'Factors Underlying the Inclination to Donate to Particular Types of Charity', *International Journal of Non-profit and Voluntary Sector Marketing*, 8(1), 1229

Berry, L.L. and Parasuraman, A. (1991) *Marketing Services: Competing Through Quality*, The Free Press/Macmillan: New York

BITC (2004) *Brand Benefits*, Business in the Community: London

Blois, K.J. (1987 and 2003) 'Marketing for Non-profit Organisations', in Baker, M.J. (ed.) *The Marketing Book*, Butterworth Heinemann: London

Blyth, B. (1989) 'Marketing Research', in Thomas, M.J. (ed.) *Marketing Handbook*, 3rd edn, Gower: Aldershot

Booms, B.H. and Bitner, M.J. (1981) 'Marketing Strategies and Organisation Structures for Service Firms', in Donnelly, J. and George, W.R. (eds) *Marketing of Services*, American Marketing Association: Chicago, 47–51

Borden, N.H. (1964) 'The Concept of the Marketing Mix', *Journal of Advertising Research*, 4 (2) 2–7

Brophy, M. (1992) 'Foreword', in McQuillan, J., *Charity Trends 1992*, CAF: Tonbridge

Bruce, I. (1973) 'How to Use Public Relations in the Social Services', in *Report of a Working Group on Public Relations in the Social Services*, United Nations: New York

Bruce, I. (1985) 'Policy Guidelines for a Development Programme', *New Beacon*, January, RNIB: London

Bruce, I. (1991) 'Employment of People with Disabilities', in Dalley, G. (ed.) *Disability and Social Policy*, Policy Studies Institute: London

Bruce, I. (1992) 'Using Market Research as a Tool in National Campaigning', *Review of the European Blind*, 3 (LXXVII), European Blind Union: Berlin

Bruce, I. (1993) 'Social Marketing', in Bruce, I. (ed.) *Charity Talks on Successful Development*, VOLPROF, Centre for Voluntary Sector and Not-for-Profit Management, City University: London

Bruce, I. (1994) *Meeting Need – Successful Charity Marketing*, ICSA: Hemel Hempstead

Bruce, I. (1995) 'Do Not-for-profits Value their Customers and Their Needs?', *International Marketing Review* 12(4), 77–84

Bruce, I. (1998) *Successful Charity Marketing*, ICSA/Prentice Hall: Hemel Hempstead

Bruce, I. and Baker, M. (2001) *Access to Written Information – A Survey of 1000 People with Sight Problems*, RNIB: London

Bruce, I. and Baker, M. (2003) *Employment and Unemployment among People with Sight Problems – A Survey of 1000 People*, RNIB: London

Bruce, I. and Raymer, A. (1992) *Managing and Staffing Britain's Largest Charities*, VOLPROF, Centre for Voluntary Sector and Not-for-profit Management, City University Business School: London

Bruce, I., Castillejo, D., Cornford, C., Gosford, C. and Routh, F. (1974) *Patronage of the Creative Artist*, Artists Now: London

Bruce, I., McKennell, A. and Walker, E. (1991) *Blind and Partially Sighted Adults in Britain: The RNIB Survey*, HMSO: London

Burnett, K. (1992 and 2002) *Relationship Fundraising*, 2nd edn, White Lion Press: London

Burnett, K. (1996) *Friends for Life – Relationship Fund-raising in Practice*, White Lion Press: London

CAF (1992 and 2005) *Charity Trends*, 15th and 26th edn, CAF: Kent

Chamberlin, E.H. (1938) *The Theory of Monopolistic Competition*, Harvard University Press

Charity Finance (2004) 'Charity Shops Survey 2004', *Charity Finance Magazine*, September

Chase, R.B. (1978) 'Where Does the Customer Fit into a Service Organisation?', *Harvard Business Review*, November/December, 137–142

Chew, C. (2003) 'What Factors Influence Positioning Strategies in Voluntary and Non-profit Organisations? Towards a Conceptual Framework', *Local Governance*, 29(4) 288–323

Clarke, P. and Mount, P. (2001) 'Nonprofit Marketing: the Key to Marketing's "Mid-life Crisis"?' *International Journal of Nonprofit and Voluntary Sector Marketing*, 6(1), 76–91

Conway, T. (1997) 'Strategy Versus Tactics in the Not-for-profit Sector: A Role for Relationship Marketing', *Journal for Non-profit and Voluntary Sector Marketing*, 2(1), 42–51

Copeman, C.C., Bruce, I., Forrest, A., Lesirge, R., Palmer, P. and Patel, A. (2004) *Tools for Tomorrow – a Practical Guide to Strategic Planning for Voluntary Organisations*, NCVO: London

Corporate Intelligence on Retailing (1992) *Charity Shops in the UK*, Corporate Intelligence Research: London

Cowell, D. (1984) (1995 2nd edn), *The Marketing of Services*, Heinemann: Oxford

Coxall, W.N. (1985) *Parties and Pressure Groups*, 2nd edn, Longman: London

Cravens, D.W. and Piercy, N.F. (1994) 'Relationship Marketing and Collaborative Networks in Service Organisations', *International Journal of Service Industry Management*, 5(5), pp. 39–53

Cronin J.J. and Taylor S.A (1994) 'SERVPERF versus SERVQUAL', *Journal of Marketing*, 58, 125–131

Crosier, K. (1975) 'What Exactly is Marketing?', *Quarterly Review of Marketing*, winter

Crosier, K. (2003) 'Promotion', in Baker, M.J. (ed.) *The Marketing Book*, Butterworth Heinemann: Oxford

Dauncey, T. (2005) 'The UK's Legacy Promotion Campaign', *International Journal of Non-profit and Voluntary Sector Marketing*, 10(1)

de Chernatony, L. (2003) 'Brand Building', in Baker, M.J. (ed.) *The Marketing Book*, Butterworth Heinemann: Oxford

Deacon, D., Fenton, N. and Walker, B. (1995) 'Communicating Philanthropy: The Media and the Voluntary Sector in Britain', *VOLUNTAS*, 6(2), 119–139

Deacon, D., Golding, P. and Walker, B. (1994) *Voluntary Activity in a Changing Communications Environment*, ESRC Fund Report, Loughborough University: Loughborough

Deakin, N. (1996) *Meeting the Challenge of Change: Voluntary Action into the 21st Century; Report of the Commission on the Future of the Voluntary Sector*, NCVO: London

Deakin, N. (2001) 'Putting Narrow-mindedness out of Countenance', in Anheier, H.K. and Kendall, J. (eds) *Third Sector Policy at the Crossroads: An International Nonprofit Analysis*, Routledge: London

Diamantopoulos, A. (2003) 'Pricing', in Baker, M.J. (ed.) *The Marketing Book* Butterworth Heinemann: Oxford

Dibb, S., Simkin, L., Pride, W.M. and Ferrell, O.C. (1991, 4th edn 2003) *Marketing Concepts and Strategies*, Houghton Mifflin: Boston

Dixon, M. (1997) 'Small and Medium Sized Charities Need a Strong Brand Too', *International Journal of Nonprofit and Voluntary Sector Marketing*, 2(1) 52–57

Doyle, P. (1991 and 2003) 'Managing the Marketing Mix', in Baker, M.J. (ed.) *The Marketing Book*, Butterworth Heinemann: Oxford

Drucker, P. (1990) *Managing the Non-Profit Organisation*, Butterworth Heinemann: Oxford

Dwyer E.R., Schurr P.H. and Oh, S. (1987) 'Developing Buyer-Seller Relationships', *Journal of Marketing*, 51, 11–27

Eiglier, P. and Langeard, E. (1977) *A New Approach to Services: New Insights*, Report 77/115, Marketing Science Institute: Boston

Embley, L.L. (1993) *Doing Well While Doing Good*, Prentice Hall: Englewood Cliffs: NJ

Espy, S. (1993) *Marketing Strategies for Non-profit Organisations*, Lyceum Books: Chicago

ESRC (2005) *Charitable Giving and Donor Motivation*, ESRC Seminar Series, ESRC: Swindon

Eurostat (1988) Commission of the European Community (epp.eurostat.cec.eu.int)

Evans, K.R. and Schultz, R.J. (1996) 'Towards an Understanding of Public Purchaser and Salespersons Interaction Activities', *Journal of Non-profit and Public Sector Marketing*, 4(4), 55–75

Farsides, T. (2005) *'How Can We Help' rather than 'Give Us Your Money'*, ESRC: www.esrcsocietytoday.ac.uk

Fenton, N. (1995) 'Charities, Media and Public Opinion: The Ideology of Welfare', in *Researching the UK Voluntary Sector*, NCVO: London

Field, F. (1982) *Poverty and Politics*, Heinemann: London

Fine, S.F. (1990) *Social Marketing: Promoting the Causes of Public and Non Profit Agencies*, Allyn and Bacon: Needham Heights

FitzHerbert, L. and Rhoades, L. (1997) *The National Lottery Year Book*, Directory of Social Change: London

Ford, D. (1996) 'Obtaining Legacies Face to Face', *Journal of Non-profit and Voluntary Sector Marketing*, 1(3), 203–212

Foxall, G.R. (1987) 'Consumer Behaviour', in Baker, M.J. (ed.) *The Marketing Book*, Heinemann: London

Foxall, G.R. (2003) 'Consumer Decision Making: Process, Level and Style' in Baker, M.J. (ed.) *The Marketing Book*, Butterworth Heinemann, Oxford

Gabor, A. (1980) *Pricing Principles & Practices*, Heinemann: London

Gaskin, K., Vlaeminke, M. and Fenton, N. (1996) *Young People's Attitudes to the Voluntary Sector*, Loughborough University: Loughborough

George, W.R., Kelly, J. Patrick and Marshall, Claudia E. (1983) 'Personal Selling of Services', in Berry, L.L., Shostack, G. Lynn and Upah, G.D. (eds)

Emerging Perspectives on Services Marketing, American Marketing Association: Chicago

Greengross, S. (1993) Accountability, in Bruce, I. (ed.) *Charity Talks on Successful Development*, VOLPROF, Centre for Voluntary Sector and Not-for-Profit Management, City University Business School: London

Gronroos, C. (1997) 'Value-driven Relational Marketing: From Products to Resources and Competencies', *Journal of Marketing Management*, 13, 407–419

Gronroos, C. (1980) *An Applied Service Marketing Theory*, Working Paper No. 57, Swedish School of Economics and Business Administration: Helsinki

Gwin, J.M. (1991) Constituent Analysis, *European Journal of Marketing*, 24(7), 43–48

Halfpenny, P. and Saxon-Harrold, S. (1991) *Charity Household Survey 1989/90*, CAF: Tonbridge

Hankinson, G. (2004) 'Repertory Grid Analysis', *International Journal of Nonprofit and Voluntary Sector Marketing*, 9(2), 145–154

Hankinson, P. (2000) 'Brand Orientation in Charity Organisations', *Journal of Non-profit and Voluntary Sector Marketing* 5(3), 207–220

Hankinson, P. (2002) 'The Impact of Brand Orientation on Managerial Practice: A Quantitative Study of 500 Fundraising Managers', *International Journal of Non-profit and Voluntary Sector Marketing*, 7(1), 30–44

Hannagan, T. (1992) *Marketing for the Non-profit Sector*, Macmillan: London

Harker, D. (1993) 'The NGO Finance Annual Survey of Charity Shops', *NGO Finance*, 3(1)

Harrison, T. (1987) *A Handbook of Advertising Techniques*, Kogan Page: London

Harrow, J. (2005) 'Mechanisms and Values in the Delivery of the Patchwork of Public Services' in Dibben, P., Wood, G. and Roper, I. (eds) *Contesting Public Sector Reforms: Critical Perspectives, International Debates*, Palgrave Macmillan: London

Hems, L. and Passey, A. (1996) *The UK Voluntary Sector Statistical Almanac 1996*, NCVO: London

Henley Centre (1996) *Survey of Public Attitudes*, Henley Centre/NCVO: Henley

Hibbert, S. (2005) *Building Understanding of Non-donors: An Application of Neutralisation*, Working Paper Series, Nottingham University Business School: Nottingham

Hibbert, S. and Horne, S. (1996) 'Giving to Charity: Questioning the Donor Decision Process', *Journal of Consumer Marketing*, 13(2), 4–13

Hill, E., O'Sullivan, C. and O'Sullivan, T. (1995) *Creative Arts Marketing*, Butterworth Heinemann: Oxford

Hinton, N. (1993) 'Planning for Growth', in Bruce, I. (ed.) *Charity Talks on Successful Development*, VOLPROF, Centre for Voluntary Sector and Not-for-Profit Management, City University Business School: London

Hiscock, H.E. (1991) *Trading by Charities*, Charities Advisory Trust: London

Holwegger, K. (1996) 'The RNID's Customer Care Initiative', *Journal of Non-profit and Voluntary Sector Marketing*, 1(2), 105–120

Horne, S. (2000) 'The Charity Shop: Purpose and Change', *Journal of Non-profit and Voluntary Sector Marketing*, 5(2), 113–125

Horne, S. and Laing, A. (2002) 'Editorial: Non-profit Marketing – Ghetto or Trailblazer', *Journal of Marketing Management*, 18, 829–832

Horne, S. and Moss, M. (1995) 'Box Collection Schemes: Analysis of Box Performance and Site Locations', *Journal of Non-profit and Public Sector Marketing*, 3(2), 47–62

Horne, S. and Moss, M. (1996) 'Charity Box Collection Schemes', *Journal of Non-profit and Voluntary Sector Marketing*, 1(3), 263–273

Hudson, M. (2002) *Managing Without Profit: The Art of Managing Third Sector Organisations*, 2nd edn, Directory of Social Change: London

Institute of Philanthropy (2004) *Who Are the Givers?*, Institute of Philanthropy: London

Jas P., Wilding K., Wainwright S., Passey A. and Hems L. (2002) *The UK Voluntary Sector Almanac 2002*, NCVO: London

Johne, A. (1996) 'Succeeding at Product Development Involves More than Avoiding Failure', *European Management Journal*, 14(2), April

Johne, A., and Storey, C. (1998) 'New Service Development', *European Journal of Marketing*, 32 (3.4) , 184–251

Jones, L. (2000) 'Market Orientation – A Case Study of Three UK Opera Companies', *International Journal of Non-profit and Voluntary Sector Marketing* 5(4), 348–364

Joseph, K. (1971) Speech to Age Concern England AGM, in *Introducing Age Concern*, Age Concern: London

Kay, J.A. (1993) *Foundations of Corporate Success*, Oxford University Press: Oxford

Kay-Williams, S. (2000) 'The Five Stages of Fundraising: A Framework for the Development Fundraising', *Journal of Non-profit and Voluntary Sector Marketing*, 5(3), 220–241

Keaveney, P. and Kaufman, M. (eds) (2001) *Marketing for the Voluntary Sector*, Kogan Page: London

Kendall, J. (2003) *The Voluntary Sector*, Routledge: London

Kendall, J. and Knapp, M. (1996) *The Voluntary Sector in the UK*, Manchester University Press: Manchester

Kingham, T. and Coe, J. (2005) *The Good Campaigns Guide*, 2nd edn, NCVO: London

Kotler, P. and Andreasen, A. (1991) *Strategic Marketing for Non-Profit Organisations*, 4th edn, Prentice Hall: Englewood Cliffs, NJ

Kotler, P. and Andreasen, A. (1995) *Strategic Marketing for Non-Profit Organisations*, 5th edn, Prentice Hall: Englewood Cliffs, NJ

Kotler, P. and Fox, K.F.A. (1985) *Strategic Marketing for Educational Institutions*, Prentice Hall: Englewood Cliffs, NJ

Kotler P. and Levy, S.J. (1969) Broadening the Concept of Marketing, *Journal of Marketing*, 33, 10–15

Kotler, P., Armstrong, G., Saunders, J. and Wong, V. (1996 and 2002) *Principles of Marketing: The European Edition*, Prentice Hall: Hemel Hempstead

Kotler, P., Roberto, E.L. and Lee, N. (2002) *Social Marketing,* Sage: London

Lamb, B. (1997) *The Good Campaigns Guide*, NCVO Publications: London

Leat, D. (1993) *Managing Across Sectors*, VOLPROF, Centre for Voluntary Sector and Not-for-Profit Management, City University Business School: London

Le Goff, F. (2004) 'Arms Control Campaign', *Third Sector*, 27 October

Liao, M., Foreman, S. and Sargeant, A. (2001) 'Market versus Societal Orientation in the Non-profit Context', *International Journal of Non-profit and Voluntary Sector Marketing*, 6(3), 254–268

Lindsay, G. and Murphy, A. (1996) 'A Systemic Approach to the Application of Marketing Theory for Charitable Organisations', *Journal of Non-profit and Voluntary Sector Marketing*, 1(3), 252–262

Lovelock, C.H. and Weinberg, C.B. (1984) *Marketing for Public and Non-Profit Managers*, John Wiley: New York

Lovelock, C.H. and Weinberg, C.B. (1989) *Public and Non-profit Marketing*, 2nd edn, The Scientific Press: Redwood City, CA

Luck, D. J. (1969) 'An Idea Too Far', *Journal of Marketing* 33, 53–55

Lynn, P. and Davis Smith, J. (1991) *The 1991 National Survey of Volunteering in the UK*, The Volunteer Centre: Berkhamsted

MacFadyen. L., Stead, M. and Hastings, G. (2003) 'Social Marketing' in Baker, M.J. (ed.) *The Marketing Book*, Butterworth Heinemann: Oxford

Maple, P. (2003) *Marketing Strategy for Effective Fundraising*, Directory of Social Change: London

Martin, J., White, A. and Meltzer, H. (1989) *Disabled Adults: Services, Transport and Employment*, OPCS Survey Report 4, HMSO: London

Maslow, A. (1943) *Motivation and Personality*, Harper & Row: New York

McCarthy, E.J. (1981) *Basic Marketing*, 7th edn, Richard D. Irwin: Homewood, IL

McKechnie, S. (1993) 'Pressure Group Work', in Bruce, I. (ed.) *Charity Talks on Successful Development*, VOLPROF, Centre for Voluntary Sector and Not-for-Profit Management, City University Business School: London

McNeal, J.U. and Zeren, L. (1981) 'Brand Name Selection for Consumer Products', *MSU Business Topics*, spring

Miller, C. (1991) 'Lobbying: The Development of the Consultation Culture, in Jordan, G. (ed.) *The Commercial Lobbyists*, Aberdeen University Press: Aberdeen

Mitchell, R.K., Agle, B.R. and Wood, D.J. (1997) 'Towards a Theory of Stakeholder Identification and Salience: Defining the Principle of Who and What Really Counts', *Academy of Management Review* 22, October

Mitchell, V.W. (1998) 'Segmenting Purchasers of Organisational Professional Services: A Risk-based Approach', *Journal of Services Marketing*, 122(2), 83–98

NCVO (1996) *Meeting the Challenge of Change, Report of the Commission on the Future of the Voluntary Sector*, chaired by Nicholas Deakin, NCVO: London

NCVO (1997) *Charitable Giving by the General Public and the National Lottery*, NCVO Research Department: London

O'Malley L. and Tynan, C. (2003) 'Relationship Marketing', in Baker, M.J. (ed.) *The Marketing Book*, Butterworth Heinemann: Oxford

O'Sullivan, C. and O'Sullivan, T. (1996) 'Naivety and Relationship Marketing in Non-profit Organisations', *Journal of Non-profit and Voluntary Sector Marketing*, 1(1), 32–40

Oxfam (1992) *The Oxfam Review 91/2*, Oxfam: Oxford

Oxfam (1993) *Newspaper Fundraising*, insert leaflet, September, Oxfam: Oxford

Palmer, P. (2002) *The Good Financial Guide for the Voluntary Sector*, NCVO: London

Palmer, P., Wise, D. and Penney D. (1999) 'Selling Goods and Services by Charities', *International Journal of Non-profit and Voluntary Sector Marketing*, 4(2), 121–134

Parasuraman, A., Zeithaml V. and Berry, L. (1988) 'SERVQUAL: A Multi-item Scale for Measuring Consumer Perceptions of Service Quality', *Journal of Retailing* 64 (spring) 12–40

Parminter, K. (1997) 'Successful Campaigning: Winning Friends and Influencing People', *Journal of Non-profit and Voluntary Sector Marketing*, 2(1), 18–22

Passey, A. and Hems, L. (1997) *Charitable Giving in Great Britain 1996*, NCVO: London

Paton, R. (1996) 'What's Different About Non-profit and Voluntary Sector Marketing? A Research Agenda', *Journal of Non-profit and Voluntary Sector Marketing*, 1(1), 23–31

Paton, R. (2002) *Managing and Measuring Social Enterprise*, Sage: London

Pentreath, R. (1994) 'Yorkshire Bitter Can Seriously Improve Your Skydiving', *Sport Parachutist, Journal of the British Parachute Association*, December 1993/January 1994, 9

Pharoah, C. and Welchman, R. (1997) *Keeping Posted – A Survey of Current Approaches to Public Communication in the Voluntary Sector*, CAF: West Malling

Pharoah, C., Walker, C., Goodey, L. and Clegg, S. (2004) *Charity Trends 2004*, CAF: West Malling

Pidgeon, S. (1996) 'Stand By Your Brand, if You Are Aware of It', *Third Sector*, 27 June

Pidgeon, S. (2005) 'Legacy Fundraising', *Journal of Non-profit and Voluntary Sector* (special issue), 10(1), 1–63

Piercey, N.F. (2003) 'Marketing Implementation, Organizational Change and Internal Marketing Strategy' in Baker, M.J. (ed.) *The Marketing Book*, Butterworth Heinemann: London

Pigou, A.C. (1932) *The Economics of Welfare*, Macmillan: London

Porter, M.E. (1980) *Competitive Strategy: Techniques for Analysing Industries and Competitors*, The Free Press/Macmillan: New York

Porter, M.E. (1985) *Competitive Advantage: Creating and Sustaining Superior Performances*, Collier Macmillan: London

Posnett, J. (1992) 'Income and Expenditure in Charities in England and Wales', in *Charity Trends 1992*, CAF: Tonbridge

Pyne, A.E. and Robertson, D.R. (1997) 'Charity Marketing – More Focus on the Beneficiary', *Journal of Non-profit and Voluntary Sector Marketing*, 2(2), 154–162

Rados, D.L. (1981) *Marketing for Non-Profit Organisations*, Auburn House: Dover, MA

Rees, P. (1998) 'Marketing in the UK and US Not-for-profit Sector: The Import Mirror View', *The Service Industries Journal*, 18(1), 113–131

Reichheld, F.F. (1996) *The Loyalty Effect*, Harvard Business School Press: Boston

Reichheld, F.F. and Sasser Jr, W.E. (1990) 'Zero Defections: Quality Comes to Services', *Harvard Business Review*, September-October, 301–307

Rodger, L.W. (1987) *Marketing the Visual Arts*, Scottish Arts Council: Edinburgh

Sargeant, A. (2004) *Marketing Management of Non-profit Organizations,* 2nd edn, Oxford University Press: Oxford

Sargeant, A. (2005) 'The Final Gift: Targeting the Potential Charity Legator', *International Journal of Non-profit and Voluntary Sector Marketing*, 10(1)

Sargeant, A. and Jay, E. (2004) *Fundraising Management: Analysis, Planning and Practice*, Routledge: London

Sargeant, A. and Lee, S. (2002) 'Improving Public Trust in the Voluntary Sector', *Journal of Non-profit and Voluntary Sector Marketing*, 7(1), 68–83

Sargeant, A. and Stephenson, H. (1997) 'Corporate Giving: Targeting the Likely Donor', *Journal of Non-profit and Voluntary Sector Marketing*, 2(1), 64–79

Saxton J. (2003) 'Is That a Business or a Charity I See?', *Public Agenda, Times*, 21 October

Saxton, J. (1996a) 'Strategies for Competitive Advantages in Non-profit Organisations', *Journal of Non-profit and Voluntary Sector Marketing*, 1(1), 50–62

Saxton, J. (1996b) 'Five Direct Marketing Strategies for Non-profit Organisations', *Journal of Non-profit and Voluntary Sector Marketing*, 1(4), 299–306

Scott, D. (1993) 'Fighting Cancer with More than Medicine', in *The Annual Review of Cancer Relief*, Macmillan Fund: London

Sewell, C. and Brown, P.B. (1990) *Customers for Life*, Doubleday: New York

Shenfield, B. and Allen, I. (1972) *The Organisation of Voluntary Service*, PEP: London

Shostack, G.L. (1977) 'Breaking Free from Product Marketing', *Journal of Marketing*, 41(2) American Marketing Association: Chicago

Shostack, G.L. (1982) 'How to Design a Service', *European Journal of Marketing*, 16(2)

Simon, H. (1989) *Price Management*, Elsevier: Amsterdam

Spillard, P. (1987) 'Organisation for Marketing', in Baker, M.J. (ed.) *The Marketing Book*, Heinemann: London

Stern, V. (1993) 'The Influence of Rapidly Changing Government Policy', in Bruce, I. (ed.) *Charity Talks on Successful Development*, VOLPROF, Centre for Voluntary Sector and Not-for-Profit Management, City University Business School: London

Tapp, A. (1996) 'Charity Brands: A Qualitative Study of Current Practice', *Journal of Non-profit and Voluntary Sector Marketing*, 1(4), 327–336

Taylor, M. (1992) 'The Changing Role of the Non-profit Sector in Britain: Moving Towards the Market', in Gidron, B., Kramer, R.M. and Salamon, L.M. (eds) *Government and the Third Sector*, Jossey-Bass: San Francisco

Teas, R.K. (1994) 'Expectations as a Comparison Standard in Measuring Service Quality', *Journal of Marketing*, 58, 132–139

Thomas, M. (1980) 'Market "Segmentation"', *Quarterly Review of Marketing*, 6(1)

Vargo, S.L. and Lusch, R.F. (2004) *Journal of Marketing*, 68, pp1–7

Walker, C. and Pharoah, C. (2002) *A Lot to Give: Trends in Charitable Giving for the 21st Century*, Hodder and Stoughton: London

Walker, E., Tobin, M. and McKennell, A. (1992) *Blind and Partially Sighted Children in Britain: The RNIB survey*, HMSO: London

Wenham, K., Stephens, D. and Hardy, R. (2003) 'The Marketing Effectiveness of UK Environmental Charity Websites Compared to Best Practices', *International Journal of Non-profit and Voluntary Sector Marketing*, 8(3), 213–223

Wensley, R. (1990) 'The Voice of the Consumer', *European Journal of Marketing* 24(7) 49–60

Wilding, K., Collins, G., Jochum, V. and Wainwright, S. (2004) *The UK Voluntary Sector Almanac*, 5th edn, NCVO Publications: London

Wilson, A. (1984) *Practice Development for Professional Firms*, McGraw-Hill: Maidenhead

Wilson, D. (1984) *Pressure: The A-Z of Campaigning in Britain*, Heinemann: London

Wolfenden, J. (1977) *The Future of Voluntary Organisations*, Croom Helm: London

Zeithaml, V.A., Bitner, M.J. and Gremler, D.D. (2006) *Services Marketing: Integrating Customer Focus Across the Firm*, 4th edn, McGraw-Hill, New York

Zeithaml, Valarie A., Parasuraman, A. and Berry, Leonard L. (1985) 'Problems and Strategies in Services Marketing', *Journal of Marketing*, spring, 33, 146, American Marketing Association: Chicago

Zeithaml, V.A. and Bitner, M.J. (2003) *Services Marketing*, 3rd edn, McGraw Hill, New York

Zerbinata, S. and Souitaris, V. (2005) 'Entrepreneurship in the Public Sector', *Entrepreneurship and Regional Development* 17(1), 43–64

Index